Public Sector Financial Management

This series brings together cutting edge research in public administration on the new budgeting and accounting methodologies and their impact across the public sector, from central and local government to public health care and education. It considers the need for better quality accounting information for decision-making, planning and control in the public sector; the development of the IPSAS (International Public Sector Accounting Standards) and the EPSAS (European Public Sector Accounting Standards), including their merits and role in accounting harmonisation; accounting information's role in governments' financial sustainability and crisis confrontation; the contribution of sophisticated ICT systems to public sector financial, cost and management accounting deployment; and the relationship between robust accounting information and performance measurement. New trends in public sector reporting and auditing are covered as well. The series fills a significant gap in the market in which works on public sector accounting and financial management are sparse, while research in the area is experiencing unprecedented growth.

More information about this series at
http://www.palgrave.com/gp/series/15782

Vesna Vašiček · Gorana Roje
Editors

Public Sector Accounting, Auditing and Control in South Eastern Europe

palgrave
macmillan

Editors
Vesna Vašiček
Faculty of Economics and Business
University of Zagreb
Zagreb, Croatia

Gorana Roje
Ministry of State Assets
Zagreb, Croatia

Public Sector Financial Management
ISBN 978-3-030-03352-1 ISBN 978-3-030-03353-8 (eBook)
https://doi.org/10.1007/978-3-030-03353-8

Library of Congress Control Number: 2018962248

This Palgrave Macmillan imprint is published by the registered company Springer Nature Switzerland AG
The registered company address is: Gewerbestrasse 11, 6330 Cham, Switzerland

Foreword I

The present book on *Public Sector Accounting, Auditing and Control in South Eastern Europe* provides a structured analysis of the respective Public Financial Management Functions *in Croatia, Poland, Romania, Serbia, Slovenia, the Federation of Bosnia and Herzegovina, the Former Yugoslav Republic of Macedonia and the Republic of Srpska*. It covers four member states of the European Union, two candidate countries as well as a potential candidate country. The structure of the analysis in general follows the structure used in other titles of the series, in particular *Public Sector Accounting and Auditing in Europe: The Challenge of Harmonization*, edited by Isabel Brusca, Eugenio Caperchione, Sandra Cohen and Francesca Manes Rossi.

Public Financial Management is a critical part of good governance and, as studies such as the one of the IMF in 2012 shows, an enabler for financial stability and economic growth. Accounting, Auditing and Control are critical parts of any state of the art, integrated Public Financial Management System. Therefore, the book addresses a topic, which is of much broader relevancy than it looks like at first glimpse. In fact, successful implementation of such systems and subsystems is critical at societal level. As the example of Switzerland shows, the investment into such systems is considerable, but easily amortized almost immediately, simply by assets found, not even taking into consideration the more indirect effects.

While Public Financial Management is usually conceptualized at national level, there is a strong trend for international convergence. Best practise is defined by international standards, of which some are a prerequisite for the accession to the European Union, such as ESA10, and some others have become a generally accepted reference point, such as IPSAS. As the book shows, all countries are making strong reference the international standards.

However, the book also shows that such international standards are often more difficult to implement than it seems. Environmental factors are different in each country, but the experience shows that they are in many cases challenging. There are often delaying a project or creating additional complexity and increasing the cost. The only way to mitigate such risk is by making sure that political sponsorship is strong and from the top level. Also, it needs to be acknowledged that even in the most advanced countries such as New Zealand, Public Financial Management systems are evolving over time. It is therefore often more important to keep the reforms going than to resolve all issues upfront.

Another important factor is the integration of the various Public Financial Management subsystems. The organizations structure within the Ministry of Finance are often making such an integration difficult, but the most important long term benefits come from the integration of budgeting, accounting, auditing and financial statistics. Although such an integration initially seems to increase the complexity, in the longer run it actually helps to manage and limit it effectively.

Finally, it seems important to stress the usefulness of comparative, yet descriptive work by scholars. While such work certainly does not use the latest statistical methodology, practitioners in contrast very often use it as a basis for their conceptual work. It is therefore of high practical usefulness and relevancy. But even scholars often need a descriptive, factual basis for theory building and testing, therefore such work is a very important contribution even from a more scholarly perspective.

Bottom line, the editors of that book, Vesna Vašiček and Gorana Roje, have delivered an excellent piece of work, together with the authors of country specific chapters.

Winterthur, Switzerland

Prof. Dr. Andreas Bergmann
Zurich University of Applied Sciences; 2010–2015 Chair of the International Public Sector Accounting Standards Board (IPSASB)

References

Brusca, I., Caperchione, E., Cohen, S., & Manes Rossi, F. (2015). *Public Sector Accounting and Auditing in Europe: The Challenge of Harmonization.* London: Palgrave Macmillan. 10.1057/9781137461346.

IMF. (2012). Fiscal Transparency, Accountability, and Risk.

Foreword II

This comparative analysis of accounting, auditing and control systems in public sectors of seven South Eastern European countries, four of which are EU Member States (Croatia, Slovenia, Poland and Romania), two candidate countries (Serbia, the Former Yugoslav Republic of Macedonia) and one potential candidate country (Bosnia and Herzegovina is represented by two entities the Federation of Bosnia and Herzegovina and the Republic of Srpska) is a valuable overview of the current state of public sectors and acts as an important contribution to the exchange of knowledge and experiences, on which further developments of these systems in the observed countries and their surroundings can be based.

Accounting systems in the observed countries are developed differently, with double entry accounting implemented and analytical data kept in all the countries in order to allow for monitoring public spending not only in economic terms, but also by organization, and in most of the countries by programmes (projects and activities). Enhancement of the accounting system is the objective in all the countries, in order to obtain quality, timely, comprehensive and accurate information on public spending, achieved results and realized objectives, based on which managers in the public administration can make decisions on the budget, as well as activities and projects being implemented.

The accounting systems in the countries covered in this book show heterogeneity as far as use of the accounting basis is concerned, ranging from a cash basis, through different modifications of accrual accounting, to a full accounting basis use. However, the objective of all the countries is implementation of accrual based accounting and International/ European public sector accounting standards (IPSAS/EPSAS) in order to enhance the reporting systems.

The comparative analysis in this book shows that awareness of the importance of communicating information on public spending to the public is very high and that all the countries want to increase transparency, being aware that that is the basis for building trust in states and institutions, and trust is the basis for attracting investment and improving the business climate, without which achieving economic growth and development is impossible.

It is interesting to note that auditing systems have been well established in all the countries and that external audit, organized through state audit offices, has a long standing tradition. Establishment of the internal audit commenced about 15 years ago, somewhat earlier in Member States, and several years later in non-member countries. All the countries are working on improving the quality and achieving better functioning of the internal audit, whose role in improvement of business processes and management functions is more developed in Member States, which have been implementing this function for a longer time. The state of play with regard to establishment of the complete Public Internal Financial Control (PIFC) system, internal audit is part of which, is similar.

It is not at all simple to provide an overview of systems in different countries in a way in which they can be comparable and in which conclusions on the state of play and perspectives can be brought, and the authors and editors of this publication managed to achieve that, so before you is a unique piece of work showing how accounting, auditing and control systems in South Eastern European countries can be further developed.

This publication can also serve as the basis for designing projects for the use of technical assistance provided within the framework of the European Strategic and Investment Funds (ESI funds) for Member States, and within pre-accession funds (IPA) for candidate countries, whose objective is not only enhancement of the accounting, reporting and control environment, but also enhancement of the functioning and transparency of the public administration, as well as reduction of irregularities and the level of corruption.

Zagreb, Croatia

Ivana Maletić, M.Sc.
Croatian Member of the
European Parliament

Preface

This publication is the result of the cooperative work of authors from Bosnia and Herzegovina (represented by two entities: the Federation of Bosnia and Herzegovina and the Republic of Srpska), Croatia, Poland, Romania, Serbia, Slovenia, and the Former Yugoslav Republic of Macedonia. The authors and editors are all distinguished researchers and experts in the area of public sector accounting and auditing in their respective countries.

The underlying motivation for writing this volume is that to our knowledge there is no literature in English that provides comparative insights into public sector accounting, auditing and control systems in or among the selected South-Eastern European (SEE) countries. The hope is for this publication to extend the outreach to researchers and experts as well as to practitioners in South East Europe and thus expand the reach of the CIGAR (Comparative International Governmental Accounting Research) network.

The South-Eastern European countries encompassed by this publication have since the 1990s witnessed changes to their social and economic environment and have undergone a transition process that has also had an impact on their public sector accounting systems. These countries, regardless of having similar starting points, have followed their own paths with varying degrees of intensity and pace, and this publication shows the differences and similarities in the level of development they have achieved and in the current state of professional and legal regulation of their public sector accounting, auditing and control systems.

The role of public sector accounting, auditing and control is growing in the context of the New Public Management (NPM) concept of development, accountability and public finance sustainability. Public sector accounting, auditing and control has become a subject of great interest for the professional and scientific audience, but also a subject of general public interest as well. The area of accounting, auditing and control is under the significant influence of national authorities and is affected both by national characteristics and by the international environment that requires harmonisation with the international regulatory framework and standard-setting processes. Converging with these demands, requirements and expectations is no easy task. Therefore, this volume explores the extent to which the experiences of other states or international standard-setters and authorities have been applied and implemented in the process of developing public sector accounting, auditing and control systems in the selected SEE countries. In considering the challenges of future developments, this publication also takes into the account that the countries under study are either EU Member States or are candidate or potential candidate countries for accession to the EU. Thus, the selected countries have considered the application of an accrual accounting basis in public sector accounting systems, as well as the potential application of IPSAS/EPSAS.

The publication presents the case studies of seven SEE countries (four of them EU Member States) on the current practice of public sector accounting, auditing and control. It is structured to include this introduction, the main body which represents an overview of the selected countries (one country per chapter, so that there are eight chapters in total, since Bosnia and Herzegovina is represented by two entities), and a conclusion.

Contributions from each country—the main chapters of this book—are methodologically structured so that the contents are comparable and allow for the similarities and differences in the achieved degree of development to be clearly seen. In this way, the factors that have affected the paths taken and the degree of development achieved can also be identified. The major headings within each chapter are unified across all chapters and are organised as follows:

The territorial organisation, scope of the public sector and distribution of public revenues contains an overview of the organisation of the country and its territorial structure, the coverage of the public sector and the main features of public funding in the observed country.

The formulation and execution of central government and local and regional self-government budgets includes an overview of the regulatory and institutional framework of budget formulation (preparation), as well as the budget execution methodology. Data classification systems and budget execution variants, including the treasury subsystem, are presented under this heading.

Accounting and financial reporting presents the features of accounting and financial reporting. Emphasis is on the choice of the accounting basis/bases and on the measurement and evaluation rules that arise from the choice of the accounting basis. The features of financial reporting are also presented, with focus on the existence of a dual reporting system and the presentation of general purpose financial reporting features, and budget execution reporting.

The second and third sub-chapters provide a complete overview of the characteristics of the budget process, from budget planning through budget execution to budgetary accounting, with attention given to the links between these processes and corresponding documents.

Audit and other oversight (supervision) in the public sector presents the types and features of budget spending oversight. An overview is given of the regulatory, institutional and execution framework for state audit, budget oversight, internal audit and internal control in the public sector.

Each chapter ends with a sub-chapter titled *Challenges in the Further Development of Public Sector Accounting and Auditing*, commenting on the state of play, the potential need for improvement, and the notion of a future development path.

This volume might be of special value and use to the following groups: academics and students and other researchers in their efforts to conduct comparative research in this field; experts and practitioners (accountants, accounting and finance managers, state auditors, internal auditors, statisticians and other affiliated professions); decision-makers (managers), the Ministry of Finance, government practitioners, politicians; and national and international academic associations and professional bodies engaged in the development of accounting standards. This book is thus dedicated to all students, scholars, public servants and practitioners who share an interest and passion for public sector accounting and auditing and public sector financial management and the desire to make them work for the better governance of the public sector.

It is hoped that this publication will also be valuable to IPSASB and Task Force EPSAS, the European Commission—Eurostat, as a contribution to the literature in the sense that it provides an overview of the state of play and outlines further development paths of the public sector accounting, auditing and control systems of the selected countries. It also provides an overview of the obstacles and incentives for the application of international and/or European accounting standards for the public sector.

This publication also forms part of the initiative of several researchers (the principal investigator and several team members) working on Project no. 8509, "Accounting and Financial Reporting Reform as a Means of Strengthening the Development of Efficient Public Sector Financial Management in Croatia" which was awarded Croatian Science Foundation financing for 48 months (from August 2014 to August 2018). Six contributors to this book are members of the aforementioned project. The book is thus the result of the project and we would hereby like to thank the Croatian Science Foundation for co-financing the costs of preparing the book for publication.

The work on this publication includes the cooperation of 14 authors with long-term scientific research and teaching experience. We sincerely thank them for contributing to this publication with their valuable knowledge, for their cooperation with public servants and practitioners, and for their insights into public sector accounting, auditing and control practices in their home countries.

We also thank the reviewers, Ivana Maletić, M.Sc., Croatian Member of the European Parliament, and Professor Andreas Bergmann, ZHAW School of Management and Law (Switzerland), who contributed to the final quality of this publication by providing suggestions and comments and confirmed the relevance and justification of such a publication. Special thanks also go to Mr. Mark Davies, for his language revision.

We hereby also thank the editors of Palgrave Macmillan *Public Sector Financial Management* series whose book, titled *Public Sector Accounting and Auditing in Europe: The Challenge of Harmonization*, has definitely inspired us to commence the work on this edition, and the publisher Palgrave Macmillan who recognised the importance of the edition and hence assured that the book is also publicly available in hard copy, as well as all others who have contributed to this publication.

We hope that readers will enjoy this book and will find it a useful means to enrich their knowledge of public sector accounting, auditing and control in SEE countries.

Zagreb, Croatia

Vesna Vašiček
Gorana Roje

Contents

Notes on Contributors

Atanasko Atanasovski is an Associate Professor in Accounting at the Faculty of Economics, Ss. Cyril and Methodius University in Skopje. His research focuses on accounting quality, financial reporting regulation in emerging countries, international financial reporting standards, corporate disclosure and transparency, integrated reporting, corporate governance and internal controls. His academic and research work has been presented at various international conferences and published in scientific journals. He is ACCA affiliate.

Bobana Čegar is the economist at International Monetary Fund in Bosnia and Herzegovina. She is also a senior assistant at the Faculty of Economics, University of Banja Luka (The Republic of Srpska, Bosnia and Herzegovina). She has more than five years of teaching experience in accounting. Currently, she is pursuing her Ph.D. studies at the University of Belgrade, Faculty of Economics and has authored or co-authored papers on the topic of "Accounting and Public Sector".

Biljana Josipović Rodić is currently completing her doctoral studies in the area of public sector accounting at the Faculty of Economics, University of Belgrade. She holds a Certificate for professional accountants, from Serbian Association of Accountants and Auditors. She participated in various domestic conferences and symposiums and is also the author of several papers in the field of accounting and financial reporting in the public sector. Currently, she works in "Telekom Serbia" as an associate fellow for controlling.

Tatjana Jovanović is an Assistant Professor in economics of the public sector at the Faculty of Administration, University of Ljubljana, Slovenia. She has more than 10 years of teaching experience in the field of taxation and accounting. Her research focuses on taxation, public sector accounting and public sector performance management. Her research work is presented at several international conferences and she is the author and co-author of several research papers in scientific and professional journals.

Jelena Jurić is a teaching assistant at the Faculty of Economics, University of Mostar, the Federation of Bosnia and Herzegovina, Bosnia and Herzegovina. She is currently enrolled in doctoral studies at the Faculty of Economics, University of Mostar. She participated in various Erasmus+mobilities, various projects, conferences, seminars and workshops and is the author and the co-author of numerous research papers. Her research focuses on public sector accounting and finance, and cost management.

Magdalena Kowalczyk holds an adjunct position in the Department of Accounting at the Faculty of Management at Poznan University of Economics and Business, and is a Senior Lecturer at The President Stanislaw Wojciechowski Higher Vocational State School in Kalisz, Poland. Her current research interests are in the field of public sector accounting, New Public Management and Corporate Social Responsibility in public sector. She has 17 years of teaching experience in the field of accounting and is the author of several papers in the area of public sector accounting.

Maja Letica is an Assistant Professor in Management and Accounting Department at the Faculty of Economics, University of Mostar, The Federation of Bosnia and Herzegovina, Bosnia and Herzegovina. She has over 10 years of teaching experience in the field of accounting and management. Her research focuses on managerial accounting and performance management in private and public sector and her work has been presented at various international conferences and published in scientific journals.

Zoran Minovski is a Full Professor of accounting at the Faculty of Economics, Ss. Cyril and Methodius University in Skopje, The Former Yugoslav Republic of Macedonia. His research is in accounting with a particular focus on public sector accounting and accounting for non-profit organizations, budget accounting and accounting of budget users, fund accounting, financial accounting and reporting in accordance with IPSAS, financial reporting under the SNA, financial reporting by system of GFS and management accounting. His work was presented at international conferences and published in scientific journals.

Jelena Poljašević is an Associate Professor at the Faculty of Economics, University of Banja Luka, The Republic of Srpska, Bosnia and Herzegovina. She is the chair of master study program titled Finance, accounting and auditing in the public sector. Her teaching and research field encompasses financial reporting, financial statement consolidation, public sector reporting and auditing, international reporting standards settings for private and public sector and risk assessment. Jelena Poljašević is the author of many papers and the co-author of several books on public sector accounting, accounting basis of financial reporting, auditing and financial statements analysis.

Gorana Roje is a Head of Division at the Ministry of State Assets, Croatia. She is currently pursuing her doctoral studies, with a focus on the role of accounting information in public sector assets management. Her research is focused on international and comparative public sector accounting and financial reporting, international public sector accounting standards setting, and public sector asset management. She was a research assistant at the Institute of Economics Zagreb. Her work has been presented at various international conferences and published in scientific journals.

Duško Šnjegota is a Full Professor at the Department of Accounting and Business Finance, at the University in Banja Luka, Faculty of Economics. With over eighty scientific and professional papers he participated in the work of recognized scientific and research organizations professional meetings, at home and abroad. In his career he held the position of the Assistant Minister of Finance in the Department of Accounting and Auditing (Government of Republic of Srpska), and the position of Auditor General in Supreme Office for the Republic of Srpska Public Sector Auditing.

Adriana Tiron-Tudor is a Full Professor in Accounting at the Faculty of Economic Studies and Business Administration, Babes-Bolyai University, Cluj-Napoca, Romania. She has a vast teaching experience in the field of accounting and auditing. Her research focuses on public sector accounting financial management and auditing, accounting and financial reporting, international accounting standards, accounting profession evolution, ethics and education. She was a member of IPSASB for the period 2012–2017, and she continues to be a member of PSC at Accountancy Europe, (former FEE) and Romanian EPSAS Task force.

Davor Vašiček is a Full Professor in Accounting at the Faculty of Economics and Business, University of Rijeka, Croatia. He has well over 20 years of managerial and business advising experience, and more than 10 years of teaching experience in the field of accounting. His research focuses on financial and managerial accounting for public sector entities and non-profit organisations. His work has been presented at many international conferences and published in various scientific journals. He currently holds the position of Vice-Rector for Financial Management at the University of Rijeka.

Vesna Vašiček is a Full Professor in Accounting at the Faculty of Economics and Business, University of Zagreb, Croatia. She has more than 30 years of teaching experience in the field of accounting. Her research focuses on accounting for non-profit organisations and public sector (budgetary) accounting and financial reporting, international public sector accounting standards setting, managerial accounting and public sector performance management. In her career she held the position of Chief Treasurer (MoF, Croatia) and the position of a Vice-Rector for Financial Management at the University of Zagreb.

List of Tables

CHAPTER 1

Public Sector Accounting, Auditing and Control in Croatia

Vesna Vašiček and Davor Vašiček

1.1 Territorial Organisation, Scope of the Public Sector and Distribution of Public Revenues

1.1.1 Territorial Organisation

The Republic of Croatia is a South Eastern European country which gained independence and international recognition after separating from former Yugoslavia in the last decade of the twentieth-century. Since 1 July 2013, Croatia has been a full member of the European Union.

According to the 2011 population census, the Republic of Croatia has a population of 4,264,889, living in 6756 cities or towns and municipalities. It has a total surface area of 88,073 km^2, out of which 56,594 km^2 are on land, while territorial and internal waters cover 31,479 km^2. This

V. Vašiček (✉)
Faculty of Economics and Business,
University of Zagreb, Zagreb, Croatia
e-mail: vvasicek@efzg.hr

D. Vašiček
Faculty of Economics and Business,
University of Rijeka, Rijeka, Croatia

V. Vašiček and G. Roje (eds.), *Public Sector Accounting, Auditing and Control in South Eastern Europe*, Public Sector Financial Management, https://doi.org/10.1007/978-3-030-03353-8_1

makes Croatia one of the more sparsely populated European countries, with an average of 75.8 inhabitants per km^2. Croatia's large territorial waters are due to the fact that the country has more than 6200 kilometres of coastline, including more than 1200 islands. In addition, its oddly shaped territory is framed by no less than 2370 km of land borders, which is also uncommon for such a relatively small country (Central Bureau of Statistics 2014: 44, 111).

One of the most important events for Croatia in the process of gaining independence was the adoption of the Constitution of the Republic of Croatia, passed in the Parliament on 12 December 1990. This constitutional act is the basis of Croatian territorial organisation and has been in effect ever since. In 1992, Croatia adopted the Act on the Areas of Counties, Cities and Municipalities in the Republic of Croatia[1] (Official Gazette of the Republic of Croatia, 86/2006), and corrections and amendments for the period 2008–2015,[2] based on which the organisational structure was organised at two levels: the central level (central government) and levels of local and regional self-government.

According to the aforementioned Act on the Areas of Counties, Cities and Municipalities in the Republic of Croatia, the Republic of Croatia is divided into 20 counties and the City of Zagreb which has the status of both a county and a city. There is also a level of local government consisting of 556 units: 128 cities/towns and 428 municipalities. The Act on Local and Regional Self-Government (Official Gazette of the Republic of Croatia, 19/2013) determines the scope and structure of local and regional self-governments, their bodies, control over their acts and work, and other important issues.

Local governments, cities and municipalities perform tasks related to: improving settlements and housing, physical and urban planning, utility services, child care, social welfare, primary healthcare, preschool and primary education, culture, physical education and sport, consumer protection, protection and improvement of the natural environment, fire

[1] All laws, regulations, decrees, appointments and official decisions passed in the Parliament or adopted by the Government are published in Croatian language and are released in the public domain by the eponymous public company, titled Narodne novine which is the official gazette (or newspaper of public record) of the Republic of Croatia, available at www.nn.hr.

[2] Official Gazette of the Republic of Croatia, 125/2006, 16/2007, 46/2010, 145/2010, 37/2013, 44/2013, 45/2013, 110/2015.

and civil protection, transport on their territory, and other tasks in line with relevant acts. In addition, large cities have the obligation to maintain public roads, to issue construction and location permits, along with other documents related to construction, the implementation of physical planning documents, and other activities in line with relevant acts.

Units of regional self-government and counties perform tasks of regional importance and, by aiming for balanced development, attempt to align the interests of counties with the interests of the municipalities and cities/towns that belong to them. These tasks relate in particular to education, healthcare, physical and urban planning, economic development, transport and transport infrastructure, the maintenance of public roads, the planning and development of educational, health, social and cultural institution networks, the issuance of construction and location permits, along with other documents concerning construction, the implementation of spatial planning documents for county areas outside large towns, and other activities in line with relevant legislation.

1.1.2 Central, Local and Regional Government Financing

The territorial and administrative autonomy of local and regional self-government units is accompanied by a level of financial independence as well. The Act on the Financing of Local and Regional Self-Government Units (Official Gazette of the Republic of Croatia, 117/1993, 69/1997, 33/2000, 73/2000, 127/2000, 59/2001, 107/2001, 117/2001, 150/2002, 147/2003, 132/2006, 73/2008, 25/2012, 147/2014, 100/2015) regulates the financial issues of the governmental activities of counties, municipalities and cities/towns (hereinafter: local government units). This act defines the financial relations between central government and local government units regarding the distribution of joint tax revenues and the rights of local units related to the collection of tax and non-tax revenues within their jurisdiction.

The Croatian system of public finance is highly centralised. Most public needs are financed through the state budget, which in turn constitutes the vast majority of total public expenditure. For example, according to data on the execution of state and local unit budgets in 2015, local government units accounted for only 16.1% of total budgetary spending, while the central government spent the remaining 83.9% (Ministry of Finance 2017).

The financing of local government units has developed in two phases: the first phase, starting in 1992 and lasting until 2001, and the second phase from 2001 until today. During the first phase, local government units had a specific position as a consequence of the armed conflict which took place then. This meant that certain local units were granted the status of Areas of Special State Concern (Official Gazette of the Republic of Croatia, 86/2008, 57/2011, 51/2013, 148/2013, 76/2014, 147/2014, 18/2015), which brought privileges in the distribution of funds and a specifically developed system of state support.

Decentralisation began in early 2001, following an analysis of the fiscal capacity of municipalities, cities/towns and counties with regard to primary and secondary education, healthcare and social welfare institutions, and network funding. It was decided to decentralise the public services of primary and secondary education, healthcare, social welfare and firefighting, with the transfer of jurisdiction, powers and responsibilities from central government to the level of counties, the City of Zagreb and a number of other cities (larger towns and county centres). This decentralisation process is prescribed by special acts, as well as in annual regulations of the government of the Republic of Croatia, which regulate the minimum standards for the financing of decentralised services.

In order to secure funds for the newly acquired expenditures of these decentralised functions, an additional portion of income tax was transferred to local units. The portion of income tax intended for local units has been gradually increased since 2001. Furthermore, an equalisation fund was established for those units of local government which were regarded as not being able to cover the expenditures of these decentralised functions, even with the added portion of tax incomes. These units have had the right for the difference to be covered by the equalisation fund which forms part of the state budget. Therefore, responsibility for the execution of decentralised functions has been and still is divided between central and local levels.

1.1.3 Scope of the Public Sector

In order to adequately track public finances and the expenditure of the central state and units of regional and local government, appropriate statistics and accounting systems had to be put in place. The scope of the public sector in the Republic of Croatia is primarily prescribed by the Budget Act (Official Gazette of the Republic of Croatia, 87/2008, 136/2012, 15/2015). According to this Act, the public sector consists of the central state budget, the budgets of local and regional self-government units and extra-budgetary users of local and regional self-government units. The central budget is the state budget that includes both budgetary and extra-budgetary users of the state budget, while the budgets of local and regional self-government units encompass only budget users. Budget users are state bodies and institutions, minority self-government councils and local self-government units whose personnel and material expenditure is secured in the budget. Extra-budgetary users are extra-budgetary funds, companies and other legal persons in which the state, local government units, or both hold enough shares to have managerial rights. These definitions, however, did not allow for a correct and unambiguous assessment to establish which legal entities are or are not budgetary users, which is essential to determine the scope of the public sector for state statistical needs. This was solved with the introduction of the Register of Budgetary Users and Extra-budgetary Users which unambiguously and consistently classified all budgetary users and extra-budgetary users of the state budget and budgetary users and extra-budgetary users of the budgets of local and regional government units. Identification of state budget and local and regional self-government budgetary users, as well as extra-budgetary users, lies under the jurisdiction of the Ministry of Finance, along with the criteria of keeping the registry of budgetary users, prescribed annually by the Ordinance on Defining Budgetary and Extra-budgetary Users of the State Budget, Budgetary and Extra-budgetary Users of the Budget of Local and Regional Government Units and the Means of Conducting the Registry of Budgetary and Extra-budgetary Users (Official Gazette of the Republic of Croatia, 128/2009, 142/2014).

The methodological framework used in setting the criteria for the introduction of the registry was the one defined in GFS 2001 and ESA 95, with ESA 2010 being introduced in 2014. According to these criteria, budgetary users of the state budget are:

1. Those founded by the Republic of Croatia;
2. Those who acquire revenues from the state budget and/or by public authority, the law or other legislation, where that income is more than 50% of the users' total income revenues;
3. Those who are listed in the registry (Ordinance on Defining Budgetary and Extra-budgetary Users of the State Budget, Budgetary and Extra-budgetary Users of the Budget of Local and Regional Government Units and the Means of Conducting the Registry of Budgetary and Extra-budgetary Users).

Budgetary users of the state budget are ministries, other state administration bodies (i.e. agencies, regulatory bodies) and institutions within the systems of higher education (universities), healthcare (public hospitals), social welfare and culture (in the part where they are state budget users).

Basic groups of local and regional self-government budget users are institutions related to decentralised public functions (elementary and secondary schools, foster-care facilities, student accommodation, social service centres, public fire brigades, health institutions, cultural institutions (culture centres, libraries, museums), day-care centres and other institutions (city-borough councils, local committees, minority self-government council representatives).[3]

The status of extra-budgetary users of state and local and regional self-government budgets is granted to:

1. units in which the Republic of Croatia and/or local and regional self-government units have a decisive management role;
2. units funded by mandatory insurance contributions and/or earmarked revenues and receipts;
3. units listed in the registry (Ordinance on Defining Budgetary and Extra-budgetary Users of the State Budget, Budgetary and Extra-budgetary Users of the Budget of Local and Regional Government Units and the Means of Conducting the Registry of Budgetary and Extra-budgetary Users).

Budgetary users listed in the registry are obliged to abide by a unified legal framework based on the Budget Act and accompanying laws, whereby both state and local budget users apply the same regulation.

[3]Registry of Budgetary and Extra-budgetary Users - Registar proračunskih i izvanproračunskih korisnika, Narodne novine 68/2015.

The Registry of Budgetary and Extra-budgetary Users listed 727 state budget and 2935 local budget users in 2015. The data from the registry are published annualy in the Official Gazzete of the Republic of Croatia and are available to the public on the website of the Ministry of Finance. The obligation of updating and maintaining the registry has been entrusted to the Financial Agency (FINA) by the Ministry of Finance.

The aformentioned Official Gazzete publishes:

- the list of budget users of the local and regional self-government budget;
- lists of budget users of the state budget;
- lists of extra-budgetary users of the local and regional self-government budget;
- lists of extra-budgetary users of the state budget.

1.2 Formulation and Execution of Central Government and Local and Regional Self-Government Budgets

In defining the budget and budgetary relations in Croatia, the starting points are determined by the Budget Act (Official Gazette of the Republic of Croatia, 87/2008) and the Amendments to the Budget Act (Official Gazette of the Republic of Croatia, 136/2012, 15/2015). The budget processes relate to budget formulation, adoption, budget execution and supervision of the budget and are prescribed for the central budget and the budgets of local and regional government (hereinafter: local government), with differences appearing in the application of the budget, as a consequence of differences in the level of public authorities and the size and structure of their budget. Thus, the Budget Act is applied equally to both the state budget and the budgets of local government, as well as to their budgetary and extra-budgetary users. The system is unified and prescribes the application of the same rules for all users. Therefore, it does not include the specifics of individual sectors (for example, education, healthcare, or the judiciary) nor does it allow specific exemptions.

1.2.1 Formulation of the Central Government and Local Government Budgets

The budget is the most important financial instrument of central and local government. Budget item (revenues, receipts, expenses and expenditures) forecasts have the function of executing the priorities, objectives and tasks of central and local governments and their bodies.

At the level of general government, (sub) types of budget documents differ depending on the level of government that prepares and approves the budget. They include:

- The state budget adopted by the Croatian Parliament;
- The budgets of local and regional self-government units adopted by county assemblies and city/town councils, as well as by representatives of local authorities: the county budget and the city and municipal budget;
- The financial plans of budget and extra-budgetary users (central or local budgets), which form an integral part of the budgets from which they are financed.

The formal structure of the budget at all levels is based on the same legislation and implementing documents, with the mentioned budget documents being comparable and suitable for consolidation. In accordance with the legal obligation, the Ministry of Finance consolidates the budgets of local government and publishes data on the general (consolidated) budget of the Republic of Croatia (comprising both the budgets of central government and local government).

In the preparation and acceptance of the budget, central government and local government have a legal obligation to apply budgetary principles, classifications, programming and three-year strategic planning, as well as to ensure that the budget is publicly announced.

The budget is accepted on the basis of a fiscal year, which in Croatia corresponds to the calendar year that begins on 1 January and ends on 31 December. But the budget is planned for a three-year period. The budget is adopted and executed in compliance with the principles of budgetary unity and accuracy, annuality, equilibrium, unit of account, universality, specification, sound financial management and transparency (the Budget Act).

The principle of transparency implies that all important budget information must be available to the general public and presented in an understandable and clear manner. There is a legal obligation to publicly announce the budgets of central government and local government, as well as to publicly announce reports on the execution of the budget.

Budget classifications determined in the Budget Act and the Ordinance on the Budget Classifications (Official Gazette of the Republic of Croatia, 6/2010, 120/2013) are used as a framework for systematic bookkeeping, the reporting and monitoring of revenues, receipts, expenses and expenditures of the responsible authority, as well as the objectives, purpose, type, location and source of funding. The Regulations prescribe the names of each classification, attribute numeric codes and determine how these interconnect. The defined classifications include: organisational classification, programme classification, functional classification, economic classification, classification by location, and classification by sources of funding.

Establishing a system of budget classification is extremely important in consolidating the data used for monitoring public finances and the expenditures of general government. A standardised approach to processing and presenting data at all levels of government contributes to the comparability of data, credibility and transparency, as well as better understanding by users.

The budget consists of a general and a special part that show budget spending by organisational, programme and economic classification and by source of funding.

A new budgetary system in the Republic of Croatia introduced programme planning (the Budget Act 2003) and strategic planning (the Budget Act 2008), which represented an innovative approach to budget preparation. Budget documents, based on programmes, should reflect policies and the priorities of budget users, which form part of content-rounded programmes, activities and projects, and develop a functional monitoring system for the evaluation of achievement, based on objective indicators. Despite the rather formal application of programme planning and the limitations of, and obstacles to, its implementation, there has been a series of improvements facilitating and creating conditions for integrated budget planning, combining budget strategic planning, a programme budget and performance indicators. In short, the model of the programme budget used in Croatia was upgraded and supplemented with three-year strategic planning, which, in fact, meant an effect-based budget.

The strategic priorities and policy objectives of central government and local government should have a direct bearing on the allocation of budgetary funds.

1.2.2 Budget Execution and Budget Execution Reporting

The execution of the budget during the year relates to continuous revenue collection and the execution of expenses that are established in the budget. Budget expenditures can be used for specific purposes determined by the budget.

One possible form of organising public revenue and expenditure management is the Treasury. In the Republic of Croatia, the State Treasury was established as part of the Ministry of Finance, and, depending on the development of local government units and their willingness to accept the operating system of the Treasury, local treasuries were established. The State Treasury works on the principle of a single and unique cash account, through which all transactions of the state budget are executed. The Treasury is a "complex system of administration of activities, which are realised through the collection and spending of state (public) money and conducted through the Treasury Single Account. The Treasury is often recognised as a centralised model of execution of the budget" (Vašiček 2002:

136). "The basic functions of the Croatian State Treasury are: budget preparation, budget execution, cash management, budget implementation, financial planning and forecasting, management of government bank accounts, revenue management, government reporting, budget accounting and public debt management" (Ministry of Finance 2007: 17).

Execution of the budget within the treasury system has implications for the use of budget execution reports and accounting records. The Treasury focuses on cash flows and uses cash basis accounting to control the execution of the budget.

The reporting system is separated into two sets of reports: the semi-annual and annual budget execution reports, as prescribed in the Budget Act and the Ordinance on Semi-annual and Annual Budget Execution Reports (Official Gazette of the Republic of Croatia, 120/2013) and financial reports pursuant to the Ordinance on Financial Reporting in Budget Accounting (Official Gazette of the Republic of Croatia, 3/2015, 93/2015, 135/2015).

Budget execution reports are produced to make the government accountable for the execution of the budget and are subject to approval by Parliament.

The Budget Act prescribes that the state budget and local government budgets need to draft an annual and semi-annual budget execution report. Semi-annual and annual budget execution reports need to contain the following:

- general section of the budget consisting of revenues and expenditures at the level of the section of economic classification;
- special section of the budget divided by organisational and programme classification and by level of section of economic classification;
- report on loans borrowed in domestic and foreign currency and capital markets;
- report on the use of budgetary reserves;
- report on issued state guarantees and expenditures pursuant to state guarantees;
- explanation of macroeconomic indicators;
- explanation of generated revenues and receipts, expenditures and outlays;
- general budget deficit.

Semi-annual and annual budget execution reports of extra-budgetary users need to contain the following:

- general section of the financial plan containing the Revenue and Expenditure Account and the Financing Account at the level of the section of economic classification;
- special section of the financial plan by organisational and programme classification and the level of the section of economic classification; and
- explanation of generated revenues and receipts, expenses and expenditures.

The annual budget execution reports must also include a report on the implementation of the public debt management strategy (the Budget Act).

The Ordinance on Semi-annual and Annual Budget Execution Reporting prescribes the content of the reports. These reports are closely related to the execution of the budget and their structure follows the content and structure of the budget itself. It is clear that the budget planning shown on a cash basis and reports on budget execution must follow the same budget basis. Due to the fact that the accounting basis has changed and that expenses began to be recognised on an accrual basis, it was necessary to adjust financial reporting on account of the differences in the bases between budgeting and accounting. In conditions of using a different basis in budgeting and accounting, semi-annual and annual budget execution reports need to be shown on a budgetary basis, with financial statements emphasising the differences in the data which occurred due to the application of different bases.

The application in practice of the aforementioned dual system (financial statements and budget execution reports) regarding the presented normative frameworks adversely affects comparisons of budgetary information and accounting information on budget execution. The current practice of reporting does not put sufficient emphasis on the differences arising from the application of a different basis, which results in a certain lack of understanding and lack of transparency in reporting. These problems are also addressed in the findings of the State Audit Office, whose Annual Report on the execution of the State Budget of the Republic of Croatian for 2014 shows that the assessment of general government deficit, based on different accounting bases used by budgetary and extra-budgetary users, is not reliable (State Audit Office 2015: 3).

1.3 Accounting and Financial Reporting

1.3.1 Budgetary Accounting

According to the Budget Act, Title IX, budgetary accounting is employed to govern business records, accounting documents and data processing, the content of accounts in charts of accounts, the recognition of revenues, receipts, expenses and expenditures, the estimation of balance sheet items, value adjustment, financial reporting and other issues pertaining to budgetary accounting (the Budget Act). The budget and the budgetary users whose signature is listed in the Register of Budgetary and Extra-budgetary Users are obliged to apply budgetary accounting and financial reporting. Extra-budgetary users are obliged to apply financial reporting in compliance with budgetary accounting.

Budgetary accounting is conducted based on the principle of double-entry bookkeeping and according to the schedule of accounts in the chart of accounts, which means that the content of accounts and the rules for recording transactions are prescribed. The Budget Act states that budgetary accounting should be based upon generally accepted accounting principles: accuracy, verity, reliability and individual presentation of business events, and on International Public Sector Accounting Standards. However, budgetary accounting is not based on the direct application of International Public Sector Accounting Standards. The Ordinance on Budgetary Accounting and the Chart of Accounts (Official Gazette of the Republic of Croatia, 124/2014, 115/2015, 87/2016) established the chart of accounts, rules of measurement and evaluation, as well as rules for recording transactions and events, which make the budget accounting framework unified and uniformly defined for all reporting entities.

Budgetary accounting is based on the modified accrual basis, with the specificity of the financial statement elements of recognition and measurement.

Regulations define an asset as a resource controlled by the budget as a result of past events, and from which benefits of business activity are expected (Ordinance on Budgetary Accounting and the Chart of Accounts).

Assets are initially recognised in the case of purchase, construction, or finance lease at cost of purchase, or in the case of free-of-charge receipts (grants) by estimated value.

During the acquisition of fixed assets, capitalisation of the acquisition cost is not applied. Rather, acquisition costs are fully recognised as expenses of the reporting period in which they occur. At the same time, the value of fixed assets is recognised directly in the amount of the acquisition value and in favour of own resources.[4]

According to the above-mentioned regulation, the depreciation of fixed assets is to be determined and reported individually, on a timeline basis and with the application of prescribed, average, annual rate adjustment (reduction) values. The accumulated depreciation and impairment of assets directly debits the balance sheet item titled own resources to reflect the new lower value of the assets. The basis for the write-off of fixed assets is their initial or revealed acquisition cost (purchase value or estimated value).

Changes in the value (revaluation) and/or in the volume of assets and liabilities, as well as events that affect assets and that are not the result of actions or transactions, nor are directly affected by elements of success, are published in a special report (Report on Changes in the Value and Volume of Assets and Liabilities). Changes in value (revaluation) are usually the result of inflation or changes in the market value of the assets. Changes in volume are usually the result of an extraordinary initial recognition and derecognition of assets and due to other changes in the quantity and quality of the already recognised assets.

Liabilities are outstanding liabilities of the budget and budgetary users, which arise from past events, and an outflow of resources is expected for their settlement. Liabilities are classified by purpose and maturity. According to maturity, liabilities can be classified as short- or long-term liabilities.

Disclosure of information on the status, structure and changes of obligations are unified for all budgetary users, as prescribed by the Ordinance on Financial Reporting in Budgetary Accounting (Official Gazette of the Republic of Croatia, 3/2015, 93/2015, 135/2015) and in the manner of the Balance Sheet and special reports on obligations (Report on Liabilities). Additionally, changes in the value and volume of liabilities are published in a special report (Report on Changes in the Value and Volume of Assets and Liabilities).

[4]The own resources item is the residual interest in the assets of the reporting entity after deducting all its liabilities.

Revenues, regardless of their character, are defined as an increase in economic benefits during the reporting period, solely in the form of inflows of cash and cash equivalents. This undoubtedly indicates that the recognition of revenues deviates from accrual basis use, i.e. it maintains the use of the cash basis.

This refers mainly to revenues from non-exchange transactions which include tax revenues, mandatory insurance contributions, aid transfers, and revenues from charges and fees.

Revenues from exchange transactions, such as revenues from sales of products and goods or provided services, as well as revenues from the sale of assets, from the time of delivery until the time they are collected, are recognised as an asset (in the form of a receivable) and deferred revenue. Only at the collection of the recognised receivable are the conditions for the recognition of these revenues met in the total income for the reporting period.

The economic benefits which flow to budget users in the form of grants (received non-financial assets) from general government entities, increases in the value of non-financial assets which were caused by revaluation, and the reduction of commitments due to the write-off are not recognised as revenues, but are directly recognised as own resources. The economic benefits which flow to budget users in the form of grants (received non-financial assets) from entities outside general government are recognised as revenues from donations at the estimated value, while in the meantime recognising the expenses as formed from the purchase of these non-financial assets. The effect of these transactions on the financial result is therefore neutral.

Expenses are defined as decreases in economic benefits in the form of a reduction of assets or increase in liabilities. Expenses are fundamentally classified as operating expenses (i.e. current expenditures) and expenses for the acquisition of non-financial assets (i.e. capital expenditures).

The application of a modified accrual basis in the recognition of expenditure in practice means:

- operating expenses are recognised when they occur (on the basis of the transaction in the reporting period to which they relate, regardless of the payment);
- the expense for acquiring non-financial fixed assets is not capitalised. Instead, they are presented as expenses in their full amount within the reporting period in which the acquisition was executed. This

means that asset depreciation is not systematically presented as a depreciation expense. However, the assets are monitored through balance sheets and corrected through source of ownership during the prescribed period of use. Related to this, donations of non-financial assets are also not recognised as expenses, but also directly burden own resources;
- the expenses of short-term non-financial assets and inventories which are supplied to perform regular activities are recognised directly and in full at the time of purchase, regardless of actual consumption. Expenses are recognised on the basis of actual consumption exclusively in the health, trade and manufacturing sectors;
- borrowing costs are not capitalised and are fully recognised as an expense in the period in which they occur;
- unrealised losses (expenses) arising from changes in the market (fair) value of financial assets, foreign exchange gains and similar situations are not recognised as expenses, but rather as equity, or as a deferred expense;
- the costs of long-term provisions are also not recognised as an expense.

Disclosure of information on the amount and structure of recognised and deferred revenue and expenses is to be carried out uniformly for all budget users, in the manner prescribed by the Ordinance on Financial Reporting regarding the Reports on Revenues, Expenses, Receipts and Expenditures.

The specificity of the Croatian accounting system is the inclusion of financial receipts and expenditures which are not characterised as revenues or expenses in the income statement. These are receipts and expenditures related to financial assets and borrowing. This special feature is the result of efforts to enable the integrated accounting system to simultaneously use both a cash and accrual accounting basis. This approach allows for the dual role of accounting to be achieved: accounting for financial reporting and reporting on budget execution which is mostly carried out on a cash basis.

Receipts from financial assets and borrowing include: received repayment (returns) on equity loans, receipts from issued securities, receipts from the sale of stocks and shares in equity, borrowings and loans and receipts from the sale of securities in the portfolio.

Acquisition of financial assets and repayment of loans include outlays for: outstanding loans, investments in securities, shares and other equity, principal repayment of borrowings and loans and the repayment of principal on securities issued.

Own resources are remaining assets after deducting all liabilities, which include:

- own resources from the budget and other sources;
- operating results (classified according to the formation of the three categories, which are surplus/deficit of income of business, surplus/deficit of income of non-financial assets, surplus/deficit of revenue from financing);
- accrued business revenues;
- accrued revenues from sales of non-financial assets.

Accrued revenues are recorded on an accrual basis in the reporting period and express the value of cash flows that will follow the collection of receivables on those grounds. After the payment of related receivables in adequate amounts, they are recognised as revenues of the reporting period, as already described.

Establishing the financial result for the year is done in a way that revenues and expenses and receipts and expenditures match with respect to their character, and intermediate results are defined in relation to revenues and expenses from operations, revenues and expenses from non-financial assets (investment activity), and receipts and expenditures from financial assets (financing).

The determined result, defined as the difference between revenues and expenses and receipts and expenditures, is transferred as the structured financial results for the year to the balance sheet position corresponding to the same results for previous periods. The cumulative financial result is then determined, ending with the reporting period.

A positive result (surplus of revenues/receipts) represents the financial potential for business in the next period, while negative results (lack of revenues/receipts) represent the obligation for coverage in future periods.

1.3.2 Financial Reporting

Financial reporting is prescribed as mandatory, with the Ordinance on Financial Reporting in Budgetary Accounting prescribing the form and content of financial reports, the periods covered by the reports, as well as liabilities and deadlines for their submission. The mentioned legislation defines a universal analytical financial reporting framework. The prescribed form and content of financial reports enable the consolidation of financial reports, with the use of uniform accounting policies for all similar transactions and events.

Financial reports are drafted on the following forms:

- Balance Sheet—Form BIL;
- Report on revenues, expenses, receipts and expenditures—Form PR-RAS;
- Report on expenditure according to functional classification—Form RAS-FUNKCIJSKI;
- Report of changes in the value and volume of assets and liabilities—Form P-VRIO;
- Report on liabilities—Form OBVEZE.

An analysis of the content and structure of these reports shows that, with the *balance sheet* as the fundamental financial statement of financial position, two additional reports are drawn up, containing elements of the balance recorded as specific requirements: Reports on Liabilities, and Reports of Changes in the Value and Volume of Assets and Liabilities.

The specifics of recognising liabilities are evident on the balance sheet, where liabilities are classified according to the sources of the liabilities, rather than the usual criteria of the maturity date. Monitoring of the maturity of liabilities is conducted by a special report—*Report on Liabilities*, in which the liabilities are listed by maturity dates, in order to detect matured and unpaid obligations.

The Report of Changes in the Value and Volume of Assets and Liabilities is drawn up to monitor changes in the assets and liabilities that have no impact on the revenues, expenses, receipts and expenditures of the reporting period and are not accompanied by cash flows, but are still reflected in the value of assets and liabilities.

The *Report on Expenditure According to Functional Classification* presents expenditures through the functional classification according to the Ordinance on Budgetary Classifications. The *Report on Revenues and Expenses, Receipts and Expenditures* presents all types of revenues and expenses, both from operations and transactions in non-financial assets (revenues from the sale of non-financial assets, expenditure for the purchase of non-financial assets) and receipts and expenditures from transactions of financial assets and liabilities (receipts from financial assets and borrowing and expenditures for financial assets and repayment of loans).

The Report on Revenues and Expenses, Receipts and Expenditures combines the recognition of revenues and expenses on both an accrual and cash basis.

1.4 Audit and Other Oversight (Supervision) in the Public Sector

Oversight of the budget and budget entities in Croatia is organised in the following forms: state audit, budgetary oversight, internal audit and *internal control systems* (financial management and control).

Implementation of oversight puts emphasis on monitoring the execution of the budget in relation to the planned amount, as stated in the budget planning process. Ministers are responsible for the internal oversight of transactions of revenues/receipts and expenses/expenditures of ministries and budgetary users who are under their jurisdiction and the Ministry of Finance is responsible, in addition to the above, for internal oversight of borrowings.

Oversight of the execution of the budget is based on the accounting data presented in the form of financial statements, whose content is legally prescribed. The obligation and presentation of financial statements is a form of oversight and is based on accounting procedures and accounting data.

Oversight of the execution of the budget and the audit of the budget represent the end of the budget cycle. The results of the oversight and audit of the budget ensure the reliability of data on budget execution and provide valuable data for corrective actions.

1.4.1 State Audit

State audit is a retrospective and external supervision of budgetary users in Croatia, conducted by the State Audit Office. The State Audit Office was established by the State Audit Office Act (Official Gazette of the Republic of Croatia, 80/2011) and for its work, it reports to the Croatian Parliament.

> For the purposes of this Act, audit shall mean the examination of documents, papers, reports, internal control systems and internal audit, accounting and financial procedures and other records to verify that financial reports present a true and fair financial position and results of financial activities in

> line with the accepted accounting standards and principles. The audit shall also mean a procedure of examination of financial transactions in terms of legal utilisation of funds. The audit shall also include an assessment of the economy and efficiency of operations, as well as an assessment of how effectively the general objectives or the objectives of individual financial transactions, programmes and projects are being met. (State Audit Office Act)

Audits are carried out in accordance with procedures laid down by the framework of the International Organisation of Supreme Audit Institutions (INTOSAI). This framework consists of documents adopted by the Congress of the International Organisation of Supreme Audit Institutions, with the aim of regulating the professional standards of Supreme Audit Institutions.

According to the auditing standards of INTOSAI, there are two types of audits: a regularity or financial audit, and a performance audit. The review process is determined by the auditing standards, and after completion of the audit, auditors should give their opinion. The auditors' opinion describes all the revised business events, according to the facts established by the audit and it gives orders, recommendations and opinions aimed at removing illegalities and irregularities and improving operations. An audit opinion on the financial statements and operations of the audited entity may be an unmodified opinion or a modified opinion. The latter may be a qualified opinion, an adverse opinion or a disclaimer of an opinion.

The State Audit Office Act stipulates that state revenues and expenses, financial reports and financial transactions of state sector bodies, local and regional self-government units, legal entities funded from the state budget, legal entities founded by the Republic of Croatia or a local and regional self-government unit, and companies and other legal entities where the Republic of Croatia, or a local or regional self-government unit, is a majority shareholder or holds a majority stake, as well as all institutions that use funds from the European Union and other international organisations or institutions that fund public needs, shall be subject to audit. The audit of the Report on the State Budget Execution shall be carried out every year.

The audit is performed by audit teams of Certified State Auditors. These are people with university degrees who become certified state auditors after passing the prescribed examination. Candidates take the Certified State Auditor Examination in accordance with the Certified State Auditor Examination Programme passed by the Auditor General.

1.4.2 *Budgetary Oversight*

Budgetary oversight is in its basics the inspectorial supervision, carried out by the State Treasury of the Ministry of Finance. Budgetary oversight inspectors of the Ministry of Finance are authorised to perform this form of budgetary oversight.

Budgetary oversight is inspectorial supervision of the legality, purposiveness and timeliness of the use of budgetary funds, the timely and comprehensive collection of revenues and receipts under the purview of budget users and bodies of local and regional governments, and inspectorial supervision of adherence to and enforcement of laws and other regulations pertaining to budgetary funds and funds from other sources, regardless of whether they concern revenues/receipts, expenses/expenditures, refunds, assets or liabilities. Budgetary oversight encompasses oversight of accounting, financial and other operating documents and an inspection of operating premises, buildings, physical articles, goods and other items in compliance with the purpose of inspectorial supervision (Ordinance on Budget Oversight—Official Gazette of the Republic of Croatia, 71/2013).

According to the Ordinance on Budget Oversight, the Ministry of Finance conducts budgetary oversight of budgetary users and extra-budgetary users of the state budget, local and regional governments and their budget users and extra-budgetary users, companies and other legal and natural persons who receive funds from the budgets and financial plans of extra-budgetary users, as well as oversight of the use of credit funds based on guarantees from the State and local and regional governments that are subject to oversight.

If the budgetary oversight inspector determines that the funds are not paid into the budget or are used contrary to the law or the budget, the budgetary oversight inspector decides on ordering payments or repayments to the budget, and in cases where there is reasonable suspicion of a criminal act or offence, criminal or misdemeanour charges are filed against the competent authorities. If the budgetary oversight discovers irregularities for which penalties are not prescribed, the use of appropriate budgetary oversight measures is required for the elimination of these irregularities.

1.4.3 *Internal Audit and Internal Control Systems*

Internal audit is responsible for providing professional and objective opinions and recommendations on management and control systems, in order for them to function on the principles of best financial management. The primary goal of internal audit is not to test the accuracy and fairness of the financial reports, but rather to give a review of the entire business, the effectiveness of the organisation, the efficiency of business functions, a functioning information system and to test business decision-making. "Internal auditing is an independent, objective, assurance and consulting activity designed to add value and improve an organization's operations. It helps an organization in accomplishing its objectives by bringing a systematic, disciplined approach to evaluation and improving the effectiveness of risk management, control and governance processes" (Allen and Tommasi 2001: 267).

The scope of internal audit, in particular, is to give opinions on internal control systems and propose recommendations on improving the system of internal control, as well as to monitor the implementation of the given recommendations.

> The control is broadly defined as a process designed to provide reasonable assurance of effective and efficient performance of activities, reliable financial reporting and compliance with established laws and regulations. (OECD 2005: 2)

> Internal control may be defined as the organization, policies and procedures used to help ensure that government programmes achieve their intended results; that the resources used to deliver these programmes are consistent with the stated aims and objectives of the organizations concerned; that programmes are protected from waste, fraud and mismanagement; and that reliable and timely information is obtained, maintained, reported and used in decision making. (Allen and Tommasi 2001: 260)

Adjustment of internal financial controls in the public sector to European standards, which is carried out in order to reform public administration and train its administrative capacity, represents for any government one of the priority areas in the EU accession process. Croatia has conducted a number of activities to build Public Internal Financial Control Systems (PIFCS). Taking organisational factors and the sustainability of PIFCS into consideration, the Croatian Government adopted several strategic documents, amended and modified the regulatory framework, and conducted a series of activities to improve the implementation of the system by budget users.

The PIFCS development strategy has been redefined and then adopted by the Croatian Government on multiple occasions. With these policy documents, the Croatian Government has clearly stressed the importance and significance of the implementation of PIFCS in the Republic of Croatia and pushed for the integration of PIFCS in other related reform processes in the Croatian public sector (Stepic 2009).

The passing of the Budget Act in 2003 was the first time that the obligation of establishing internal audit and basic elements of financial management and internal controls was prescribed. In order to encourage the development of PIFCS and strengthen the legal obligations for their implementation, the Public Internal Financial Control Act (Official Gazette of the Republic of Croatia, 141/2006) was adopted at the end of 2006. During 2015, Parliament adopted the new Public Internal Control Act (Official Gazette of the Republic of Croatia, 78/2015). This Act prescribes the main framework for systems of financial management, financial control and internal audit, the purpose of financial management and control, financial management and control components and reporting, as well as managerial accountability.

The intention of the overall normative framework was to improve the management of public funds and to obligate the management of budgetary users to establish a system of internal controls in their units and improve business practices within their jurisdiction. Focus on the responsibility of the leadership clearly shows that the main aim of establishing internal control systems in the public sector was to improve the management processes there.

The Ministry of Finance is responsible for coordinating the establishment and development of this system, while the responsibility for coordinating implementation lies within the Central Harmonisation Units. The Ministry of Finance also authorises the work of internal auditors.

Although it is possible (fairly easy) to methodologically improve and make the systems of internal control and audit normatively uniform, actual implementation will not occur without developing instruments to introduce such systems and without recognising the interlinked processes.

Business risks which budgetary users may face are linked with all business processes, but are most prominently expressed in the financial aspect. Therefore, financial accounting becomes an area of prime interest for internal controls and audits. In this context, accounting systems are organised in such a way that they serve to provide information for the mentioned controls and audits.

Such control must not only be a corrective one, but must also become a way of preventing unwanted business practices. In this way, the role of accounting extends to predicting (forecasting) information for the purpose of outcomes management, efficiency measurement and other similar processes. A more proactive role is expected from accounting, and its functions are becoming more complex and therefore the demands put on it are also multiplying, based on the broadened spectrum of the required accounting information it now collects.

Accounting has the function of external reporting and until now has reached satisfactory levels and is continually improving. Information provided by managerial accounting is clearly necessary in laying down strategic, tactical and operational goals, the planning and oversight of plan execution, as well as reporting on execution. However, all the recent research has shown that managerial accounting which serves the function of internal reporting is not sufficiently developed (Vašiček and Dragija 2011). However, a positive trend can be seen, since the need for the development of managerial accounting has been recognised by the responsible bodies and put into the context of the sustainability of an overall reforming process. Therefore, certain encouragement for its development can be expected (Ministarstvo financija 2012).

The Public Internal Control Act obliges the management of budgetary users to establish an efficient and effective, cost-appropriate system of internal controls, but the legal framework itself does not provide complete security in terms of the actual implementation of internal controls and internal audit. Penalties for illegal and inefficient spending of budgetary funds, which is possible in terms of the absence or underdevelopment of internal control systems, are prescribed in the penal provisions of the Budget Act. In addition to the aforementioned legal framework, the Fiscal Responsibility Act (Official Gazette of the Republic of Croatia, 139/2010, 19/2014) with the accompanying Regulation on the Drafting and Submission of the Fiscal Responsibility Statement and the Report on the Application of Fiscal Rules (Official Gazette of the Republic of Croatia, 78/2011, 106/2012, 130/2013) is also prescribed with the aim of strengthening awareness of the importance of internal financial controls for public management and of its responsibility to establish such controls.

The Fiscal Responsibility Act, which integrates the provisions of the Budget Act (2008) and the Public Internal Control Act (2006), stipulates the obligation for the management of budgetary users to draw up a Fiscal Responsibility Statement on an annual basis. With the Fiscal Responsibility Statement, the management of budget users confirms that it is working in a legally secure fashion, ensures the dedicated and purposeful spending of funds, required by the legal framework of the budget, and the efficient and effective functioning of financial management and control within the budget, also required by the legal framework of internal control in the public sector. Duplication of standing legal frameworks in the field of financial management and control has its positive and negative sides. In order to improve the implementation of internal financial controls and ensure stronger interpolation in the financial system, it may be recommended to create a single normative framework to integrate the provisions of the legal framework of internal control into the public sector, and to integrate fiscal responsibility into the legal framework of the budget.

1.5 Challenges in Further Development of Public Sector Accounting and Auditing

The implementation and application of public sector accounting in the Republic of Croatia as outlined in this chapter is a significant step towards developing an international, comparable and transparent system of reporting on the finance and business operations of the government and its entities.

Taking into consideration the achieved level of economic development and other relevant elements and particularities of the national economy and the Croatian public sector, the implementation of the current system can be evaluated as optimal. However, it is necessary to continue developing it both at the macro and micro level into an efficient management instrument, notably in the context of Croatia's membership of the EU.

Based on the consistent implementation of the present public sector accounting system, specific areas/categories which need to be further developed, are identified, and classified as follows:

It is deemed important to determine precisely the adequate budget basis to be applied continuously in the process of planning and monitoring the budget execution and financial plans of the budgetary entities in relation to the applied accounting basis in accounting and financial reports of the budgetary entities.

There is no an appropriate degree of compliance with this important issue in the Republic of Croatia which often generates entropy of the reporting system at higher levels, and more often does not provide high-quality consolidation of the financial reports of related budgetary entities. Therefore, it is important to define the role of accounting precisely and to differentiate its role as an instrument to monitor the business operation of budgetary entities from its role as an instrument to monitor the budget execution and financial plan.

In addition to the above-mentioned consistency of application of an adequate accounting basis, it is also necessary to consider rationalisation of the reporting system, which is far too complex and elaborate due to the unique reporting framework for budgetary entities and reports on monitoring the budget execution.

Consistent application of a modified accrual basis in the part that concerns recognition of revenues of budgetary entities proves to be a serious weakness when reporting operating results in cases of disturbed dynamics of financing between the budget and the budget user.The expenditures of the budget users are recognised when the transaction occurs and revenues are recognised at the time of the receipt of cash characterised as revenue. With transition to the new fiscal year, each delay in revenue payment from the budget to finance expenditures of budgetary users has a negative impact on the reported operating results of the users. However, the report does not reflect the actual business operations and negatively affects high-level managements' subjective assessment of lower management. Therefore, this may result in accounting data manipulation.

The application of a modified accrual basis has certain weaknesses, which are principally connected with the quality of information on total cost management, and, consequently, with measuring the operating efficiency of some subsystems (services) in the public sector. This principally concerns capital-intensive industries, and the applied accounting basis does not provide capitalisation of expenses for acquiring fixed assets and their systematic timeline or functional allocation through depreciation to locations and bearers of expenses. As a result, there are no means to calculate the economic price of an output, particularly in public sector subsystems where outputs are precisely recognisable and measurable (i.e. in the healthcare sector). This also narrows the optimal economic choice when making decisions on how to carry out certain projects or provide services, including decisions about purchasing or hiring, doing business on one's own or using outsourcing, joining a project based on public–private partnership, etc.

In the context of public sector reform regarding improving its efficiency, there is a growing need for the development of an internal accounting system and its convergence with the external accounting system. In developing cost accounting and management accounting, it has become possible to eliminate weaknesses in the system regarding the quality and effectiveness of business decision-making management as well as specific business and financial performance indicators. Therefore, this approach will put an end to the application of a uniform, general, governmental accounting system in monitoring some public services such as healthcare and education.

In order to carry out accounting reform, the key determinants and principles of change are a gradual approach and the assessment of costs and benefits. Furthermore, EU membership has become an important argument and a stimulus to accomplish changes in the system of governmental accounting. EU membership has resulted in a number of requirements regarding reports on government finance that must be complied with. The objective of change in the regulatory framework of economic management is to achieve economic and budgetary stability in the EU. Therefore, the implementation of an accrual basis is recommended, along with an examination of the possibility of the direct implementation of the International Public Sector Accounting Standards (IPSAS) or the development of harmonised accounting standards for the public sector in the EU—known as European Public Sector Accounting Standards (EPSAS). The processes of introducing an agreed accrual basis in the accounting systems, budget planning and reporting, as well as connecting them with the accrual basis present in the system of state statistics, have been intensified both at the level of the EU and at the level of the member states.

References

Allen, R. and Tommasi, D. (Eds.). (2001). Managing Government Expenditure: A Reference Book for Transition Countries. Paris: OECD SIGMA. http://www1.worldbank.org/publicsector/pe/oecdpemhandbook.pdf. Accessed 23 September 2016.

Central Bureau of Statistics – Državni zavod za statistiku. (2014). *Statistički ljetopis Republike Hrvatske*. Avilable via http://www.dzs.hr/. Accessed 1 December 2015.

Ministarstvo financija. (2007). Strategy for the Development and Modernization of the State Treasury 2007–2011. http://www.mfin.hr/adminmax/docs/strategija2007_eng.pdf. Accessed 13 January 2017.

Ministarstvo financija. (2012). Smjernice za troškovno i upravljačko računovodstvo. Available via http://www.mfin.hr/adminmax/docs/Smjernicezatroskovniupravljackoracunovodstvo.pdf. Accessed 3 October 2015.

Ministarstvo financija. (2017). Ostvarenje poračuna JLP(R)S za Period 2010–2015. Available via http://www.mfin.hr/hr/ostvarenje-proracuna-jl-prs-za-period-2014-2015. Accessed 13 January 2017.

Ministry of Finance. (2017). Godišnji izvještaj o izvršenju Državnog proračuna za 2014. godinu. Available via http://www.mfin.hr/hr/ostvarenje-proracuna-jlprs-za-period-2014-2015. Accessed 13 January 2017.

OECD. (2005). Policy Brief: Public Sector Modernisation: Modernising Accountability and Control. Available via http://www.oecd.org/site/gov-gfg/39044829.pdf. Accessed 1 October 2015.

State Audit Office – Državni ured za reviziju. (2015). Izvješće o obavljenoj reviziji godišnjeg izvještaja o izvršenju Državnog proračuna Republike Hrvatske za 2014. godinu. Available via http://www.revizija.hr/datastore/filestore/57/drzavni_proracun_republike_hrvatske_za_2014.pdf. Accessed 13 January 2017.

Stepić, D. (2009). Strategija razvoja sustava unutarnjih financijskih kontrola u javnom sektoru Republike Hrvatske za razdoblje 2009–2011. *Riznica, časopis za računovodstvo, reviziju, financije i pravo u sustavu proračuna i neprofitnom sektoru*. RIF, Zagreb, Hrvatska.

Vašiček, V. (2002). Stanje i perspektiva razvoja računovodstvenih sustava proračuna i neprofitnih organizacija, u: Tadijančević, S., Gulin. D., Cota. B. (ur.), XXXVII. Simpozij, Pula, Računovodstvo, financije i revizija u suvremenim gospodarskim uvjetima, Hrvatska zajednica računovođa i financijskih djelatnika, Zagreb, 132–147.

Vašiček, V., & Dragija, M. (Eds.). (2011). Upravljačko računovodstvo i računovodstvo troškova u javnom sektoru – izabrane teme. Hrvatska zajednica računovođa i financijskih djelatnika, Zagreb, Hrvatska.

Useful Sites

www.nn.hr.
www.mfin.hr.
www.revizija.hr.

CHAPTER 2

Public Sector Accounting, Auditing and Control in Poland

Magdalena Kowalczyk

2.1 Territorial Organisation, Scope of the Public Sector and Distribution of Public Revenues

The notion of "public sector" appeared in Poland after World War II along with the territorial reform of the country. The introduction of local government reform in 1991 which resulted in the separation of state resources and local government resources constituted the basis for the further development of the public sector following the experiences of western countries (Rudzka-Lorentz 2008: 146).

The process of creating a new finance system in Poland began in 1989 with the election and formation of a new government under the leadership of T. Mazowiecki. This process can be divided into 6 stages:

- Stage I (1989–1991) refers to the formation of the foundations for the public finance system in its present form: re-establishment of a state budget as an autonomic and basic fund; gradual separation of fiscal and monetary areas; arrangement of the state financial

M. Kowalczyk (✉)
Poznań University of Economics and Business, Poznań, Poland
e-mail: magdalena.kowalczyk@ue.poznan.pl

V. Vašiček and G. Roje (eds.), *Public Sector Accounting, Auditing and Control in South Eastern Europe*, Public Sector Financial Management, https://doi.org/10.1007/978-3-030-03353-8_2

system—liquidation of a complex financial economy by means of a special purpose fund; formation of financial basics for local government (communes) operations and development; establishment of a category (amount) of public debt for which the government is held responsible.

- Stage II (1992–1993) refers to the tax reform that constituted the most important process in the formation of a modern public finance system.
- Stage III (1994–1996) refers to actions aimed at creating the institutional foundations for streamlining public expenses.
- Stage IV (1997–1999)—a crucial period for forming the public finance sector in Poland. The stage reflects the period of intensive work on: a new Constitution of the III Republic of Poland; an act on public finance; a new administrative division of the country; reform of the pension system; reform of the healthcare system; reform of the healthcare education system; reform of the education system; adoption of the tax ordinance. The intensive work on all the above actions resulted in the adoption of appropriate legal acts and significantly influenced the form of the public finance system in Poland.
- Stage V (2000–2008) refers to intensive work on adjusting the Polish financial system to EU requirements. Other important changes relate to the introduction of notes on internal audit in public finance entities, the Act on Public Finance and the introduction of changes to budgetary classification so that state budget settlements coming from EU resources were distinguished from other budgetary resources.
- Stage VI (2009–until present) refers to the public finance system undergoing reforms in response to the state doctrine, etc. The most important changes to public finance, as of 2009, include: the adoption of a new Act on Public Finance in 2009; the implementation of the National Long-Term Financial Plan on the basis of the Act on Public Finance; the separation of EU resources and national resources in the state budget; the introduction of managerial control; changes of tax rates for direct and indirect taxpayers (Owsiak 2017: 532–543).

Table 2.1 presents the stages of the development of the public finance sector in Poland according to T. Lubińska.

Table 2.1 Stages of the development of public finance

No.	*Period*	*Scope of reforms*
1.	Tax reform 1992–1993	Personal and Corporate Income Tax, Value Added Tax
2.	Reform on decentralisation of public tasks 1992, 1999	Communes (PL: gminy), districts (PL: powiaty), local government "voivodeships" (PL: województwa samorządowe)
3.	Reform of the education system 1999	6 years of basic education (primary school) + 3 years of gymnasium (lower- secondary education) + 3 years (secondary school)
4.	Reform of social insurance 1999	2-pillar social insurance system
5.	Reform of healthcare 1999	Separation of financing healthcare services from the state budget
6.	Integration with the European Union 2004–2006, 2007–2013	Fiscal consolidation—requirements of the Maastricht treaty on the deficit and public debt
7.	European Union Funds 2004–2006, 2007–2013	Radical changes to the structure of expenses
8.	Reform—tasks-oriented budget 2006–2013	Implementation of a task-oriented budget at the central level

Source Author's elaboration based on Lubińska (2010: 86)

The formation of new local government units—districts (PL: powiaty) and "voivodeships" (PL: województwa) on 1 January 1999 led to the fact that at present in Poland there is a 3-level system of local government. In terms of the tasks of particular local governments and the territorial scope of their activities, the government of a commune and district is considered as local government, while "voivodeship" government is seen as a more regional one. Table 2.2 presents the structure of public administration in Poland (Rudzka-Lorentz 2008: 146).

The basic territorial division of the country includes 2489 communes (including 65 cities with the rights of a district), 308 districts and 16 "voivodeships". After the changes introduced in 2003, there were 2478 communes (including 65 cities with the rights of a district), 314 districts and 16 "voivodeships" (Rudzka-Lorentz: 146).

Table 2.3 presents the structure of the public finance sector in Poland.

Budgetary units at both the state and local government level constitute basic organisational units of both the government sub-sector and the local government sub-sector. Budgetary units at both the state and local government level are characterised by their form of relation with

Table 2.2 Structure of public administration'

Criteria of distinguishing the type of administration	*Present administrative structures*
Level of organisation	
National	Central administration Public administration
Regional	Central administration in "voivodeship" (Polish: województwo) Local government administration of "voivodeship"
Local	Local government administration of district (Polish: powiat) Local government administration of commune (Polish: gmina)

Source Hausner (2003: 168)

Table 2.3 Structure of the public sector

Specification	*Public sector entities*	*Organisational units*
Government sub-sector	State Treasury Public universities Public cultural institutions Public film institutions Executive agencies Budget policy institutions Independent public healthcare units PAN (Polish Academy of Sciences) Other legal persons established on the basis of separate acts on carrying out public tasks	State budgetary units State special purposes funds which do not have legal personality National Healthcare Fund (NFZ) Other units
Local government sub-sector	Local government territorial units Unions of local government units Local government culture institutions Independent public healthcare units	Local government budgetary units Local government budgetary establishments
Social insurance sub-sector	ZUS (Social Insurance Fund)	KRUS (Agricultural Social Insurance Fund)

Source Zysnarska (2014: 13)

the budget—the gross method—which means that the expenses of the units constitute budget expenses and the income of the units constitute budget incomes. The units do not have any legal personality: their financial system is based on a financial plan that includes planned incomes and expenses. Such a method of financing is related to units providing services free of charge or for a small fee that does not cover the costs of operation. Table 2.4 gives examples of state and local government budgetary units.

Budgetary establishments of local government constitute a more flexible organisational form of the local government sub-sector. The Act on Public Finance of 27 August 2009 liquidated budgetary establishments at the government sub-sector level.

Table 2.4 State and local government budgetary units

State budgetary units' disposal of the state budget	*Local government budgetary units' disposal of the local government budget*
Offices of key state bodies such as: Polish President''s Office, Sejm (the lower chamber of the Polish Parliament), Senate	**At the level of commune:**
All offices of state and local government administration	Commune offices (cities)
Law enforcement control offices (Highest Chamber of Control, regional chambers of account)	Primary schools, groups of schools of economics and administration
Courts, public prosecutor's office and tribunals	Social welfare centres in a commune
Prisons and jails	Some preschools
Organisational units subject to the Ministry of National Defence and Ministry of Internal Affairs and Administration	**At the level of district:**
Primary schools, gymnasiums, upper-secondary schools and post-secondary schools	County
Educational care facilities, pedagogical counselling centres	Vocational schools, groups of schools and high schools
Social assistance centres	Social assistance centres
National and landscape parks	Road authorities
Training and advice units	

Source Author's elaboration based on Winiarska (2016: 13–14)

Budgetary establishments of local governments perform their activities for a charge. A financial schedule that includes planned revenues and expenses is the basis of their financial management. Revenues earned by local government establishments must cover all the costs of their operations. According to Article 14 of the Act on Public Finance of 27 August 2009,[1] own tasks performed by local governments can be used by local government budgetary establishments in terms of:

- managing housing and commercial premises;
- roads, streets, bridges, public squares and managing traffic;
- waterworks and the water supply system, the sewage system, disposal and cleaning of municipal waste water, maintenance of sanitary equipment, landfills dumping grounds and neutralising municipal waste, electricity supply, heat and gas supply;
- local public transport;
- marketplaces;
- community green areas and trees;
- physical culture and sports, including maintenance of recreational areas and sports equipment;
- keeping different exotic and national animals, especially breeding endangered species in order to protect them outside their natural habitat;
- cemeteries (Act on Public Finance of 27 August 2009).

Activities performed previously by state budgetary establishments may be carried out by other organisational forms, for example: an executive agency or budgetary sector institutions.

Table 2.5 presents characteristics of such organisational forms.

Executive agencies, budgetary sector institutions, administrators of purpose-oriented state funds and state legal persons are obliged to prepare task-oriented financial plans for the budgetary year and also for two subsequent years (Act on Public Finance of 27 August 2009).

[1] Dz. U. Nr 157 poz. 1240. Dz. U. is the abbreviation for Dziennik Ustaw Rzeczypospolitej Polskiej, the Official Gazette of the Republic of Poland.

Table 2.5 Public finance sector organisations

No.	*Organisational form*	*Characteristics*
1.	Executive agency	According to the Act on Public Finance, this is a state legal personality created on the basis of a separate act in order to execute state tasks The basis of the financial management of an executive agency is an annual financial plan, including: – incomes from own activities; – state budget subsidies; – settlement of costs; – resources for capital expenses; – resources provided for other entities; – receivables and liabilities at the beginning and end of year; – financial resources at the beginning and end of year An executive agency is obliged yearly to make payments of financial surplus to the state budget, to the account of current incomes of the state budgetary unit operating for the minister controlling this agency Examples: Military Property Agency, Military Housing Agency, State Treasury Agricultural Property Agency, National Science Centre, National Centre for Research and Development
2.	Budgetary sector institution	This constitutes a unit of the public finance sector formed to carry out public tasks that: – executes payable distinguishable tasks; – covers the costs of activities and liabilities from gained incomes The basis of the financial management system of budgetary sector institutions is a yearly financial plan including: – incomes from performed activities; – state budget subsidies; – settlement of costs; – resources for capital expenses; – financial results; – receivables and liabilities; – financial resources at the beginning and end of year Assets of budgetary sector institutions may include: real estate with transferred ownership, assets—equipment lent by a body that functions as a founding body, assets bought for own resources Examples: Service Bureau of the President of Republic of Poland, Judiciary Purchasing Centre, Central Sports Centre, Shared Services Centre, Centre for Information Technology

(continued)

Table 2.5 (continued)

No.	*Organisational form*	*Characteristics*
3.	Purpose-oriented state fund	This is formed on the basis of a separate act; its revenues come from public resources and its costs are incurred by means of the execution of separate state tasks. It has no legal personality and has a separate bank account at the disposal of a minister by means of the act founding the fund or other body specified in the act. The basis of the financial management fund is a yearly plan. The purpose-oriented state fund can give out loans to local governments if the act so provides Examples: Social Insurance Fund, Pension Fund, Temporary Retirement Fund, Guaranteed Employment Benefit Fund, Labour Fund, National Fund for the Rehabilitation of People with Disabilities
4.	State and local government legal persons	These are formed by means of a separate act. The basis for their financial management is a financial plan including: revenues from carried-out activities, state budget subsidies and local government budget subsidies, costs, resources for capital expenses, resources provided for other entities, receivables and liabilities at the beginning and end of year, financial resources at the beginning and end of year Examples of state legal persons: Agency for Technology Assessment, Social Insurance System, Polish Tourist Organisation, Polish Centre for Accreditation, Polish Film Institute

Source Author's elaboration based on the Act on Public Finance of 27 August 2009 (Heciak 2014: 29–34)

2.2 Formulation and Execution of Central Government and Local and Regional Self-Government Budgets

2.2.1 Financial Management and Public Finance

The budgetary system in Poland consists of the state budget, the local government budget, including the commune budget, the district budget and the local government "voivodeship" budget. The functioning principles of the state budget and local government budget are almost identical. This is due to the fact that Poland has adopted a doctrine on uniform public authorities, and in particular financial uniformity (Owsiak 2017: 564–565).

The legal foundations of the Polish budget are specified by the following legal acts: the Polish Constitution, the Act on Public Finance, budgetary acts on a yearly basis, acts related to the budget and executive laws prepared by the Minister of Finance, the Board of Ministers or specific ministers. The Polish Constitution forms the basic principles of the budgetary sector and specifies the deadlines of budgetary work (Marczakowska-Proczka 2008: 96). Table 2.6 presents the structure of state budgetary expenses in Poland.

There is Long-Term Financial State Planning prepared for the particular budgetary year and three subsequent years at the central government level in Poland. This includes the Convergence Programme on strengthening supervision and coordination of economic policy, specifying the aims and indicators of its execution, in terms of the main functions of the state.

This constitutes the basis for the preparation of the budgetary act for the subsequent year (Article 103 of the Act on Public Finance). Table 2.7 presents the detailed characteristics of Long-Term Financial Planning.

The Budget Act constitutes the basis of financial management in the specific year. The budgetary act passed for the period of one calendar year specifies:

- the aggregate amount of projected tax and non-tax national budget revenue;
- the aggregate amount of planned national budget expenditures;

Table 2.6 Structure of state budgetary expenses

No.	*Type of expenses*	*Purpose*
1.	Subsidies and grants	– Purpose subsidies – Specific subsidies – Specified-user subsidies
2.	Services for the benefit of physical persons	These include state budget expenses aimed, directly or indirectly, according to separate laws, at physical persons, and do not constitute remuneration for provided work
3.	Current expenses of budgetary units	– Remunerations and salaries of persons employed in state budgetary units and contributions from remuneration and salaries; – Purchase of goods and services; – Maintenance costs and other expenses related to the functioning of the budgetary units and performance of their statutory tasks; – Costs of tasks delegated to entities that are and are not part of public finance, excluding non-governmental organisations
4.	Capital expenses	– Expenses for the purchase and takeover of shares and payment of contributions to companies; – Investment expenses of state budgetary units and purpose-oriented subsidies for financing and subsidising costs of investments performed by other units
5.	Expenses for administrating State Treasury debt[a]	These include in particular expenses for interest and discounts of state securities, interest on credits and loans and fees related to securities and guarantees granted by the State Treasury and also costs related to the issuing of securities
6.	Expenses for performance of programmes	Expenses from EU resources financed by a share of EU funds
7.	EU's own resources	These include: – a share to inflows from customs, agricultural and sugar fees; – resources calculated on the basis of tax on goods and in accordance with the methodology resulting from EU regulations; – resources calculated on the basis of gross national income; – interests and fines for untimely or incorrectly calculated payments

Source Author's elaboration based on Articles 124, 125 of the Act on Public Finance
[a]The term State Treasury debt refers to central government sector debt

Table 2.7 Characteristics of long-term financial state planning

No.	*Characteristics*	*Description*
1.	Definition	This is a plan of national budget incomes and expenditures and revenue and outgoings, prepared for four budgetary years
2.	Structure	This covers state functions together with the goals and indicators of their execution and includes: – the goals of the mid-term development strategy of the country; – the directions of social and economic policy
3.	Scope	Divided by specific budgetary years, it states: – basic macroeconomic indicators; – directions of fiscal policy; – projected national budget income and expenditures; – amount of national budget deficit and loan needs and sources of financing them; – projected income and expenditure of the European resources budget; – European resources budget outturn; – consolidated forecast of public finance budget balance; – amount of national debt
4.	Core issue	This is the basis for preparing the budget project for the next budgetary year

Source Articles 100–105 of the Act on Public Finance

- the amount of planned deficit in the national budget together with sources covering it;
- the aggregate amount of projected budgetary revenue from European resources;
- the aggregate amount of planned budgetary expenditures from European resources;
- European resources budget outturn;
- the aggregate amount of planned national budget incomes;
- the aggregate amount of planned national budget spending;
- the planned income and expenditure balance of the national budget;
- the liability limit due to assumed credits and loans and issued securities (Article 109, 110 of the Act on Public Finance).

According to Article 211 of the Act on Public Finance, the local government budget represents a yearly plan of revenues and expenses.[2] The local government budget is for a budgetary year that usually reflects one calendar year. The budgetary act, constituting the basis of local government financial management in the specific budgetary year, specifies:

- the aggregate amount of planned incomes of the local government budget, distinguishing current and capital incomes;
- the aggregate amount of planned expenditures of the local government budget, distinguishing current and capital expenditures;
- the amount of the planned local government budget deficit or surplus together with sources covering the deficit or allocation of the surplus;
- the aggregate amount of the planned incomes of the local government;
- the aggregate amount of the planned spending of the local government;
- the limit of liabilities due to taken credits, loans and issued securities;
- the amount of expenditures payable in the specific budgetary year, according to a concluded agreement, resulting from securities and guarantees granted by local government;
- special provisions for local government budget execution in the budgetary year, resulting from separate acts;
- the authority of auxiliary units to administer financial management in terms of the commune budget;
- other provisions that must be included in the budgetary act result from resolutions by decision-making bodies of local government (Article 212 of the Act on Public Finance).

Table 2.8 presents the structure of the local government budget.

In terms of local governments, the basis for financial management is also the budgetary act prepared for the calendar year and the long-term financial forecast. Local governments prepare a long-term financial forecast that must be realistic and must specify at least the following issues for each year of the forecast:

[2] In Poland, the local government budget is a yearly plan of income (e.g. from taxes), expenses (e.g. for salaries, services), revenues (e.g. receiving a bank loan), spending (e.g. repayment of a bank loan).

Table 2.8 Structure of the local government budget

Current budget—incomes	*Current budget—expenditures*
Taxes	Personnel expenses
Public fees	Material expenses
Purpose-oriented and general subsidies	Debt administration
Capital incomes (without incomes from the sale of assets)	Transfer of surplus to investment budget
Investment budget—incomes	*Investment budget—expenditures*
Incomes from the sale of assets	Investment expenditures
Incomes from investment subsidies	Payment of credits and loans, purchase of securities
Incomes from credits and loans	Covering of deficits from previous years
Transfers from the current budget	Transfers to the current budget

Source Surówka (2013: 34)

- current incomes and expenditures of the local government budget, including for debts, guarantees and securities;
- capital incomes, including incomes from the sale of assets and capital expenditures of the local government budget;
- the financial result of the local government budget;
- the allocation of surpluses or the manner of financing deficits;
- incomes and expenditures of the local government budget, taking into account debts incurred and projected to be incurred;
- the amount of local government debt and the manner of financing its payment;
- the amount of current and capital expenditures resulting from the limits of expenditures for planned and performed activities carried out by local governments (Article 226 of the Act on Public Finance).

Long-term financial planning must contribute to the reasonable management of public resources. The structure of the National Long-term Financial Forecast and Local government Long-term Financial Forecast indicates that their founding is task-oriented planning that constitutes a modern method of managing public finances. The application of a task-oriented budget in budgetary planning is supposed to facilitate the more effective use of public resources (Winiarska and Kaczurak-Kozak 2013: 20).

The reform of Polish public finance towards a task-oriented budget in the government sector was introduced in 2006. At present, the task-oriented budget covers the entire public finance sector, excluding local government and the National Health Fund (Winiarska and Kaczurak-Kozak 2013: 21).

2.2.2 *Execution of the State Budget and Local Government Budget*

Financial flows in the state budget are related to the execution of the state budget and local government budget. A budgetary unit is the basic organisational unit. Table 2.9 presents a structure of the budgetary sector in Poland.

The government sector consists of a 3-level division of budget administrators. It includes:

1. main administrators, that is, state budgetary units which constitute a separate part of the state budget, e.g. ministers, "voivodes" or other units with the importance of main administrators;
2. 2nd-level administrators, that is, state units that are directly subject to the main administrators;
3. 3rd-level administrators, that is, state budgetary units that are subject to a higher level administrator or directly subject to the main administrators.

The main administrator of the local government is the board (of a district, "voivodeship"), and budgetary units subject to the board are 3rd-level administrators. These units can constitute administrators of the 2nd-level if they are involved in the execution of government administration tasks. The "voivode", mayor and president of a city function as boards of the commune (Winiarska 2016: 13).

Budget execution is performed on a cash basis, according to which budget incomes and expenses of a particular year include only those that occurred in the form of inflows or outflows of financial resources to specific bank accounts. This principle is broken down in the register of budget execution of the local government and includes expenses that do not expire at the end of the budgetary year (Zysnarska 2010: 107).

Table 2.9 Structure of the budgetary sector in Poland

Distinguishing feature	*Government sub-sector*	*Local government sub-sector*
– Public sector entities	– State treasury	– Local government units – Connections between local government units
– Organisational units	– National budgetary units	– Local government units

Source Zysnarska (2014: 14)

2.3 Accounting and Financial Reporting

2.3.1 Public Finance Accounting

Public finance units keep accounts in compliance with the provisions of the Act on Accounting[3] and also take into account provisions specified in the Act on Public Finance. This signifies that provided that the Act on Public Finance does not state otherwise, the public finance sector applies the provisions of the Act on Accounting (Maciejewska and Wojtczak 2012: 43).

Budgetary accounting covers operations of cash and actual budgetary and non-budgetary expenses and all the economic occurrences taking place during the execution of the state budget and the execution of the local government budget (of a commune, district, "voivodeship"). The accounting system is influenced mainly by principles of public finance, finance investment and also the preparation, execution and control of the budget (Hellich 2005: 64–65).

Budgetary accounting can be divided into three types, specified in Table 2.10.

Special regulations concern charts of accounts for the state budget, local government budget, local government budgetary establishments, purpose-oriented state funds and state budgetary units that have their registered offices outside the territory of the Republic of Poland and provide that:

- incomes and expenses are stated in the payment period, irrespective of the yearly budget that they consider;
- all the stages of settlements preceding the payments of incomes and expenses and in terms of expenses and costs—also resources;
- interests due to untimely payments shall be calculated and registered not later than the end of each quarter;
- the assessment of assets and liabilities expressed in foreign currencies shall be done not later than the end of the quarter (Act on Public Finance, Article 40).

Special provisions of accounting concern, pursuant to the Act on Public Finance:

[3]Dz. U. z 2016, poz. 615.

Table 2.10 Description of types of budgetary accounting

No.	*Budgetary accounting*	*Description*
1.	Accounting of state budget and local government budget execution	This system of budgetary accounting focuses on the economic processes of accumulating and spending financial resources. The accounting rules of budget execution facilitate the specification of the budget execution outcome in the form of budget surplus or deficit and its settlements with other local government units, the state budget and tax offices
2.	Accounting of budgetary units and local government budgetary establishments	Accounting of budgetary units and local government budgetary establishments concern: – the register of accumulating and spending financial resources; – settlement of accounts; – register of fixed assets and current assets; – register of incomes and related costs, profits and extraordinary losses; – register of incomes and expenses; – register of funds and financial result
3.	Accounting for taxes and fees and tax-free budgetary receivables	This part of budgetary accounting concerns the accounting register of taxes and fees due and collected and also supervision over the timely payment of liabilities and liquidation of overpayments

Source Author's elaboration based on Filipiak (2009: 139)

1. the register of budget execution;
2. the register of task-oriented budget execution;
3. the register of fixed assets belonging to the State Treasury or local governments;
4. the assessment of particular assets and liabilities;
5. preparation of financial reports and the recipients of these reports.

The executive act on these principles relates to the provisions specified in the Resolution by the Minister of Finance of 5 July 2010 on special principles of accounting and charts of accounts for the state budget, local government budget, budgetary units, local government budgetary establishments, purpose-oriented state funds and state budgetary units that have their registered offices outside the territory of the Republic of Poland.

The principles of accounting were specified to provide the transparency of the charts of accounts and the nature of activities carried out by the unit.

In compliance with the provisions of the Act on Public Finance, the organisation of budgetary accounting is uniform for specific units of public finance. This requirement is stated in the obligation to apply the same chart of accounts (individually for the state budget, local government budget and budgetary units and local government budgetary establishments) and a uniform budgetary classification.

Since 1999, the Act on Public Finance has used the notion of a detailed classification of incomes,[4] expenses,[5] revenues,[6] spending[7] and resources from the European Union budget and other foreign sources (Winiarska and Kaczurak-Kozak 2013: 51).

Budgetary classification is formed for cognitive, informative, operational and legal purposes. The cognitive purposes of the budgetary classification relate to the need to determine the origin of resources constituting budget incomes and ways of spending them. At the same time, it helps in determining the size of the incomes and expenses structure in a clear manner—thus, it achieves its informative purposes. Operational purposes result from the need to plan the budget and its execution in general and partial amounts. It is based on subjective, objective and specific criteria. In Poland, there are four main types in the state budget incomes and expenses classification, which are: parts, sections, chapters and paragraphs (Podstawka 2017: 147).

2.3.2 *Financial Reporting in Local Government*

Financial reporting in the public sector provides basic information on the resources of units of local government and flows of their revenues and expenses. Information included in the reports constitutes a source of data crucial for taking financial decisions that contribute to the optimal managing of public finance and achieving the best effects from the efforts (principle of effectiveness). However, in order to understand whether the goal is achieved, it is necessary to have some knowledge of the occurrences taking place in the unit (and its surrounding) (Kaczurak-Kozak, in Winiarska 2016: 110).

[4] i.e. income from taxes.

[5] i.e. salaries expense or purchase of services.

[6] e.g. when local government receives a bank loan.

[7] e.g. when local government pays back the loan.

Public finance units prepare financial reporting according to the act on accounting. Thus, Table 2.11 presents the scope of reporting and further changes introduced in the period 2001–2010 in terms of local governments, local government budgetary establishments and budgetary units.

The balance sheet in the execution of the local government budget is a report on financial resources, receivables, budget settlements and net assets and liabilities. The basis for its preparation is the balances of accounts covered in the "plan of accounts for the local government budget". The balance sheet on the budget execution is prepared by the body which is responsible for budget execution, that is, a mayor (city mayor, president), the board of the district and the board of the local government "voivodeship" (Zysnarska 2011: 110). Detailed data on the amounts of executed budget incomes and expenses can be found, according to budgetary classification, in a yearly report on the execution of the local government budget.

Thus, all the organisational units comprising the specific unit of the local government prepare financial reporting, including:

- balance sheet;
- profit and loss statement;
- statement of changes in the fund.

The balance sheet of budgetary units and local government budgetary establishments that comprise a specific unit of local government is prepared on the basis of reporting prepared for commercial entities. Naturally, some components of the balance sheet prepared for local government organisational units are different from those prepared by commercial entities. This results from the nature of their operations (Kowalczyk 2017: 69).

According to a resolution of the Minister of Finance on special principles of accounting and charts of accounts for the state budget, local government budget, budgetary units, local government budgetary establishments, purpose-oriented state funds and state budgetary units, the profit and loss account can contain the following types of operations:

- basic operational activities;
- other operational activities;
- finance and investment activities;
- obligatory burdening of the financial result.

Table 2.11 Changes to financial reporting during the period 2001–2010 in local government

Reporting period	*Financial reporting levels*	*Types of financial statements*
After 2001	Organisational units of the local government	Balance sheet
	Local government units	Aggregate balance sheet, which is a total of individual balance sheets
	Board of the local government unit	Consolidated balance sheet of the local government unit
After 2006	Organisational units of the local government	– balance sheet – profit and loss account—comparative option – statement of changes in the fund
	Local government units	– board of the local government unit prepares consolidated financial report separately for budgetary units, budgetary establishments, and – auxiliary enterprises[a] of the budgetary units
	Board of the local government unit	Consolidated balance sheet according to the assumption that a local government unit is the dominant unit
After 2010	Organisational units of the local government	– balance sheet – profit and loss account—comparative option – statement of changes in the fund
	Local government units	– balance sheet on the execution of the local government budget – aggregate balance sheet covering data resulting from the balance sheet of budgetary local government units and budgetary establishments of local government – aggregate profit and loss account of budgetary local government units and budgetary establishments of local government – aggregate statement of changes in the fund covering data resulting from statement of changes in the fund of budgetary local governments and budgetary establishments of local governments
	Board of the local government unit	Consolidated balance sheet according to the assumption that a local government unit is the dominant unit

Source Kowalczyk (2015: 254–255)

[a]This could mean, for example, that the school has its own auxiliary enterprises, such as dormitories and a lunchroom

The first part of the profit and loss account relates to the unit's basic operational activities. In terms of public finance, the profit and loss account is prepared only as a comparative option. This means that the costs of operational activities are grouped by type—depreciation, consumption of materials and energy, outside services, remunerations, social insurance and other benefits, taxes and fees and other costs by type.

The second part presents revenues and costs related to operational activities—e.g. sale of fixed assets. This part is significantly influenced by the application of the precautionary principle in the assessment of operational assets, e.g. making write-downs. The third part of the account presents revenues and costs connected with financial and investment operations. As of 1 January 2016, there has been no 4th part of the profit and loss account demonstrating the financial results of so-called extraordinary occurrences in the units (Świderska 2003: 10–62).

The profit and loss account, similarly to other components of the financial reporting of local governments, was founded on the basis of profit and loss accounts prepared by commercial entities. Due to the above, some entries that can be seen in the present form of the profit and loss account do not always reflect the nature of the public sector. However, it is necessary to underline that it is constantly being modified and adjusted to the specifics of local government (Kowalczyk 2017: 79).

The last component of financial reporting prepared by budgetary units and local government budgetary establishments is a statement of changes to the fund and, in the case of private sector entities, also called a statement of changes to share capital.

The unit's fund, in public finance, reflects the value of the fixed and current capital of the organisational unit. Changes occurring in the fund are of significant importance for the users of financial reporting as they present reasons for its growth and decrease in the specific reporting period (Kowalczyk 2017: 80).

Aggregate financial reporting, constituting the balance sheet, profit and loss account and statement of changes to the fund, is prepared on the basis of received financial reporting from units comprising the specific local government.

The commune office, and also budgetary units and local government budgetary establishments that are subject to local government, prepare individual financial reporting on the basis of their own financial and accounting systems. Individual financial reports constitute the financial reporting of the local government. However, the diversity of tasks performed by subjective organisational units means that the financial data presented in the financial reporting of the office, and also of budgetary units and local government budgetary establishments, may vary in terms of the presented contents. Non-comparable economic issues may include, for example, the presentation of revenues in the profit and loss account of:

- education institutions that conduct financial management in the form of budgetary units (in high schools, revenues are occasional, mostly as revenues from budget incomes);
- urban financial management in the form of local government budgetary establishments (in a municipal water service, these will take the form of revenues from the sale of products).

Thus, as this considers different tasks that are performed by means of organisational units of local government, the data is not comparable (Wojtczak 2013: 149).

A crucial component of the methods of preparing aggregate reports is, as stated in paragraph 19 and 20 of the resolution by the Minister of Finance of 5 July 2010, the requirement of carrying out mutual aggregate exclusions and settlements between units. In other words, after totalling particular entries of individual reports, some entries need to be eliminated in the form of corrections that eliminate mutual settlements between units.

2.3.3 Budgetary Reporting in Public Finance

Budgetary reporting is the main and most important source of information about budget execution and its compliance with the law, and at the same time is a main tool of managing state finances and local government finance. It also constitutes the basis for preparing a yearly report on the budget execution of local government (Bakalarska 2005: 10).

Information included in budgetary reporting provides a significant source of reliable data that helps make comparisons in terms of budgetary incomes and expenses within different periods and also helps to create future budgets. In terms of the preparation of budgetary reports, there are certain principles that guarantee a relevant quality of information included there (Zysnarska 2014: 182).

The reports are prepared mostly to satisfy outside recipients (budgetary administrators, the Minister of Finance, the Regional Chamber of Accounts and the Supreme Chamber of Control). Information provided by budgetary reporting may also be used to make internal analyses or for supervising the execution of the financial plan.

Budgetary reporting includes the following reports on:

- local government budget execution;
- the execution of financial plans of budgetary units;
- revenue and expenses on the accounts;
- the execution of financial plans of local government budgetary establishments;
- the execution of financial plans of executive agencies;
- the execution of financial plans of budgetary sector institutions;
- purpose-oriented state financial resources;
- balance of bank accounts of local government;
- the execution of financial plans of the Social Insurance Institution;
- structural expenses incurred by public finance (Resolution of the Minister of Finance of 16 January 2014 on budgetary accounting).

Table 2.12 presents the types of budgetary reporting prepared in public finance.

At the end of year, the board of the local government prepares a yearly report on budget execution. Data from yearly reports provide information on the degree of budget execution and are very important for administrative purposes. The report on the budget execution of local governments is of prime importance for managing its finances and it needs to meet huge requirements. Data included in the reports must be of the highest utility. A yearly report on the budget execution of local government constitutes the most important report submitted by an executive body. It is the basis for obtaining a vote of acceptance by this body. Data included in the report provide a detailed analysis and evaluation of whether the execution is correct. A yearly report needs to provide at least the details specified in the binding regulations and must include:

- budgetary incomes and expenses of local government, in particular specified in the budgetary act;
- changes to the plan of expenses for financial programmes with a share of resources from the EU budget and of non-refundable

resources from the aid granted by member countries of the European Free Market Association EFTA; and non-refundable resources from foreign sources, other than those already mentioned;
- the extent of executing long-term projects (Act on Public Finance of 27 August 2009, Article 269, paragraph 1, points 2 and 3).

Additionally, the board of local government provides information on the status of local government assets, including data on:

- ownership rights belonging to the local government;
- other property rights other than ownership titles, including in particular limited property rights, the rights of perpetual usufruct, the rights of receivables, the rights to shares in companies, held shares;
- changes to the condition of public assets;

Table 2.12 Types of budgetary reporting

No.	*Type of budgetary reporting*	*Description*
1.	Individual reporting	Prepared by managers of budgetary units; the data consider operations taking place in these units. Individual reports are handed over to higher-level units and are aggregated to make aggregate reports
2.	Aggregate reporting	Aggregate reports are prepared by: – *Second level administrators of the state budget and administrators of budgetary parts* who have subordinated units—on the basis of individual reports by the subordinated units and own individual reports – *Administrators of state budget resources transferring subsidies for tasks of government administration and other tasks delegated to the local government unit by means of acts*—on the basis of Rb-50 reports received from local government units – *Directors of revenue offices*—on the basis of revenue office individual reports, tax bodies
3.	Composite reporting	A characteristic feature of composite reports is that they consider only local government
4.	Consolidated reporting	Consolidated (composite and aggregate) reports that consider reports on structural expenses (Rb-WSa, Rb-WSb). A characteristic feature of these reports is the need to eliminate flows of financial resources inside and outside the sector

Sources Author's elaboration based on Heciak (2014: 310–312)

- revenues from the execution of ownership rights and other property rights;
- information on occurrences influencing the condition of local government assets (Article 267 of the Act on Public Finance of 27 August 2009).

There are two types of audit in the Polish public finance sector: external and internal audit. The first one is carried out independently of the unit's management by external organisations in order to examine the unit's condition, especially financial ones. In terms of state administration, external audit means audit carried out by organisations that are independent government institutions, e.g. Supreme Chamber of Control (NIK), or independent self-government institutions NIK, Regional Accounting Chamber (RIO).

Internal audit, according to Article 272 of the Act on Public Finance, is an independent and objective activity aimed at supporting a minister or a manager of a specific department in the execution of goals and tasks by means of systematic evaluation of managerial control and advisory activities.

2.4 Audit and Other Oversight (Supervision) in the Public Sector

2.4.1 External Audit in Public Sector

Budget execution is subject to government and administrative control. The first is carried out by the Sejm and the Supreme Chamber of Control (NIK) which is subordinate to the Sejm. The second is executed by the Minister of Finance. The results of the control performed by the Minister of Finance are presented to the Board of Ministers and the Supreme Chamber of Control by means of periodic reports. The Supreme Chamber of Control analyses yearly reports on the execution of the state budget and evaluates the results of control performed during the budgetary year (Podstawka 2017: 156).

The organisation and the functioning of NIK are set out in the Constitution of the Republic of Poland and in the Act on NIK of 23 December 1994. NIK is subordinate to the Sejm and is headed by a president, who is appointed by the Sejm for a six-year term of office. NIK's basic task is to conduct audits related to the execution of the state budget. It also audits public spending and the management of public assets by state and local governmental bodies and economic entities (businesses). Every year, NIK submits three key documents to the Sejm: its analysis of the execution of the state budget and monetary policy guidelines, its opinion on the vote of approval for the government and its annual activity report. The Mission of the Supreme Chamber of Control is to promote economic efficiency and effectiveness in the public service for the benefit of the Republic of Poland. The vision of NIK is that of a Supreme Audit Institution with widely recognised standing, whose reports are a reliable and sought source of information for bodies of the state and for the general public (Annual Report SAO 2012).

Thus, control of the financial management of communes, districts and local government "vovideships" and their unions and associations, and also local government organisational units that have legal personality, is carried out by the regional chamber of audit on the basis of compliance with the laws (legality) and the compliance of documents with the actual state (reliability). Control of the financial management of local government in terms of government administration, performed by local government units on the basis of acts or conducted agreements (so-called delegated tasks), is executed also with reference to usefulness and economic efficiency. The chambers also keep control over supervisory reports on the execution of the local government budget in terms of accounting and formal issues (Ruśkowski 2008: 246).

The Act on Regional Chambers of Audit was passed by the Sejm on 7 October 1992 and came into force on 1 January 1993. Defining the powers of the RIOs, the Act authorised them "to audit the financial management of communes, counties and provinces, as well as intercommunal unions and other local legal entities", and "to supervise the legal acts of local authorities and their unions in financial matters" (Country Report of Poland 2011).

As a supervisory body, the regional chambers of audit may step into the activity of local government only in cases clearly specified by law. The supervision of regional chambers of audit is carried out by reviewing the legality of resolutions and directives passed by local government bodies concerning:

- the procedure of passing the budget and changes therein;
- implementation of the budget including budget modifications;
- contraction of debts;
- allocation of subsidies;

- local taxes, fees and charges;
- the vote of approval for the local executive for its budget execution;
- long-term financial forecasts and changes therein (Article 11 of the Act on Regional Chambers of Audit of 7 October 1992).[8]

2.4.2 *Internal Audit and Internal Control System*

The economic management of public resources at the executive level is controlled by decision-making bodies. In the case of the state budget and other funds at the central level, control is exercised by the Sejm of the Republic of Poland. In terms of local governments, boards of communes, districts and the regional council of a "voivodeship" monitor the management of public resources. Decision-making authorities are supported by specialised controlling institutions that are authorised by the laws. Taking into account central authorities, it is the Supreme Chamber of Audit that performs this function, and in the case of local governments it is the regional chambers of accounts (Owsiak 2017: 610).

Internal audit in Polish public finance has been functioning since 1 January 2002. The obligation of setting legal regulations on financial control and internal audit was the result of accession negotiations for Polish membership of the European Union. The Act on Public Finance with its amendments—Chapter 6 "Internal audit and internal audit coordination in public finance"—constitutes a legal act of the highest rank. Thus, the resolutions of the Minister of Finance of 1 February 2010 on performing and documenting internal audit and the resolution of the Minister of Finance of 29 December 2009 on the audit committee are executive acts (Kostur 2012: 55–57).

The purpose of audit carried out in a specific unit is to examine internal operations by means of assurance tasks and advisory activities. Assurance tasks signify a set of actions taken to provide independent and objective evaluation. Therefore, advisory activities mean activities different from assurance tasks which are taken by an internal auditor, the nature and scope of which are agreed upon with the unit's manager and the main purpose of which is to improve the unit's operations (Heciak 2014: 341).

The Minister of Finance specifies detailed standards of internal audit for all units of the public finance sector. In these terms, Poland follows international standards of internal audit as professional practices (Owsiak 2017: 611).

[8] Dz. U. z 2016 r., poz. 561.

Another stage in the improvement of the allocation system of public resources was the introduction in 2009, by means of the Act on Public Finance, of managerial control over institutions. Implementation of this act was in compliance with the arising determination to introduce modern methods of management to the public sector. It was also desired from the point of view of the purpose-oriented allocation of EU resources by different projects (Owsiak 2017: 613).

Managerial control is defined as "a scope of activities undertaken to ensure execution of goals and tasks in accordance with law and in an effective, economic and timely manner". The purpose of managerial control is in particular to ensure:

- compliance of the operations with the law and internal procedures;
- the effectiveness and productivity of operations;
- the reliability of statements;
- the protection of resources;
- the enforcement and promotion of ethical principles of conduct;
- the effectiveness of the information flow;
- risk management (Article 68 paragraph 2 of the Act on Public Finance).

The provision of adequate, effective and efficient managerial control is the responsibility of:

- the minister in the government administration departments managed by him or her;
- the town mayor, city mayor, president of the city, president of the board of local government;
- the manager of the unit.

Managerial control is coordinated with internal audit pursuant to Article 71 of the Act on Public Finance and includes:

- promoting standards of managerial control, in compliance with international standards;
- cooperation with national and foreign organisations;
- cooperation with internal audit committees (Article 71 of the Act on Public Finance).

2.5 Challenges in Further Development of Public Sector Accounting and Auditing

Over the last 20 years, many important reforms have been undertaken in public sector accounting with the goal of adapting it to changes brought about by the introduction of the New Public Management philosophy. The New Public Management (NPM) concept has significantly influenced the shape of present public sector accounting in Poland. The introduction of the accrual basis makes it possible to develop financial reporting, but it also requires it to adjust the changes to the plan of accounts of local government units. However, it is worth underlining that in Poland budgeting reporting is given priority over financial reporting.

The research on the IPSAS implementation in other countries indicates the insignificant implementation advancement, despite the reasonably long period of discussion regarding the application and implementation. In addition, the progress of EPSAS development is considerably delayed in comparison to the original proposals and plans. These factors, among others, have remarkably influenced the possibilities of IPSAS/EPSAS implementation in Poland (Siewieczek and Tkocz-Wolny 2017: 104–105).

It is quite problematic to implement the International Public Sector Accounting Standards in Poland, for several reasons, as follows. The Bureau of Research, the Chancellery of the Sejm, prepared in 2013 the Opinion on the report from the Commission to the Council and the European Parliament 'Towards the implementation of harmonized public sector accounting standards in the Member States. The usefulness of the International Public Sector Accounting Standards for Member States' (COM [2013] 114 final). Though the European Commission report was positively addressed in the Opinion, it pointed out that the process of implementing harmonised accounting standards might take longer than the European Commission assumes, due to the differentiated arrangements across countries. In addition, the implementation of these standards to streamline the governance process in the public sector may result in fewer benefits than it was firstly anticipated. Even more there is a concern that further actions towards the European Commission's proposals' application would require verification of whether or not the proposed reforms materially affect the principle of proportionality and the principle of subsidiarity (Szpringer and Łacny 2013: 4).

The level of familiarity with IPSAS contents in Poland is relatively low. The lack of their translation into Polish constitutes a crucial limitation in the process of their popularisation. Given that understanding the IPSAS themselves is not easy, it is even more difficult to adapt the general English text to the nature of the Polish public sector. The translation of IFRS into Polish, partially used for the purpose of IPSAS translation, is not most adequate, since IPSAS refers to public finance units that are not referred to, in IFRS.

In addition, there is a considerable dispersion of accounting rules in public finance in Poland which is another factor enhancing the aforementioned difficulties. Consequently, the application process requires intense activities, strong coordination and longer period of implementation, if it is to result in lowering the cost of this process (Siewieczek and Tkocz-Wolny 2017: 104–105).

In Poland, it is possible to use the procedures of preparing and presenting financial reports stated in IPSAS. However, in order to do that it is necessary to adjust the current examples of reports and estimates to those specified in the standards. Implementation of EPSAS in the EU countries, including Poland, shall significantly influence, among others, on the financial reporting of public finance units (Siewieczek and Tkocz-Wolny 2017: 104–105; Wrona et al. 2018: 66).

2016 Report of the Minister of Finance, titled "Assumptions of the budgetary system reform", indicates that polish government sector lacks the financial statement that would constitute an equivalent of the local government financial statement that includes the data from financial statements of budgetary local governments and establishments. It is especially important in terms of current activities timing at standardisation of public sector accounting in EU (Ministry of Finance 2016: 34).

One of the first steps towards the implementation of EPSAS in Poland is the enacted obligation to prepare the financial statement of the state's budget. The first statement (the balance sheet) will be prepared for the financial year 2018 (The Resolution of the Minister of Finance and Development as of 13 September 2017, on accounting and chart plans for the state budget, budgets of local government units, budgetary units, self-government budgetary establishments, state earmarked funds and state budgetary units based outside the Republic of Poland). However, according to A. Siewieczek and K. Tkocz, the slow process of implementing IPSAS/EPSAS makes the process of implementing EPSAS quite distant. No actions have been undertaken on the government level to adjust/implement these standards to national resolutions. It is worth underlining that Poland is one of the countries where financial reporting of the public sector relies mainly on the memorial principle which signifies that the basic concept of implementing IPSAS loses its significance. Thus, IPSAS/EPSAS implementation in Poland will require quite high adjustment of the expenditures, mainly in terms of training aimed at spreading the detailed knowledge on IPSAS/EPSAS (Siewieczek and Tkocz-Wolny 2017: 104–105). The biggest obstacle related with future IPSAS/EPSAS application in Poland is high costs of implementation. Another issue is the lack of adequate relation between the complexity of standards and the size of the unit, as well as the issue of satisfying the accounting and reporting needs of not all but some of the users (Siewieczek 2015: 128–129).

Internal auditing as institutional control, in contrast to functional management control (a system of management control), focuses on the overall weaknesses of the management system, including the control and effectiveness of risk management, and not only on specific cases of error. On the other hand, management control ensures that tasks are carried out in a lawful, economical and timely manner. For this purpose, management control requires the use of prevention, detection and correction mechanisms. The new approach to public finance audits in the public finance sector, in connection with the adoption of the NPM concept, will have an effect on the further extension of internal audit tasks and the increased role assigned to the internal audit tasks (Adamek-Hyska and Szczepankiewicz 2016: 16–18).

The implementation of an internal audit depends on the nature of the sector and thus it is much differentiated. The obligation to carry out audits in the units of public finance sector for which the budget is over PLN 40 mln has limited the control and supervision in these units and has not influenced on the increase of management quality. This solution has increased the possibility of financial and legal risk in the processes that lack systematic controls. Finally, an important issue that has not been addressed is the set of criteria of evaluating the audit by means of indicators. Elaboration of a group of objective, transparent indicators shall allow for evaluating the internal audits of public finance units by different evaluating bodies (Sojka 2017: 193–194).

References

Adamek-Hyska, D., Szczepankiewicz, E. I. (2016). New Public Management wyzwaniem dla rachunkowości, kontroli zarządczej i audytu wewnętrznego w sektorze finansów publicznych. Studia Ekonomiczne, Zeszyty Naukowe Uniwersytetu Ekonomicznego w Katowicach, Nr 307, Katowice.

Annual Report Supreme Audit Office (NIK). (2010). Warsaw.

Bakalarska, B. (2005). *Komentarz do zmian w sprawie sprawozdawczości budżetowej*. Gdańsk: ODDK.

Country Report of Poland. (2011). *Regional Public Sector Audit in Poland*, pp. 1–8.

Filipiak, B. (Ed.). (2009). *Metodyka kompleksowej oceny gospodarki finansowej jednostki samorządu terytorialnego*. Warszawa: Difin.

Hausner, J. (Ed.). (2003). *Administracja publiczna*. Warszawa: Wydawnictwo Naukowe PWN.

Heciak, S. (2014). *Finanse i rachunkowość sektora publicznego*. Przewodnik dla nie finansistów: PRESSCOM, Wrocław.

Hellich, E. (2005). Treść ekonomiczna zdarzeń gospodarczych. *Prace Naukowe Akademii Ekonomicznej we Wrocławiu*, pp. 63–71.

Kostur, A. (2012). *Metody i procedury audytu wewnętrznego w jednostkach sektora finansów publicznych*. Katowice: Uniwersytet Ekonomiczny w Katowicach.

Kowalczyk, M. (2015). Ewolucja rachunkowości budżetowej w Polsce [Evolution of Budgetary Accounting in Poland]. In J. Krasodomska & K. Świetala (red.), Współczesne uwarunkowania sprawozdawczości i rewizji finansowej [Present Conditions of Reporting and Audit]. Kraków: Uniwersytet Ekonomiczny w Krakowie.

Kowalczyk, M. (2017). *Podstawy analizy ekonomiczno—finansowej w jednostkach samorządu terytorialnego*. Warszawa: Difin.

Lubińska, T. (2010). *Budżet a finanse publiczne*. Warszawa: Difin.

Marczakowska-Proczka, J. (2008). *System budżetowy państwa, w: System finansowy w Polsce, tom 2*. Warszawa: PWN.

Maciejewska, I., & Wojtczak, M. (2012). *Badanie sprawozdań finansowych jednostek sektora finansów publicznych*. Warszawa: Krajowa Izba Biegłych Reidentów.

Owsiak, S. (2017). *Finanse publiczne*. Warszawa: PWN.

Podstawka, M. (Ed.). (2017). *Finanse*. Warszawa: PWN.

Report of the Minister of Finance. (2016). *Assumption of the budgetary system reform*. pp. 1–45.

Rozporządzenie Ministra Rozwoju i Finansów z dnia 13 września. (2017). r. w sprawie rachunkowości oraz planów kont dla budżetu państwa, budżetów jednostek samorządu terytorialnego, jednostek budżetowych, samorządowych zakładów budżetowych, państwowych funduszy celowych oraz państwowych jednostek budżetowych mających siedzibę poza granicami Rzeczypospolitej Polskiej, Dz.U. 2017, poz. 1911.

Rudzka-Lorentz, C. (2008). *System finansowy jednostek samorządu terytorialnego w: System finansowy w Polsce, tom 2*. Warszawa: PWN.

Ruśkowski, E. (2008). Finanse samorządu regionalnego i lokalnego w. In Z. Strzelecki (Ed.), *Gospodarka regionalna i lokalna*. Warszawa: PWN.

Siewieczek, A. (2015). W kierunku standaryzacji rachunkowości jednostek sektora publicznego – perspektywa europejska, Studia Ekonomiczne. *Zeszyty Naukowe, Uniwersytet Ekonomiczny w Katowicach, Nr, 252,* 118–130.

Siewieczek, A., & Tkocz-Wolny, K. (2017). Ocena możliwości implementacji IPSAS do systemu rachunkowości podmiotów sektora publicznego w Polsce. *Zeszyty Teoretyczne Rachunkowości, tom, 94*(150), 81–108.

Sojka, K. (2017). Analiza funkcjonowania audytu wewnętrznego w Polsce w aspekcie obowiązujących regulacji prawnych. *Finanse, Rynki Finansowe, Ubezpieczenia, 3*(87/1), 187–195.

Supreme Audit Office. (2012). *Annual report 2011*. Warsaw, pp. 1–37.

Surówka, K. (2013). *Samodzielność finansowa samorządu terytorialnego w Polsce*. Warszawa: PWE.

Świderska, G. K. (2003). *Rachunkowość zarządcza i rachunek kosztów*. Warszawa: Difin.

Szpringer, Z., & Łacny, J. (2013). Opinion on the Report from the Commission to the Council and the European Parliament "Towards the Implementation of Harmonized Public Sector Accounting Standards in the Member States. Usefulness of International Public Sector Accounting Standards for Member States". COM/2013/114/FINAL. Bureau of Research, Chancellery of the Sejm.

Winiarska, K. (Ed.). (2016). *Sprawozdawczość finansowa i budżetowa jednostek sektora finansów publicznych*. Warszaw: Wolters Kluwer.

Winiarska, K., & Kaczurak-Kozak, M. (2013). *Rachunkowość budżetowa*. Warszawa: Oficyna Wydawnicza a Wolter Kluwer business.

Wojtczak, M. (2013). Wytyczne w zakresie sporządzania sprawozdania finansowego o charakterze łącznym w JST. In: M. Łyszczarz & G. Dragon (Eds.), *Vademecum skarbnika jednostki samorządu terytorialnego*. Warszawa: C.H. Beck.

Wrona, B., Rechul, H., & Szulc, M. (2018). Zawartość informacyjna sprawozdań finansowych jednostek sektora finansów publicznych. *Zeszyty Naukowe, Uniwersytet Ekonomiczny w Krakowie, Nr, 2*(974), 61–80.

Założenia reformy systemu budżetowego, Ministerstwo Finansów. (2016). Warszawa. 1–45.

Zysnarska, A. (2010). *Rachunkowość budżetowa w świetle koncepcji prawdziwego i wiernego obrazu*. Gdańsk: Wydawnictwo Uniwersytetu Gdańskiego.

Zysnarska, A. (2011). *Rachunkowość budżetu, jednostek budżetowych i samorządowych zakładów budżetowych*. Gdańsk: ODDK.

Zysnarska, A. (2014). *Rachunkowość budżetu, jednostek budżetowych i samorządowych zakładów budżetowych*. Gdańsk: 2014.

Useful Site

http://www.dziennikustaw.gov.pl/.

CHAPTER 3

Public Sector Accounting, Auditing and Control in Romania

Adriana Tiron-Tudor

3.1 Territorial Organization, Scope of the Public Sector and Distribution of Public Revenues

3.1.1 Territorial Organization

Romania is situated in the southeastern area of Central Europe, and shares borders with Hungary to the northwest, Serbia to the southwest, Bulgaria to the south, and the Black Sea to the southeast, Ukraine to the east and the north and the Republic of Moldova to the east. Since 1 January 2007, Romania is a full member of the European Union.

In 2016 the Romania population was 19.976.314 citizens, representing 3.9% of total EU. The population density is 91 inhabitants/square kilometres. It has a whole surface of 238.397 square kilometres and is dominated by the Carpathian Mountains in the north and centre of the

A. Tiron-Tudor (✉)
Faculty of Economic Studies and Business Administration,
Babes-Bolyai University, Cluj-Napoca, Romania
e-mail: adriana.tiron@econ.ubbcluj.ro

V. Vašiček and G. Roje (eds.), *Public Sector Accounting, Auditing and Control in South Eastern Europe*, Public Sector Financial Management, https://doi.org/10.1007/978-3-030-03353-8_3

country while the main feature in the south is the vast Danube valley, which becomes a delta as it approaches the Black Sea.

After 1989, the year that marked the fall of Communism in Eastern Europe, Romania entered in a new stage of her evolution with a political system described as a representative democracy, governed by the directly elected President and Parliament (semi-presidential system). The President of Romania mandate is five years, with the possibility of a second term. The Romanian Parliament is bicameral: Chamber of Deputies with 332 directly elected deputies and the Senate with 137 directly elected senators. Both Chambers of the Parliament have the same power (Muraru and Constantinescu 2005). The bicameral Parliament of Romania is the only one in Europe where senators and deputies are elected by the same vote system, directly by the citizens, it represents the same population and it has a common mandate of four years (Dima 2009).

Romanian territory is divided into Counties, Communes and Towns. Towns with a large number of inhabitants and being of vital economic, social, political and scientific importance at the national level or meeting the necessary conditions for development in these fields may be classified as municipalities (cities).

The 41 counties of Romania are run by county councils composed of members elected by universal, equal, direct, secret ballot for a four-year term. The council has the following attributes: supervises the implementation public administration law, it is responsible for the distribution of the public funds. There is no subordination between local councils and county council. The county councils are responsible for coordinating commune and town councils in the performance of those public services that are of countywide interest. They deal with economic development activities and establish the general orientation of spatial planning, environmental policies and county fees and taxes.

The county council president is appointed by the elected members of the council and is the legal representative of the council. He can delegate responsibilities to the two vice presidents who are appointed by the members of the county council.

The central government appoints the Prefect as a representative of the government at the County level. The Prefect role is to monitor the legality of the local and county public administration authorities' administrative acts adopted or issued and to ensure the implementation of the government strategy and programmes in their county.

County-level competencies are in the following areas: county development, land development, water supply and sewage, public transports, departmental roads, social assistance to children and education. The Romanian Counties are the administrative-territorial units at the intermediate level, while Communes, Towns and Municipalities (Cities) form the local administrative level. The local level comprises 2859 Communes (groups of villages in rural areas) and 423 towns and municipalities (cities).

The local council is the deliberative assembly. It is composed of councillors elected for a four-year term. The local council is responsible for the local authority budget approval. The mayor is elected by universal direct suffrage for a four-year term, is the executive body, and leads the local public administration. Some of the mayor responsibilities can be delegated to the vice-mayor. Local council competences are in the following areas: housing, urbanism, environmental protection, public health, waste management, local transport infrastructure, water supply and sewage system education (except academic level), administration of the local heritage, security (through the local police), administration of the parks and public gardens and other green public areas.

In Romania there are eight regional divisions (called development regions) created to better coordinate regional development as Romania progressed towards accession to the European Union, and consist of several counties each (The Law on Regional Development in Romania, The Official Gazette of Romania, no. 315/2004).[1] These correspond to NUTS II-level divisions in European Union member states, without an administrative status and a legislative or executive council or government. The deliberative body is the National Council for Regional Development (NCRD) which functions on the principle of partnership. The NCRD coordinates at the national level, the regional development policies' implementation. NCRD is composed of 15 representatives of the Government and 16 representatives of the Regional Developments Councils (RDC). The Minister for development, public works and housing chair the NCRD. The 8 RDCs are also deliberative bodies without legal personality representing the developing regions. Each of them is assisted by executive authorities, the Agencies for Regional Development (ARD). The competences of regional divisions are the preparation and implementation of the regional and operational and development programmes and funds management.

[1]The Official Gazette of Romania ("Monitorul Oficial al Romaniei") is the official legal publication of the Romanian State, and it is available at: http://www.monitoruloficial.ro/?lang=hu.

Legal acts issued by the Government, are mandatory for the local authorities. The Prefect, as representative of the government at County level, control the legality of local authorities' actions. Articles 120 and 123 of the Constitution prescribe the legal limits of the exercise of jurisdiction by the Prefect on the Local Councils, which are "the functional autonomy, the principle of administrative autonomy and decentralization as well as the principle of decentralization of public services".

In addition to the Constitution of 1991, amended in 2003, the Law no. 215/2001 on Local Public Administration (The Official Gazette of Romania, no. 776/2006), the Framework Law no. 195/2006 of Decentralization (The Official Gazette of Romania, no. 453/2006) and the Law no. 315/2004 on Regional Development (The Official Gazette of Romania, no. 577/2004) are the primary sources of legislation.

3.1.2 Central and Local Government Financing

Concerning the public finance, two laws constitute the legal framework in Romania. Law 500/2002 on public finances (The Official Gazette of Romania, no. 597/2002), amended in 2013 regulates the state finances and the state social security finances, and at the local level, for administrative-territorial units, the Law 273/2006 on local public finances (The Official Gazette of Romania, no. 618/2006) is applied. The law regulates the financial issue of governmental activities of counties, municipalities and cities (from now on local government units). This act defines the financial relations between the central government and local government units, regarding the distribution of joint tax revenues and rights of local entities on the collection of tax and non-tax revenues from their jurisdiction. Since 2010, the state and local finances and budget proposals must take into consideration and adopt the national fiscal strategy (Law no. 69/2010 on Fiscal Responsibility, The Official Gazette of Romania, no. 330/2015).

The above-mentioned legal frameworks are inter-connected. On the one hand, the Public Finances Law no. 500/2002 and the Local Public Finances Law no. 273/2006 establish the general rules of state and local finances and budgets formation, administration, elaboration, execution, actors involved and their responsibilities. On the other hand, the Fiscal Responsibility Law no. 69/2010 complements both the Public Finances law and the Local Public Finances Law, establishing the medium- and long-term fiscal discipline principles and laying down the multiannual fiscal framework and spending ceilings within which the latter two operate.

Romanian system of public finance is still highly centralized. Most of the public needs are being financed through the state budget, which in turn makes up a vast majority of total public expenditure.

The process of Romanian fiscal decentralization can be divided into three separate periods (Profiroiu and Profiroiu 2006). The first one (1991–1994) developed essential steps for the organization of the administrative structure and the financing of local public authorities. The second one (1998–2000), it was an increase in the revenues transferred to local budgets. The last one (2001 onwards), has been marked by the adoption of the Local Public Administration Law no. 215/2001, which regulates the general features of self-government and autonomy, and by the Local Public Finances Law no. 273/2006 that specifies the rules for revenues and spending at the local level. The adoption of the new Law on Decentralization no. 195/2006, which transfers new responsibilities to sub-national governments, along with the 273/2006 Law on Sub-National Public Finances and the Public Services Law no. 51/2006 (The Official Gazette of Romania, no. 254/2006), recently began a new chapter of decentralization in Romania (Profiroiu and Profiroiu 2006).

The new framework law on decentralization defines a set of principles, rules and steps that have to be respected by each ministry in the process of transferring new competencies to the local governments. The final objective was to integrate the efforts made by each line ministry involved in this process into a coherent, systematic and efficient decentralization policy. According to the new regulation, local governments are entirely responsible for human resources management in primary and secondary schools, setting up the local police service and running the local and country public health units. They benefit from additional resources to build and maintain the public road network and the decentralization of cultural and local interest religious institutions. Sub-national governments now also have the right to set energy prices as part of the changes in public utility management changes. The Law introduces some fundamental concepts for the implementation of the future transfer of administrative and financial responsibilities from central to local level, including cost and quality standards, the geographical area for beneficiaries, their organizational capacity and a more specific definition of shared, delegated and exclusive responsibilities.

With all progress concerning the local financing system decentralization, Romanian local governments remain dependent on transfers from the central government, as own revenues can cover only a small fraction of their financial needs (Profiroiu and Profiroiu 2006; Rusu and Petrisor 2017; Profiroiu et al. 2017).

Local governments administrate four major categories of revenues: current fiscal revenues (e.g. taxes on properties, land and transportation vehicles); current non-fiscal revenues (e.g. transfers and grants from the state budget); capital revenues (e.g. local assets revenues); and revenues from particular sources (e.g. taxes and unused expenses from previous years).

The principle of local financial autonomy entitles the administrative units to sufficient financial resources that local authorities can use on the basis and within limits provided by law. Local authorities have the power to establish levels of local taxes under the law. Resource allocation to balance local budgets should not affect the application of budgetary policies local authorities in their area of competence. Local budget revenues are as follows: own revenues comprised of taxes, fees, contributions and other payments, other income and allowances deducted from income tax; amounts from certain revenues of the state budget; grants received from the state budget and different budgets; donations and sponsorships; values obtained from the European Union and/or other donors. Local autonomy allows grounding, sizing and distribution of local budget expenditures on authorizing officers by purpose, i.e. the actions, activities, programmes, projects, objectives, are made by the powers conferred to local authorities; they set priorities to operate their respective local interest. Substantiation and approval of local budget expenditures are in strict correlation with the real possibilities of local budget revenue collection, estimated to be achieved.

3.2 Formulation and Execution of Central Government and Local and Regional Self-Government Budgets

3.2.1 Formulation of Central Government and Local Government Budgets

The budget processes refer to budget formulation, approval, budget execution and supervision of the budget and are prescribed for the central and local budgets, with differences appearing in the application of the budget, as a consequence of differences in the level of public authorities, size and structure of their budget.

Principles of the budgeting process enforced by Romanian laws are as follows:

- The universality principle,
- The principle of advertising budget,
- The principle of budgetary unity,
- The principle of annual budget,
- The principle of budgetary specialization,
- The principle of monetary unicity.

Romania has a robust legal framework for budget formulation, established by the Law on public finances 500/2002 and has recently been complemented by the Fiscal Responsibility Law 69/2010. The legal framework defines the budget calendar, related procedures and the role of the main players involved, including the Ministry of Finance (MOF), Line Ministries, Parliament and Fiscal Council.

The Romanian state budget is adopted on an annual basis by the Parliament acting by simple majority on the proposal of the Government. According to Article 138 of the Romanian Constitution, "the national budget includes the state budget, the state social security budget and the budgets of the administrative-territorial units". Yearly, by 15 August, the Government sends the Parliament the fiscal strategy for the next three years together with a legislative proposal on spending ceilings obligatory for the reference budgetary year and the next two years for approval. The state budget along with the state social security budget proposal drafted by the Government is transmitted to the Parliament by 15 November. The Parliament approves the state budget laws by a simple majority. In case the budget law is not authorized by mid-December, the Government must demand the examination of the budget law in the emergency procedure. If the Parliament fails to reach an agreement on the budget laws three days before the start of the next budgetary year (by 28 December) the old budget is applied until the adoption of the new budget. As well, the Constitution of Romania provides at Article 138 (5) that "no budgetary expense may be approved without a pre-established financing source".

The budget process combines a top-down and bottom-up budgeting approach. First the Government, through the MOF, centralizes the overall goals of the national budgetary frame. Then, MOF drafts the annual state budget laws, fixing the spending ceilings for the reference budgetary year. In the second stage, the MOF informs the primary ordinateurs on the macroeconomic estimates and limits within which their respective budgets are to be drafted. The primary ordinateurs send the budget proposals to the MOF which analyses their consistency with the set macroeconomic estimates, ceilings and fiscal-budgetary strategy. In the final stage, the consolidated state budget is sent to the Government and subsequently to the Parliament for approval. The local budgets are approved at the local level.

Romanian budgeting is based on line-item budget which is extensively used due to the following advantages: easy to prepare and does not require sophisticated financial skills; simple to administer, facile to understand, revenues and expenditures can be easily monitored (Lazăr and Inceu 2004). Line-item budgets list total departmental appropriations by items for which funds are to be spent, presenting a detailed destination map for each amount.

The state budget laws may be "amended later on a maximum of two times during the budgetary year but exclusively during the last six months" (Law no. 69/2010 article 15(2)).

As of 2013, the law on public finances expressly states that "the Medium Term Budgetary Framework (the 'MTBF') is the basis for the annual budget" (Law 500/2002, Section 1-1). The MTBF follows the macroeconomic and budgetary estimates of the European Commission closely. Any change in the MTBT shall be "highlighted in the annexe to the annual budget proposal and dully justified" (Law 500/2002, article 30-2 (3)).

Given the frequent Government changes noted in the past, the 2013 amendment stipulates that in case of Government change the MTBF may be updated according to the new governance priorities; however, "the changes shall be detailed and clearly specified" (Law 500/2002, article 30-5 (3)). As well, in response to prolonged electoral periods registered in the past, in case parliamentary elections are scheduled in the last three months of the annual budgetary period (October–November) "the budget must be adopted before" (Law 500/2002, article 35-1).

Local budgets are prepared by every territorial-administrative unit due to the principle of autonomy, assuring the decisional independence of local governments and the improvement in the use of local funds and financial resources. Budgetary procedure regarding local budgets is conducted on the principles stated by the named laws. Precisely, "public administration in territorial-administrative units is organized and operates under the principles of decentralization, local autonomy, devolution of public services, local governments' eligibility, legality and consultation of citizens in solving local problems of particular interest" (Law no. 273/2006). The Law no. 273/2006 establishes the following principles for budgets: universality, transparency and publicity, unity, monetary unity, annuallity, budgetary specialization and balance.

A stronger emphasis on the multiannual budgetary planning has been included as of 2010, in the form of a multiannual fiscal strategy (Law 69/2010, article 5). Later in 2013, an express medium-term budgetary framework has been introduced, to line up the national and EU budgetary frameworks (Law 500/2002, Section 1-1). The budgetary calendar substantially changed to allow proper incorporation of European Semester recommendations (Law 500/2002, Section 2). A complete transition towards the European Account System (EAS) in budget planning and reporting, notably for the public deficit calculation was adopted (Law 500/2002, article 7-1).

Regarding budgetary stability, the new legal framework limits the amendments of the budget laws to two budget rectification yearly, both allowed only in the second part of the budgetary year. Further corrections may be included just in situations of extraordinary macroeconomic imbalances.

The budget expenditure classification system in Romania allows reporting according to the international standards (ESA 95 and GFSM 2001). It includes an administrative (organizational), a functional and economic classification. There is currently no programme segment either in the budget classification or the Court of Audit (CoA).

Budget classifications are used as a framework for recording and reporting the revenues and expenses. Starting with 2014, income and expenditure accounts were opened on the Classification of the Functions of Government (COFOG) III budget classification structure (Finance Minister Order no. 720/2014, The Official Gazette of Romania, no. 396/2014).[2] Thus, the state, through its treasury, provides data validation regarding the budget execution of income and expenditure as well as the automatic validation of payments, through their inclusion within the limits of the approved budget.

[2] The order refers to the execution of the income and expenditure budget of the autonomous public institutions, of the public institutions financed entirely or partially by their revenues and by the activities which are wholly funded from their revenues.

Budget classification is "the grouping of the budgetary income and expenditure in a compulsory order and unitary criteria" (Law no. 500/2002, article 2). According to the budget classification of central and local budget revenues and expenditures, expenses are viewed from a functional and economic point of view. Government expenditure, according to with COFOG classification describes government expenditure according to 10 significant functions or purposes: (1) general public services, (2) defence, (3) public order and safety, (4) economic affairs, (5) environmental protection, (6) housing and community amenities, (7) health, (8) recreation, culture and religion, (9) education, and (10) social protection. Economic classification groups the expenditure according to their economic nature and effect. By using the economic classification, it seeks both to set trends in state policy and management analysis of the budgetary funds to micro and medium economic levels.

This current classification, contained in Annex no. 2 of the Law 273/2006 can be adapted and updated as a result of the improvement of the fiscal legislation as well as by the annual budget laws by the programmes for increasing the financial autonomy of the administrative-territorial units and decentralization of public services. It is the basis for drawing up local budgets, executing them, and drawing up the budget execution account.

The local budget expenditures are grouped according to the functional classification as follows: public authorities and external actions; other general public services; interests; general transfers between different levels of government; defence, public order and national security; education; health; culture, recreation and religion; insurance and social assistance; housing, services and public development; environment protection; general economic, commercial and labour actions; fuel and energy; agriculture, forestry, fish farming and hunting; transport; other economic actions. These categories of expenditure in local budgets are in turn divided into chapters and sub-chapters.

3.2.2 Budget Execution and Budget Execution Reporting

The legal framework for budget execution is stipulated in Law 500/2002 on Public Finance. Structurally, Romania's budget execution system resembles other continental European countries.

The Government is responsible for the realization and coordination of national fiscal budgetary policy. The MoFP conducts this activity.

The budgetary execution is organized in a three-layered system involving the primary, secondary and tertiary managers (credit holders). The primary managers dispose of and approve the public fund's expenditure. At the central level, the primary managers are usually the heads of Ministries and other central public or autonomous authorities, whereas on the local level the primary managers are the Mayors and Presidents of local councils. The secondary managers are the heads of public institutions with legal personality in the subordination of the primary managers, while tertiary managers are the heads of public institutions with legal nature in the subordination of primary or secondary managers. The primary and secondary managers assign and use the budgetary resources, whereas the tertiary ones may only use the funds allocated.

At the central Government Level, there are 75 primary credit holders with about 9000 subordinated secondary and tertiary credit holders. The primary managers are the Minister or Head of Agency, who typically internally delegates public finance functions to the secretary general. Also, there are about 3200 local government credit holders, e.g. mayors, which hold autonomously approved budgets, but use the services of the central treasury for budget execution. Each of these entities has designated financial management staff responsible for committing funds and authorizing spending within the allocated budget credit and for adequately accounting for transactions by the prevailing CoA.

Budget execution is split into four stages in accordance with the principle of duties segregation: commitment, verification, payment order and payment.

Cash is released through monthly "credit opening". Main spending authorities present each month several requests for cash releases, which should be in line with the quarterly spending limit. These requests are accompanied by a note presenting the operations that will be financed. After reviewing these requests, the "credit openings" are authorized, and release cash to central spending authorities and partly to secondary spending authorities. These "credit openings" are recorded in the Treasury payment system. Then, the authorized cash releases are distributed in cascade fashion within the line ministries or other significant spending units. This process is manual and relies on postal mail for distribution of credit openings to regional offices.

Budget execution includes the collection of revenue and making the authorized expenditure (Anghelache et al. 2017). This duty is incumbent upon the Government. The income registered in the budget is a minimum task, the attention being directed toward identifying all the revenue sources and the full collection of the sums due to the State, without committing fiscal abuses. In return, for expenses, the amounts registered in the budget represent maximum limits. The undertaking of spending above the threshold approved or for other purposes than those for which the approval was granted is a breach of the financial discipline. As regards shifting to the execution of cash accounts of the budget, i.e. to the actual collection of revenues and to the payments at the expense of the budget resources allocated, few previous operations have to be carried out. First, the annual figures approved by law for revenue and expenditure have to be assigned by quarters, depending on the juridical terms for collecting taxes and for time grading of the spending. Then the appropriations are made available, or the authorizing officers' accounts are financed opened with the State Treasury, an indispensable condition for the allowances to be used. Resource allocation may be made within the limit of the appropriations approved by legal destinations about the degree the resources previously made available are used. The authorizing officers are obliged to use the allocations received only within the limit and for the purposes approved for spending related strictly to the activity of the institution they lead. The execution of cash accounts of the budget is different for revenues and expenditure.

There is a rigorous delineation between the execution of the part of revenue and the execution of the part of expenditure by the forbiddance to make payment directly from the revenue and in agreement with the rule of non-contracting revenue and expenditure. By a public institution "financed from the budget's engaging expenditure" is understood that it undertakes to pay in the future a sum of money to a third party, natural person or legal entity. The engagement should have a legal ground. It is made when procuring goods or services by concluding a contract, issuing an order or accepting an offer. Some obligations are born from adopting a decision to appoint in the case of hiring a civil servant by a judgment with writ of execution whereby the court is obliged to make payments or the engagement can result from the laws adopted by the Parliament in respect of the introducing new pay scales for State employees which leads to the salary increase with regard to salary indexation or awarding compensations.

The validation of expenditure has two phases and presupposes the carry out of the operation engaged or set out previously and setting out of the sum due to the beneficiary. As compared with the degree of fulfilment of the obligations recorded on the occasion of a previous engagement, the amount due coincides or not with the one set out when the expenditure was engaged. The authorization of payment is made by issuing an order, or an order of payment addressed to the cashier whereby, following validation, payment of the sum due to the beneficiary is ordered. The engagement and expenditure making is approved and is made only if there is a preventive financial control stamp on that document. For the consolidated expenditure or systematic, such as payment of the civil servant's salaries or payments in the account of public debt service, payments can be made without prior verification. When implementing the revenue part the principle of separating the functions is also observed, and the operations being carried out are different about the type of revenue due to the State.

The State Treasury plays a vital role in budget execution. The State Treasury's purpose is to provide cash management, payment, accounting and reporting services to government institutions, being a significant enabler of efficient Government operations, transparency and accountability to the public. The State Treasury works on the principle of a single and unique cash account, through which all transactions of the state budget are executed. Treasury is a "complex system of administration of activities", which are realized through the collection and spending of state (public) money and conducted through the Treasury Single Account.

Execution of budget within the treasury system has its implications on the use of budget execution reports and accounting records. The Treasury focuses on cash flows and uses the cash basis of accounting to control the execution of the budget. Budget execution reporting makes the government accountable for the execution of the budget according to the approval by the Parliament at State level and the local council at a local level. The state and local government budgets are reported annually and at each trimester according to Romanian legislation.

The report on budget execution shows: (i) the commitment authorization; (ii) the initial payment budgetary credit; (iii) the revised budgetary credit; (iv) the budgetary commitments (reservation of the budgetary credit for a specific use); (v) the legal commitments; (vi) the payments; and (vii) the verified expenditures including unpaid expenditures.

The annual budget execution report comprises the revenue column provisions of initial budgets, final budget provisions and collections made, and in the expenditure initial budget appropriations, final budget appropriations and payments made. The Ministry of Public Finance (MOF) draws-up and appends to the general execution account of the

State budget and the general account of public debt. It comprises the reports of the domestic public deficit and direct foreign public debt of the State and the statement of the government guaranteed internal and external appropriations received by other legal entities.

The principal activities of the MOF in budget execution include: (i) in-year financial planning and release of funds; (ii) debt management; (iii) payment processing; (iv) accounting and reporting; (v) financial control; and (vi) support to internal audit. MOF aims to and permanently supervises the carry out of budget implementation and submits regular reports for informing the Government in respect of the balance state of the budget. To that effect, it employs the quarterly accounting statements of the authorizing officers and keeps track of the accounts in respect of the execution of cash accounts of the budget by the State treasury. At the end of the budget year, the MOF drafts the annual general report of the execution of the State budget and, respectively, the execution of cash accounts of the individual fund's budgets and the budgets of the authorizing officers, including the annexes to these. In parallel, the Treasury Information System can produce aggregate budget execution reports on a cash basis, nearly in real time.

The principle of transparency implies that all critical budget information must be available to the general public and presented in an understandable and precise manner.

Revenue recognition is performed based on types of revenue by nature and source, and the accounting for the income and expenses for the general budget is carried out according to the structure of the budgetary classification in force. Based on the financial statements presented by the leading authorizing institutions, the accounts regarding the cash implementation of the state budget, the state social insurance budget and the individual funds budgets, drawn up by the authorities legally entrusted with this task, and following the analysis and verification thereof, the MOF drafts the state budget general annual implementation account and the state social insurance budget implementation account, particular funds budget yearly implementation accounts and the budgets of the central authorizing institutions (Law 500/2002) and then submits to the government. Following the verification by the Court of Audit (CoA), the implementation accounts are approved by the parliament. MOF drafts the annual balance sheet of public institutions (Law no. 82/1991 on accounting, The Official Gazette of Romania, no. 265/1991, 495/1998). The information in the financial statements of public institutions is used for preparing financial reports by the MOF, the National Bank and the National Institute of Statistics; the reports are submitted to the Statistical Institute of the EU (Eurostat) according to the European system of national and regional accounts, and to the International Monetary Fund.

Regarding the public access to public information, the legal framework is constituted from Law no. 544/2001 on free access to general information with ulterior supplements.

The principle of transparency and publicity requires that the budget process is an open and transparent one, this being achieved by:

- publishing in the local press, on the website of the public institution or by displaying at the local public administration authority the draft of the local budget and annual account of its implementation;
- Public discussion of the local budget draft, during its approval and presentation of the annual account of the local budget execution in public meeting. Procedures for advertising and publishing the budgets of territorial-administrative units are presented in Law 273/2006, article 76, with ulterior modification.

The principal officers of local public institutions must allow the documents and information on budget (i.e. budgets' drafts, approved budgets, financial statements in budgetary implementation) be available on the websites of territorial-administrative units.

The article 1 point 2 in the Law 273/2006 refers to: local budgets of communes, towns, municipalities, districts of Bucharest, counties of Bucharest; budgets of public institutions wholly or partly funded from local budgets, as appropriate; budgets of public institutions financed from own revenues; budget of external and internal loans for which repayment, payment of interest, fees, expenses and other costs are paid from local budgets and external loans contracted by state and sub-loaned to local authorities and/or operators and public service subordinated to them; loans to local government authorities and state-guaranteed, foreign investments and/or internal contracted or guaranteed by local authorities and external grants budget.

Framework legislation for budget management has been in place since the organic budget law 500 was passed in 2002. The legal framework has more recently been reinforced, notably about macro-fiscal discipline, through the Fiscal Responsibility Law no. 69/2010. The transposition of Acquis requirements into national law resulted in changes in the internal control environment, most importantly the establishment of internal audit units across the Government (Cioban et al. 2015).

Since the beginning of the financial crisis, the Fiscal Responsibility Law 69/2010 represents the first significant change of the Romanian budgeting system. The law was adopted in late 2010 and responded to the main challenges identified by the "troika": lack of independent monitoring, the absence of a robust multiannual fiscal strategy, poor fiscal targets enforcement and weak fiscal rules. Therefore, the Fiscal Responsibility Law first puts in place an independent Fiscal Council to ensure the monitoring function. Secondly, a multiannual fiscal strategy stage is introduced. As highlighted in the budgetary calendar above, "the Government by August 15 submits the next three years fiscal budgetary strategy on an annual basis to the attention of the Parliament" (Law 69/2010, article 18). Furthermore, "the Government approves a legal proposal annually on budgetary limits for the reference budgetary year and the next two years to be adopted by the Parliament" (Law 69/2010, article 20).

In drafting the annual budget laws, the Government take into account the fiscal budgetary strategy. At the same time, the primary managers line up their budget proposals with the budgetary policy and macroeconomic estimates communicated by the MOF subject to the sanction of rejection of the budget proposal in case of failure to do so.

Fourth, strict fiscal discipline rules were introduced, backed by responsibilities and sanctions (Law 69/2010, Section XI).

3.3 Accounting and Financial Reporting

3.3.1 Accounting System

Until 2002 the accounting system for the public sector applied in Romania was characterized as being an accounting system based on cash. For Romania, in the context of European integration, the achievement of the public sector accounting reform has become an urgent necessity (Tiron-Tudor 2006). The main adjustments needed regard:

- the use of accrual systems for inventories, receivables (taxes, social contributions and interests) and payables necessary for the recognition of expenditures (and receipts) made in financial periods other than those in which the costs were incurred (Tiron-Tudor 2017).

- the recognition of full depreciation of fixed assets to ensure full incorporation into the costs of activities of the consumption, use and deterioration of fixed assets. This is often a significant cost component of capital-intensive public sector activities.
- the assessment of reasonable profits as "costs of capital" will recognize the return on investment implicit in the use of the funding of fixed and working capital by owners or by other funding sources in addition to loans.
- the re-evaluation of fixed assets to allow for inflation will result in recognition of current fixed asset values and the related ongoing costs of depreciation. It also affects the proper recognition of the return on investment, when expressed as a percentage of the real (opportunity) costs of capital.

With the intention of harmonizing the public sector accounting system with the European and international regulations, in the period 2002–2005 the reform started with as follows (Tiron-Tudor 2006):

- The induction, liquidation, ordering and payment of public institutions expenses (Order of the Minister of Public Finance (OMPF), no. 1792/2002, The Official Gazette of Romania, no. 426/2005),[3] the four stages of the budget execution of expenses are carried out by all public institutions no matter their subordination and the way of financing expenses with compulsory preobservance of procedures. Public institutions are also compelled to organize, lead the record and report the budgetary and legal arrangements starting with 2003.
- The re-evaluation and depreciation of fixed assets belonging to public institutions are introduced in the history of public administration in Romania (Government Ordinance (GO) no. 81/2003,[4] The Official Gazette of Romania, no. 624/2003, and OMPF

[3]The Order regards the approval of the Methodological policies regarding the organizing and management of the accounting of public institutions, Accounts plan for public institutions and application instructions.

[4]The Ordinance refers to the re-evaluation of the fixed assets belonging to public institutions.

no. 1487/2003,[5] The Official Gazette of Romania, no. 788/2003). By entering re-evaluation, the goal was to bring at the current cost or the entrance value actualized in correlation with the utility of goods and their market value, and by introducing the depreciation, the aim was to reflect the real value of assets and the presentation through financial statements of a real image of the patrimony.

– The organization and leading of budgetary incomes accounting (OMPF no. 520/2003 on organization and leading of budgetary incomes accounting, The Official Gazette of Romania, no. 267/2003), according to the Accounting law, that stipulates the compulsoriness of registering in accounting the rights and obligations of the public institutions when they are acknowledged, in this sense there had been until that moment a significant contradiction between the national regulation in accounting and the rules applicable to public institutions.
– The introduction of a new budgetary classification (OMPF no. 1025/2005, on the classification of public finance indicators, The Official Gazette of Romania, no. 1020/2005) appropriate starting with 2006 according to ESA 95 requirements concerning accounting, and public debt has contributed to making an essential step in the harmonization of the public sector accounting with the European and International regulations.

With the implementation of OMPF no. 1917/2005, on Accounting of Public Institutions, a unified chart of accounts is applicable for the central and local government units and all public institutions have been applying the same accounting system ever since. The public institutions (Law no. 500/2002) represent the generic name to include the Parliament, Presidential Administration, the ministries, the other specialized bodies of public administration, public authority, autonomous public institutions, as well as the institutions under their command regardless of the funding manner. Main, secondary and tertiary spending authorities of the State budget and other government entities keep their accounts using the modified accrual accounting method.

[5] The Order refers to the Methodological Norms on the revaluation and depreciation of the fixed assets in the patrimony of public institutions.

Romania has made significant steps in adopting the accounting methodologies to international standards. Also, in the period from 2003 to 2009 Romanian government implemented 18 International Public Sector Accounting Standards (IPSAS) accrual-based accounting standards (Tiron-Tudor 2011).

The new regulation, OMPF no. 1917/2005 has brought a new Chart of Accounts for public entities, revolutionizing the accounts coding method. Thus, the synthetic accounts grew up to the level of synthetic accounts of the third degree, and the latter, to report the balance to the Ministry of Public Finance (MOF), develop to analytical accounts. More specifically, any account is encoded in the system using 40 characters of which: 7 characters are compulsory for the synthetic accounts and 33 characters are mandatory for the analytical accounts. In the accounting records the use of the 40 characters is compulsory, to which may be added, optionally, additional analytics as needed. The coding method for the compulsory analytical accounts is built on an algorithm in seven steps shown below:

1. The accounting symbol according to the General Chart of Accounts 7 characters
2. Sector code 2 characters
3. Source code 1 character
4. Revenue and expenditure functional classification 6 characters
5. Expenditure economic classification 6 characters
6. Sector/subsector according to ESA 5 characters
7. Unique registration code of partners 13 characters

The new system assures data transmission to EUROSTAT at COFOG III level (for revenues— classification on chapters, subchapters, paragraphs, and for expenses—classification on chapters, subchapters, paragraphs, titles, articles, items).

Public accounting includes: budgetary revenue and expenditure accounting, reflecting the settlement of revenue and the payment of expenditure in a financial year; general accounting, based on accrual basis of establishing rights and obligations and reflecting the evolution of the financial situation and the assets, including the surplus or deficit of assets; and cost analysis accounting for approved programmes (Law 500/2002, Law 82/1991).

Public sector accounting provides information on the assets under the public institutions' administration, the execution of the revenue and expenditure budget, the result of the budgetary execution, the situation of assets and liabilities and the cost of approved programmes. Revenue and expenditure are registered in the accounting records of public institutions according to the rules of accrual accounting. Thus, the effects of transactions and other events are recognized when the said transactions and events take place as of fact, not when cash amounts or equivalents are cashed in or paid, and are consequently registered in the accounting records and reported in the financial statements of the corresponding periods. The financial records of public institutions, which are drawn up in the form of double-entry accounting, provide information to the users not only on past transactions that involved collections and payments but also on future payment obligations and the resources corresponding to future proceeds.

The public sector accounting regulation refers to the generally accepted accounting principles, sets the chart of accounts, rules of measurement and evaluation, as well as rules for recording the transactions and events. According to this regulation, all public sector reporting entities, are obliged to use a unified and uniform accounting framework, as follows:

- The assets are initially recognized in the case of a purchase, at acquisition cost, if are produced by the entity, at production cost. During the useful life of long-term assets, subsequent expenses are capitalized if the capacity of asset increases or if there are some cost reductions. If there are just some repayments, the value is recognized as expenses. The depreciation of fixed assets is to be determined and reported individually, on a time-line basis and with the application of prescribed, average, annual rate adjustment (reduction) values. The accumulated depreciation and impairment of assets diminish the value of assets in the balance sheet. The basis for the write-off of fixed assets is its initial or reassessed value (purchase value or estimated value).
- Liabilities arise from past events and outflow of resources is expected for their settlement. Purpose and maturity classify liabilities. According to timeline, debts can be classified as short or long-term obligations.

- Revenues, regardless of their character, are defined as an increase in economic benefits during the reporting period, in the form of inflows of cash and cash equivalents or not. This refers mainly to revenues from non-exchange transactions which include tax revenues, transfers, revenues from charges.
- Expenses are defined as decreases in economic benefits in the form of a reduction in assets or increase in liabilities. Expenses are fundamentally classified as operating expenses (i.e. current expenditures) and expenses for the acquisition of long-term assets (i.e. capital expenditures).
- Operating expenses are recognized when occurred (by the transaction in the reporting period to which they relate, regardless of the payment). The asset depreciation is systematically presented as a depreciation expense. Donations of long-term assets are recognized as revenue. Expenses are recognized by actual consumption. Borrowing costs are not capitalized and are fully recognized as an expense in the period in which they occurred;
- Own resources are remaining assets after deducting all liabilities, which include funds from the budget and other sources and operating result.

3.3.2 Financial Reporting

Financial reporting is prescribed as mandatory, prescribing the form and content of financial reports, periods covered by the reports, as well as liabilities and deadlines for their submission.

The set of financial statements includes: (a) the balance sheet which presents the assets and liabilities and financial situation at 31 December of the current year and previous year; (b) the revenue and expenses account revealing the economic performance at 31 December of the current year and prior year; (c) the cash-flow statement showing amounts collected and paid during the year and the final treasury position; (d) the statement of changes in capital details the increases and decreases during the year in each item of the capital accounts; and (e) reports on the implementation of the budget of the institution (OMFP 1917/2005).

The Annex to the financial statements supplements and comments on the information presented in the statements referred before and supply all the additional information prescribed by internationally accepted accounting practice where such information is relevant to the activities of a public institution. The same regulation refers to the budget execution reports that comprise: (a) the budgetary outturn account, which sets out all budgetary operations for the year regarding revenue and expenditure; (b) the Annex to the budget outturn account, which shall supplement and comment on the information given in that account.

The financial statements of public institutions are accompanied by a report on budgetary and financial management during the year.

In the balance sheet, the assets and liabilities are disclosed separately in two groups: current and non-current, depending on the period of their realization (less the one year and over one year) which permits to users the calculation of financial ratios of liquidity, risk, solvability and others. The assets are reflected in a decreasing scale of liquidity and liabilities are reflected in an increasing sale of payment date. The net assets (own equity) is calculated in balance sheet like the difference between the total of assets and sum of liabilities, and are composed by the current result and earned result, funds and revaluation reserves.

In the Romanian regulation, the balance sheet structure is fixed, very detailed for some positions. The own capital position is composed of the period result, retained earnings from previous years and provisions, without capital contributions of other public institutions.

Patrimonial outcome statement includes revenue and expenditure according to the nature of their business: operational, financial and extraordinary in a fixed structure. It discloses the patrimonial revenues, funding and expenditures during the current year. Revenue and grants are presented on types of income by their nature or source, whether earned or not. Expenditures are shown on types of expenses by nature or destination, whether paid or not. Revenues that do not involve their collection are also disclosed (e.g. income and value adjustments resumption provisions) and calculated expenditure (e.g. depreciation, provisions and value adjustments) which do not involve payment.

The patrimonial outcome account is a new statement for Romanian public institutions, the patrimonial outcome concept is not defined comprehensively by the national regulations, and it is not very well understood by the practitioners.

The public institution presents, as a separate component of its financial statements, a statement showing:

- The net surplus or deficit for the period;
- Each item of revenue and expense, which, as required by other standards, is recognized directly in net assets/equity, and the total of these items; and
- The cumulative effect of changes in accounting policy and the correction of fundamental errors dealt with under the benchmark treatments in IPSAS 3.

For cash flow statement, the Romanian regulation requires the use of only the direct method. The way in which the method is presented and explained is not similar to IPSAS 2 because it requires to use separate columns for each account opened at Treasury and banks (Tiron-Tudor 2011).

Budget execution account discloses information that can be used for better management of budget revenue and expenditure data that established rights (income), legal and budgetary commitments (at cost).

Budgetary accounts must show, for each subdivision of the budget:

- for expenditures: initial budget allocations approved, the budget allocations made to amend, the commitments made, payment of the financial year, the duties still to pay
- for income: recorded in the initial budget estimates, the estimates made in amending budgets, the rights established, the proceeds realized, the remaining registered receivable duties.

Report on budgetary and financial management during the year must submit an accurate description of the objectives to accomplish for the year, in line with the principle of sound financial management and financial situation and the events that had a significant influence on activities during the year.

Notes to financial statements, under international regulations, must contain the following information:

- the principles, rules and accounting procedures;
- explanatory notes providing additional information not incorporated in the financial statements which are necessary for an accurate picture;
- showing off-balance sheet commitments and obligations included in the balance sheet justifications that may have a material impact on assets and liabilities, financial position or results of that entity.

Romanian regulations consider that the notes are part of financial statements and contents: accounting policies and explanatory notes. Explanatory notes provide supplementary information which is not included in financial statements.

Quarterly and annual financial statements are prepared by all 14,000 spending units and consolidated by Ministry of Public Finance (MOF). The reporting process is labour-intensive and time-consuming. The State budget financial statements are verified and consolidated by principal spending authorities for their subordinated secondary and tertiary spending units. Then, they are centralized by the Finance Ministry. Similarly, local authorities' reports are consolidated by the county public finance departments.

The modernization bases of financial reporting in Romanian public institutions were set through a project funded from non-refundable external funds post-accession entitled ForExeBug (The Operational Program for the Administrative Capacity Development co-financed from the European Social Fund). Romanian Finance Ministry created simplified forms for reporting financial statements by public institutions and functionality of the electronic control and monitoring legal and budgetary commitments in the Treasury, with direct impact on improving fiscal discipline and prevention of arrears of public institutions. The new software for reporting financial statements of public institutions also provide the authorizing officers effective budget management, providing real-time information on using the approved budget in all public institutions subordinated hierarchically, ensure proper functioning of electronic mechanisms for aggregation, centralization, consolidation and reconciliation of financial data reporting entity hierarchies, funding sources and other criteria.

3.4 Audit and Other Oversight (Supervision) in the Public Sector

3.4.1 State Audit

In Romania, the Court of Accounts (CoA) conduct public finances management audit, without jurisdictional competences. The CoA's role is to contribute to the improvement of how the state and public sector financial resources are established, administered and used

(Tiron-Tudor 2007). Also, the CoA provides reports to the Parliament and deliberative bodies of the administrative and territorial units annual. The CoA's reports include:

- the CoA's comments on the execution accounts of the budgets subjected to its control;
- the conclusions resulting from the inspections ordered by the Chamber of Deputies or by the Senate or conducted at the level of self-managed commercial companies with state integrally or majority owned capital and at other legal entities subjected to the control of the CoA;
- the law infringements found and the measures taken;
- other issues which the CoA deems necessary.

The duties of the CoA involve in principal financial audit, performance audit and control. Also, CoA endorses normative regulations in the field of public finances, public accounting and of the ones mentioned explicitly by law. CoA verifies whether public funds are correctly accounted for, and spent in keeping with the applicable regulations, as well as whether due consideration is given to obtain a value for money (Stefan et al. 2015).

Audits are carried out by procedures laid down by the framework of the International Organisation of Supreme Audit Institutions (INTOSAI). According to the auditing standards of the INTOSAI, there are two types of audits: regularity or financial audit and performance audit. The review process is determined by the auditing standards, and after completion of the audit, auditor's opinion should be made (Tiron-Tudor 2007).

Court of Accounts audits the constitution, management and use of state and public sector financial resources. The audit function of the CoA is exercised using public external audit procedures set out in audit standards drafted by the international audit standards. Within its tasks established by law, the CoA carries out particular activities about all public entities. The specific activities of the CoA consist of control and public external audit. Public external audit mainly includes financial audit and performance audit. Additionally, the CoA has the task of assessing the own financial control and the internal audit activities of the legal persons falling within its competence.

As an EU Member State, for Romania, it was mandatory to establish an audit authority for non-refundable pre-accession and post-accession EU funds granted to Romania by the EU. The audit authority is the only national authority in charge of the public external audit of non-refundable funds given to Romania by the EU, by international and national legislation.

The CoA drafts an annual public report that is submitted to the parliament and which includes: observations on the budget implementation accounts controlled, the conclusions drawn based on the controls ordered by the Chamber of Deputies or by the Senate or performed on autonomous companies, wholly or predominantly state-owned companies and other legal persons subject to the control of the CoA; the infringements found and the coercive measures are taken, and other aspects considered relevant by the CoA. The CoA also drafts an annual report on the degree of implementation of the internal control system in the controlled public entities.

3.4.2 Budgetary Oversight

In Romania, there is consultation of Parliament in the preparation of the state budget. The Government prepares and submits a state budget annual draft and a separate one for state social security schemes which are forwarded to the parliament for approval. The modalities of Parliament oversight are the following:

- Analysis of the budget/finance act by the chambers in joint session and before the approval of the state budget and the state social security budget. The plenary debate is preceded by a presentation of the essential elements of both drafts as well as by a display of the joint report of the two finance committees.
- Reports on the budget/finance act by Committees. Individual or groups of parliamentarians may prepare amendments to be sent to the budget, finance and banking committees of each chamber within a maximum of five days from the date the draft budgets were received. And, then, the finance committees in a maximum of 30 days, draw up a joint report on each of the two draft budgets. The statements include both adopted and rejected amendments with a brief explanation in each case.

The Parliament exercises oversight over all public funds. The fields overseen are as follows: defence budget and budget of specialized departments.

The Parliament debates the broad lines of the economic policy that the Government must implement and grants a vote of confidence following the presentation of the Government's legislative programme. The Government is required to submit the draft budget bills to the parliament for approval by 10 October each year at the latest. There is no deadline set for the parliament to approve the budget. Consequences of failure by Parliament to adopt the budget/finance act: If the bills for the state budget and the state social security budget have not been adopted at least three days before the expiry of budget period, the figures for the state budgets of the previous year are applied until the new budgets are approved.

3.4.3 Public Internal Control System

Starting from 1990, Romania began the process of transition to a market economy. In parallel, the process of preparation to join the European Union (EU) included concerted actions aimed at reforming public management and increasing its performance. Before its accession to the EU, Romania integrated the EU acquis regarding Chapter 28 "Financial Control" in its entirety, harmonized national and EU legislation and developed the institutional infrastructure necessary for its implementation. In the domain of public administration, the MOF implemented the components of public internal control, that is, internal audit, managerial control, and managerial responsibility and accountability. The state transferred a part of its control tasks to the management of public entities and concentrated the forms of control exercised in public institutions by independent structures, shifting emphasis to management systems, internal audit and actions ensuring effective public services.

3.4.3.1 Public Internal Audit

The public internal audit is defined by Law no. 672/2002 on public internal audit (The Official Gazette of Romania, no. 856/2011) in the same manner as the Internal Auditors Institute (IIA). "Internal audit in public entities is a functionally independent and objective activity, which endorses and counsels the administrative personnel for a good management of public revenue and expenses, improving the activities of the public entity; it helps the public entity to achieve its objectives through a systematic and methodical approach, which evaluates and improves the efficiency and effectiveness of the management system based on risk management, control and administration processes."

Public internal audit in Romania is organized as follows: Public Internal Audit Committee (PIAC); Central Unit for the Harmonisation of Public Internal Audit (CHU PIA) and public internal audit (PIAS) structures within public entities directly subordinated to the manager or the collective management body. PIAS's tasks include risk management systems assessment, control and good governance, and the follow-up on the transparency and conformity with the rules of legality, regularity, efficiency and effectiveness rules.

For local public entities that are not subordinated to other public entities and have an annual budget of up to the equivalent of EUR 100,000, the public internal audit is limited to the regularity audit, performed by the territorial internal audit branches of the MOF.

The CHU PIA carry out the internal audit function, based on a protocol, for central public entities having an annual budget of up to RON 5,000,000 and that, at a local level, coordinate and offer guidance to the public entities in implementing the cooperation system for ensuring the public internal audit function. The CHU PIA issued general rules on exercising the public internal audit activity, based on the Standards of the Internal Auditors Institute (IIA), including the Internal Audit Charter.

The internal audit activity, as regulated by law, comprises assurance engagements and advisory missions (counselling). Within assurance engagements, the following types of audit are performed: regularity (conformity) audit; system audit; performance audit. Given the shift towards the consolidation of the implementation of the public internal audit function in public sector entities, the number of performance audit missions has now increased. Where, during internal audit missions, the internal auditors identify irregularities or possible damages, they must report them immediately to the public entity management and the authorized internal control structure, because they are not authorized to investigate them (Dascalu et al. 2016).

The distinct organization and the functional independence of the public internal audit department, as set out by the legislation in force, allow for a clear separation of the internal audit tasks from any of the functions exercised by the personnel of the public entity, including about the implementation of the control/managerial system.

One of the tasks of the CHU PIA (Law 672/2002), is to cooperate with the CoA and with other authorities and public financial control bodies from Romania and abroad, including the European Commission. The CoA is in charge of the external evaluation of the public internal audit activity of the verified entities. Between MOF and CoA there is a collaboration protocol by which the opportunities for cooperation and collaboration between public internal audit and external audit are explored. While safeguarding the independence and objectivity of the public internal audit and external audit, the protocol regulates the relations between the two institutions according to the complementarity principle with regard to increasing the efficiency of the audit activity, aligning the methodological framework, ensuring the professional training of the auditors and exchanging information.

3.4.3.2 Audit Committees

Public Internal Audit Committee (PIAC) operates audit committees in Romania, in accordance with Law no. 672/2002, as a consultative body organized under the CHU PIA that carries out actions with a view to defining the strategy and improving the public internal audit activity in the public sector. The main tasks of the PIAC are to endorse the strategic development directions of public internal audit, draft legislation in the field of internal audit; annual reports on public internal audit activity and submit them to the government. Also, PIAC tasks include issuing an opinion on the reports of internal audit activity assessment missions, as well as on the reports of intersectoral audit missions that are significant at a national level. PIAC assess the consequences of the non-implementation of the recommendations that were not assumed by the management of the public entities; to evaluate the cooperation agreements between public internal audit and external audit, as well as the programmes for the professional training of auditors. The new draft law provides for the establishment, at the level of those central authorizing institutions within the central public administration that has an annual budget exceeding RON 2,000,000,000, of audit committees, made up of three to seven members, with tasks similar to those of the PIAC within the MOF. The Law on public internal audit has been modified to allow for audit committees that focus on supporting the specific roles of the internal auditor. In 2010 Romania started introducing the function of internal audit at the level of local administration (town halls in rural areas) on the basis of audit partnerships. The first form of collaboration was among members of the Romanian Association of Communes (RAC). In practice, this means that a number of town halls that are members of the RAC decide to cooperate by establishing an internal audit structure to serve them. At the moment of writing this contribution there are already 12 such partnerships operational. The new Law on public internal audit also aims to cover communes that are not members of the RAC.

3.4.3.3 Coordination of the Public Internal Control System

The public entity manager has the task of ensuring the elaboration and development of internal/managerial control systems, as well as of providing an independent and functional internal audit. The coordination and harmonization thereof are assigned to the MOF, through two specialized structures, the Central Unit for the Harmonisation of Financial Management and Control Systems (CHU FMC) and the CHU PIA.

By establishing the CHU FMC, the MOF enabled the assurance, methodological guidance, coordination and supervision of the implementation of internal/managerial control systems. There is a unitary strategy in the field of financial management and internal control, with internal control standards, harmonized implementation rules, to ensure sound financial management of public funds and assets and a professional training system of the specialists involved in internal control.

The management of public entities takes the necessary measures for the elaboration and development of the internal/managerial control systems within the respective entities. Such actions mainly consist of: elaborating and/or updating the programme for the development of the entity's own internal/managerial control system; setting up the structure in charge of the monitoring, coordination and methodological guidance of the own internal/managerial control system; elaborating and/or updating formalized procedures for activities; following up on the implementation of the measures included in the development programme; performing analyses on the development of the internal/managerial control system. As of 2011, the management of each public entity elaborates an annual report on the internal/managerial control system, which represents a statement of conformity of the public entity's internal/managerial control system with the internal/managerial control standards.

The MOF, via the CHU FMC, issues and submits to the government an annual national report on internal control, which reflects the progress in the implementation of the internal/managerial control system at the level of public institutions exercising the function of principal authorizing officer for the state budget, the state social insurance budget or any special fund budget, including their subordinated public institutions.

The CHU PIA is responsible for the elaboration, management and application of a unitary strategy in the field of public internal audit and in the national monitoring thereof; development of the legislative framework in the area of public internal audit; development and implementation of uniform procedures and methodologies, based on international internal audit standards; development of the system for reporting the results of public internal audit activity; elaboration of the annual report on the public internal audit activity for the public sector; performance of audit missions of national interest; assessment of the compliance with the rules, instructions and Conduct Code for Internal Auditors by the public internal audit structures; coordination of the recruitment and professional training system in the field of public internal audit; endorsement of the appointment/dismissal of the heads of the public internal audit structures within public entities; cooperation with the CoA and other public institutions in Romania and from abroad. The PIAC operates under the CHU PIA, which carries out its activities within the MOF.

3.4.3.4 Managerial Control

The need for internal management control resides precisely in its purpose, namely achieving the objectives set by the public entity and improving the economy (minimizing the cost of resources used to produce the estimated results of an activity, while maintaining the appropriate quality of these results) and efficiency (maximizing the results of an action in relation to the resources used) of the public entity management. According to the law in our country, the internal management control is defined as "all forms of control exercised at the level of the public entity, including internal audit, established by management in accordance with its objectives and legal regulations, in order to provide economical, efficient and effective fund administration; it also includes organizational structures, methods and procedures". Designing, building, elaborating and developing the internal/managerial control, including formalized activity-based procedures is a lengthy process that requires significant efforts from the entire personnel of the entity and in particular from the employees in management positions. The goal is to create a uniform and consistent model of internal/managerial control to allow comparisons between entities of the same kind or the same entity at different times, and make it possible to highlight the results of the entity in its evolution. To this aim, the internal control management uses a set of 16 standards. These standards are grouped into five essential elements: the environment of control, performance and risk management, control activities, information and communication, evaluation and audit. They are constituted as a starting or reference point against which to assess the system and identify areas and directions of change. The five essential elements are specific to the model of internal control implemented by the Committee of Sponsoring Organisations (COSO) since 1992 in the US, which was improved later on.

3.4.3.5 Internal Financial Control

The internal control environment is structured after the Public Internal Financial Control framework, in compliance with EU requirements (Popa et al. 2016). There is a system of preventive (ex-ante) financial control performed by:

- internal financial controllers who perform ex ante financial control of all expenditure transactions (commitments, cash opening and payment order) in all ministries and central spending units,
- "delegated" financial controllers who belong to the staff of the MOF CHU for Financial Management and Control in 29 line ministries or primary spending units. They perform financial controls on transactions above a certain amount, which are generally in the range of 30,000–50,000 RON (8700–14,500 USD).

After the approval of the annual budget law, the principal spending authorities draft quarterly budget implementation plans which are reviewed by the BPGD and approved by the minister of Finance. The primary spending authorities include ministers, heads of other public bodies and specialized agencies and chiefs of autonomous public entities. Once the quarterly budget implementation plans are approved, the primary spending authorities distribute the approved budgetary credits for their budget and for their subordinated public entities or units, whose managers are secondary or tertiary spending authorities. Then, the secondary spending authorities distribute the approved budgetary credits for their budget and their subordinate tertiary spending authorities. To ensure prudent budget execution, the main spending authorities are required to allocate in their budget implementation plan 10% of approved funding to a reserve, except personnel expenditures and funds related to external liabilities, which are entirely distributed. This reserve is allocated during the second half of the year.

3.4.3.6 Managerial Responsibility and Accountability

The existing legal framework describes managerial responsibility as a process in which managers at all levels are responsible for the decisions made, and actions are taken to achieve the objectives of the public entity of which they are part. This issue involves the accountability of the managers for good financial governance and the legality of public funds and public asset management. Managerial responsibility at the level of public entities includes the management of the entity or component thereof, within the boundaries of internal or external determinations, in order to achieve the established objectives efficiently, effectively and in accordance with the legal provisions; transparent communication in this regard; and accountability for the non-fulfilment of managerial obligations, according to their respective type of legal responsibility. Responsibility is an essential obligation for all the managers in the public sector and is regulated, in all cases, by legislative acts such as laws, government decisions, authorities' rules and regulations, etc. In organizing the management actions based on the concept of managerial responsibility, the managers take the following premises into account: the general manager/authorizing officer is responsible for the optimum organization and operation of the internal control system; the internal control system of the public entity shall be based on verifications and corrective measures, on the one hand, and on independent internal and external assessments, on the other hand; the general manager/authorizing officer is responsible for achieving the objectives of the entity; the general manager/authorizing officer may delegate authority/competence without being exempted from public accountability; managerial accountability may not be invoked in the absence of the corresponding authority/competence; responsibility requires transparency and accountability. Managerial responsibility and accountability in the field of public management are regulated mainly as follows.

In accordance with the Law no. 69/2010, fiscal budgetary responsibility main objectives are: to ensure and maintain the fiscal budgetary discipline, transparency and sustainability of public finances, in the medium- and long-term; to establish a framework of principles and rules based on which the government ensures the implementation of fiscal budgetary policies leading to sound financial management of the resources; to manage public funds efficiently so as to serve the public interest in the long term. The law mentioned above establishes the responsibilities in the field of the government, the MOF and the principal authorizing officers. Thus, the law introduces into government practice the accountability statement, signed by the prime minister and the MOF, which certifies the correctness, completeness and legality of the information in the fiscal budgetary strategy, the targets or the limits for fiscal rules and the observance of the fiscal responsibility principles. The accountability statement is presented to the parliament together with the fiscal budgetary strategy and the legislative proposal for approving the limits specified in the fiscal budgetary strategy. The cited law also introduces the conformity statement, signed by the prime minister and the MOF, which confirms the conformity of the budgetary construction with the rules and targets established in the fiscal budgetary strategy. The statement is presented to the parliament together with the annual budget. An important role in the budgetary process is the role of the Fiscal Council, an independent authority in charge of providing support to the government and parliament in the drafting and development of the fiscal budgetary policies and which answers to the parliament for the correctness and accuracy of the analyses/studies/opinions and recommendations elaborated in accordance with its responsibilities.

Under Government Ordinance no. 119/1999 on internal control and financial preventive control (The Official Gazette of Romania, no. 430/1999), the MOF is responsible for the elaboration and implementation of policy in the fields of internal/managerial control and financial administration. The MOF offers methodological guidance, coordinates and supervises the implementation of internal/managerial control systems and the assurance of sound financial management in the use of public funds and the management of public assets. Internal/managerial control comprises the ensemble of control mechanisms exercised at the level of the public entity, including internal audit, established by the management in accordance with its objectives and the legal provisions in force, in order to ensure an economical, efficient and effective fund management; this also refers to the organizational structure, methods and procedures. Internal/managerial control verifies the achievement of the following general objectives:

- the regular, efficient, economical and efficient accomplishment, at a reasonable quality level, of the tasks of public institutions, as established in accordance with their mission;
- the protection of public funds against losses due to errors, misuse, abuse or fraud;
- compliance with laws, regulations and management decisions the development and maintenance of systems for the collection, storage, processing, updating and dissemination of financial and management data and information, as well as of public information systems and procedures by means of periodic reports.

Government Ordinance no. 119/1999 regulated the internal/managerial control on the use of public funds and the efficient, effective and economical management of public assets and set out the responsibilities in this area of the public institution manager. Furthermore, it regulated the responsibility of the managers of specialized departments that initiate operation projects as regards the reality, regularity and legality of the operations whose supporting documents are certified by their signature. The persons entitled to perform the financial control are accountable, according to their respective responsibility, for the legality, regularity and compliance with the ceilings of the budgetary appropriations or accrual appropriations, as applicable, of the operations for which they granted the ex ante financial control approval. The financial control of operation projects having patrimonial implications at the level of public entities takes the form of own preventive financial control, which falls within the scope of managerial responsibility. In half of the main authorizing institutions, preventive financial control is also exercised by delegated comptrollers from the MOF. Preventive financial control on behalf of the MOF at the level of these main authorizing institutions comprises a low volume of operation projects, which nevertheless imply a significant risk. The number and value of operation projects that are re-verified by comptrollers of the MOF are decreasing from one year to the next. The strategy for the development of PIFC in Romania for 2010–2013 (hereinafter referred to as the "strategy") sets out as a major objective the gradual integration of preventive financial control within the scope of managerial responsibility, to the extent that management control is capable of increasingly eliminating the risks in the administration of public funds. By Government Ordinance no. 119/1999, under a legislative initiative concluded at the end of 2010, the top management of each public entity has the responsibility to draft an annual report on the internal/managerial control system. The statement is meant to increase the awareness of institutional managers at all levels as regards their responsibilities in the implementation of internal control standards. A regulatory level after the above-mentioned ordinance is represented by the Order of the MOF no. 946/2005 (on the management and internal control system, The Official Gazette of Romania, no. 675/2005) approving the Internal Control Code, comprising the internal control standards for public entities and the development of managerial control systems. Moreover, the standards constitute a reference system for the assessment/reassessment of internal control systems and the identification of risk areas and necessary changes. At the level of each public institution, a structure was established that is usually managed by the secretary-general and is in charge of drafting/updating the development programme of the managerial internal control system, which comprises the objectives of the public entity, the actions, responsibilities, deadlines and other components of such measures. Another example of the application of the managerial responsibility principle at the level of public entities, by Order no. 946/2005, is the development of formalized procedures, which include a distinct chapter on the respective responsibilities of the different management levels involved in the process.

Managerial responsibility is also regulated by Law on accounting no. 82/1991. Under this law, the responsibility for the organization and management of the accounting devolves upon the administrator, the authorizing officer or any other person entrusted with the management of the respective entity. As a rule, the accounting is organized and managed within separate departments and run by the economic director, the accountant-general or any other person authorized for the position; accountability for any misapplication of the accounting regulations devolves upon such persons and their subordinates. The annual financial statements are accompanied by a written statement of the persons responsible for the organization and management of the accounting, in which they assume responsibility for the drafting of the annual financial statements and confirm that: the accounting policies applied for the preparation of the annual financial statements are in accordance with the applicable accounting regulations; the yearly financial statements provide a clear overview of the financial position and financial performance; the legal person carries out its activity in conditions of continuity. The general regime for the legal relations between public officers and the state or the local public administration generically referred to as work relations, is regulated by Law on The status of public officers (The Official Gazette of Romania, no. 188/1999). Public positions are assigned general tasks and responsibilities common to all public authorities and institutions, as well as tasks and liabilities that are specific to some public authorities and institutions. In general, within public institutions, the top manager or the secretary-general in charge of elaborating the policies, in conjunction with the economic manager, represents the competence level to which the endorsement of the following works is assigned: the draft budget, the revenue and expenditure budget, the organization of the ex-ante control, budgetary programming and implementation, the modification of financial indicators, the financial statements, the payrolls, etc. Thus the top manager or the secretary-general elaborates the policies regarding the institution's budget, based on the supporting activities carried out by the economic manager. The objectives, activities, tasks and main responsibilities of the management and personnel participating in the achievement of institutional objectives are established by the regulation on the organization and operation of the institution and are set out in the job descriptions.

Accountability, as regulated by Law on ministerial responsibility (The Official Gazette of Romania, no. 115/1999), refers to the political accountability of the government as a whole and of each of its members. The government is politically accountable only to the parliament, under the confidence vote it received upon investiture, and each member of the government may be held politically accountable, together with other members, for the activity and actions of the government. Besides political accountability, the members of the government may be held accountable for a civil, contraventional, disciplinary or criminal point of view, according to the general legislation in the field, notwithstanding derogatory provisions. Internal control, organized at the level of the public authority or institution, also includes the legality notice issued by the legal adviser for documents of a legal nature prior to their approval by the manager of the public institution, which is regulated by Law on the organization and practice of the profession of legal adviser (The Official Gazette of Romania, no. 514/2003).

3.5 Challenges in Further Development of Public Sector Accounting and Auditing

One of the Romania's challenges for the next period in the development of public sector accounting is the EPSAS implementation. At European level, the sovereign debt crisis has underlined the need for more rigorous, transparent and comparable reporting of fiscal data. The primary objective of implementing harmonised European Public Sector Accounting Standards (EPSAS) is to increase fiscal transparency and achieve comparability of public sector accounting and reporting systems within and across the member states.

Romania, like all UE members, respects Council Directive 2011/85/EU on requirements for budgetary frameworks of the Member States that sets out the rules on Member State budgetary frameworks necessary to ensure compliance with the Treaty obligation to avoid excessive government deficits. In this context, the idea of a unique set of accounting standards for all UE members arises. At first IPSAS issued by IPSASB were considered a possible suitable solution, but after a detailed analysis it was decided to proceed with EPSAS development for the Member States to adopt.

Working Group on EPSAS was launched in September 2015, to build on the work of the Task Forces and to establish a more permanent forum concerned with the development, introduction and operation of EPSAS in the mid-to-longer term. Romania had participated and will continue participating in this taskforce with a group of experts from Finance Ministry, Court of Accounts, academia and national accountancy professional body CECCAR. The Working Group task is to identify the key issues for EPSAS governance and standards, and to discuss how to develop and introduce suitable EPSAS structures and requirements. At national level the group of experts has analysed the possibilities of EPSAS implementation and the regulation changes requested. Romania has done important steps toward a sound governmental reporting package under FOREXBUG project.

The Romanian Finance Ministry completed the implementation of the project "Increasing the Accountability by upgrading computer system for reporting financial statements of public institutions (FOREXEBUG)". The project's objective is to increase the efficiency of central government and local administrative transparency, by providing the public institutions with modern standardized instruments for reporting and disclosing of financial statements and details on the use of public funds in accordance with budgetary classifications. The software allows automatic generation of summary reports (standard and ad hoc) based on the data collected via electronic reporting of financial statements and to improve budget management by reducing reporting burden related activities and creating the possibility for reallocation of time for analysis and decision-making activities in the area. The software allows the presentation of the main topics covered, challenges and potential benefits (i.e. main topic being defined as a standard Chart of Accounts for all public entities, with a challenge of identifying types of analytical accounts needed and improved efficiency as a result of standardization as a potential benefit or main topic being defined as the reconciliation methodology for the cash to accrual deficit, with a challenge of identifying the exceptions from the standards to be included in the reconciliation and an automated reconciliation between the cash and accrual deficit as a potential benefit.

The FOREXBUG system is to ensure proper functioning of electronic mechanisms for aggregation, centralization, consolidation and reconciliation of financial data reporting entity hierarchies, funding sources and other criteria. The main challenges for the Romania to implement the government reporting package are as follows (PWC 2013):

- roll out of the project from central to entity level,
- providing quality input into the reporting system,
- budget to actual comparison,
- ongoing and focused training for accounting professionals at all levels and across the territory so that recognizing the transactions is standardized and input is accurate and reliable.

The internal public sector audit function, in Romania is in its third stage of its evolution. The initial period (1999–2002) is marked by the regulation of the internal audit function, area of applicability for internal audit, existence of a mandate for performing the audit mission, aadoption of a risk-based approach for planning the internal audit activity). The second one (2003–2011) concerned the implementation of the internal audit function in public entities (result oriented approach) consisting of a coherent and exhaustive legal base, clear delimitation for the role and goal of public internal audit, defining the types of internal audit engagements, ensuring the organizational and functional independence, and improving the training of internal auditors.

There were some difficulties encountered in implementing the internal audit function due to the large number of territorial administrative bodies which should to ensure the implementation of the internal audit function; also great geographical dispersion, the consecutive reorganization in the architecture of the entities subordinated to the ministries, budgetary constraints and paying system inadequacy.

For the next period the major challenges for the internal public sector audit are as follows:

- Implementation of the Internal Audit Committee
- Establishing regional bodies of CHUPIA
- Endeavour for implementing the management system of quality within CHUPIA, including at the regional bodies
- Increasing the degree of automation of internal audit activities
- Rethinking of the actual system regarding the organization of public internal audit:
- Increasing budgetary thresholds used in setting the responsible with internal audit organization
- Promoting a strategy to attract in partnership the small public entities from local public administration
- Implementing an e-learning system of professional training for internal auditors

For The Romanian Court of Accounts, the challenges for the next period concern to control of the implementation of National Strategy on Public Procurements adopted by the Romania government. The primary objective of the strategy is to reform the institutional framework of the Romanian public procurement system. This reformation will be achieved through the incorporation of European directives into national law, as well as transforming the institutional framework and ensuring functionality. Under these conditions, it became necessary to strengthen the role of the Romanian Court of Accounts. The Chamber of the Romanian Court of Accounts has also approved the establishment of a directorate that will be an immediate report to the President of the Court. The measures are designed to strengthen the role of the Romanian Court of Accounts in the audit of public procurement, as well as to enhance the quality of the country's overall audit work.

References

Anghelache, G., Panait, M., & Marinescu, R. (2017, January). Analysis Model of Financial Placements and Budget Execution of Romania in 2016. *Romanian Statistical Review Supplement, Romanian Statistical Review, 65*(1), 93–105.

Cioban, A. N., Hlaciuc, E., & Zaiceanu, A. M. (2015). The Impact and Results of the Internal Audit Activity Exercised in the Public Sector in Romania. *Procedia Economics and Finance, 32,* 394–399.

Council Directive 2011/85/EU on Requirements for Budgetary Frameworks of the Member States. Official Journal of the European Union L306/41.

Dascălu, E. D. (2016). Model for Dimensioning the Audit Structures in the Public Sector. *Audit Financiar, 14*(140), 909–917.

Dascalu, E. D., Marcu, N., & Hurjui, I. (2016). Performance Management and Monitoring of Internal Audit for the Public Sector in Romania. *Amfiteatru Economic Journal, 18*(43), 691–706.

Dima, B. (2009). Structură bicamerală sau unicamerală pentru Parlamentul României? *Revista de Drept Public,* Nr. 3.

Lazăr, D. T., & Inceu, A. M. (2004). Bugetul Funcţional (Line – Item Budget) şi Metoda Buget Bază Zero (Zero Base Budgeting – ZBB). *Revista Transilvană de Ştiinţe Administrative, 2*(11), 86–91.

Muraru, I., & Constantinescu, M. (2005). *Drept parlamentar românesc.* Bucureşti: Editura All Beck.

Popa, I. G., & Nasta, N. L. (2016). Study on the Public Financial Control in Romania. *Land Forces Academy Review, 21*(1), 77.

Profiroiu, M., & Profiroiu, A. (2006). Decentralization Process in Romania. *Transylvanian Review of Administrative Sciences, 16,* E/2006.

Profiroiu, C. M., Profiroiu, A. G., & Szabo, S. R. (2017). The Decentralization Process in Romania. In J. Ruano & M. Profiroiu (Eds.), *The Palgrave Handbook of Decentralisation in Europe.* Cham: Palgrave Macmillan.

PWC. (2013). *Government Accounting and Reporting.* Available via http://ceccar.ro/ro/wp-content/uploads/2013/11/Government-accounting-and-reporting-PWC.pdf. Accessed 22 January 2018.

Rusu, C. E., & Petrisor, M. B. (2017). Overviewing of Fiscal Decentralization in Romania. *EuroEconomica, 36*(1), 78–84.

Stefan, L., & Paunica, M. (2015). Romanian Public External Audit Integration in the European Union Acquis. *Ovidius University Annals, Series Economic Sciences, 15*(1), 123–128.

Tiron-Tudor, A. (2006, April 2). *The Reform of the Romanian Local Public Governments Accounting in the Context of the European Integration.* Available at SSRN: https://ssrn.com/abstract=924100 or http://dx.doi.org/10.2139/ssrn.924100.

Tiron-Tudor, A. (2007). Performance Audit in Public Sector Entities—A New Challenge for Eastern European Countries. *Transylvanian Review of Administrative Sciences, 19E*, 126–141.

Tiron-Tudor, A. (2011). Romanian Public Institutions Financial Statements on the Way of Harmonization with IPSAS. *International Journal of Accounting & Information Management, 19*(2).

Tiron-Tudor, A. (2017). Accrual Accounting. In *Global Encyclopedia of Public Administration, Public Policy, and Governance* (pp. 1–6). Cham: Springer International Publishing.

Useful Site

http://www.monitoruloficial.ro/?lang=hu.

CHAPTER 4

Public Sector Accounting, Auditing and Control in Serbia

Biljana Josipović Rodić

4.1 Territorial Organisation, Scope of the Public Sector and Distribution of Public Revenues

4.1.1 Territorial Organisation

The Republic of Serbia is a continental country located in South Eastern Europe, in the central part of the Balkan Peninsula. The territory of the Republic of Serbia has a total surface area of 88,499 square kilometres. According to the census of 2011, the Republic of Serbia has a population of 7,186,862. The number of households amounted to 2,487,886. The average population density in Serbia is 92.6 inhabitants per square kilometre.[1]

[1]Demographic Yearbook in the Republic of Serbia, 2014, Statistical Office of the Republic of Serbia, Belgrade, 2015.

B. Josipović Rodić (✉)
Telekom Serbia a.d., A Joint Stock Telecommunications Company, Belgrade, Serbia
e-mail: biljana.josipovic@mts.rs

V. Vašiček and G. Roje (eds.), *Public Sector Accounting, Auditing and Control in South Eastern Europe*, Public Sector Financial Management, https://doi.org/10.1007/978-3-030-03353-8_4

The territorial organisation of the Republic of Serbia is regulated by the Law on Territorial Organisation adopted in the National Assembly in 2007 (Official Gazette of the Republic of Serbia, no. 129/2007[2]). The territorial organisation of the Republic of Serbia involves territorial units of local self-government and autonomous provinces as forms of territorial autonomy. Territorial local government units are municipalities, towns and the city of Belgrade as the capital city of the Republic of Serbia. In Serbia there are 30 areas, 29 administrative districts, 24 cities, 198 municipalities, 6158 villages and 193 urban settlements.[3]

In Serbia, the Regulation on Administrative Districts prescribes administrative districts and some of their names, areas and seats. An administrative district is defined as a regional centre of public administration which includes district regional units of government which are formed in its area.

The Law on Local Self-Government (Official Gazette of the Republic of Serbia, no. 129/2007) defines the jurisdiction and powers of the territorial units of local self-government. Municipalities are responsible for the budget and final accounts, the performance and development of communal activities, urban plans, the maintenance of residential buildings, public parks, public spaces, the development of building land, environmental protection, local economic development, the protection of natural resources, the establishment of institutions and organisations in the field of primary education, culture, primary healthcare, physical culture, sports, child protection and tourism, monitoring and ensuring the functioning of these institutions and organisations, establishing institutions of social protection, ensuring the promotion and care of tourism development on its territory, the organisation and performance of activities concerning the protection of cultural property, providing funds for financing and co-financing programmes and projects in the field of culture of importance for the municipality and the creation of conditions for the work of museums, libraries and other cultural institutions founded by municipalities,

[2]Official Gazette of the Republic of Serbia is the English translation of the Službeni glasnik Republike Srbije, which is the public record where all laws, regulations, decrees, appointments and official decisions passed in the Parliament or adopted by the Government are published in Serbian language and are released in the public domain, available at http://www.slglasnik.com/.

[3]http://webrzs.stat.gov.rs/WebSite/repository/documents/00/02/07/26/Statisticki_kalendar_2016.pdf. Accessed 2 October 2017.

organising protection against natural and other disasters and fire protection, protection and regulation of agricultural land, property management of the municipality and the use of assets owned by the state, the development of various forms of self-help and solidarity with persons with special needs, ensuring the exercise, protection and promotion of human rights, taking care of public information of public interest, and other affairs of direct interest for citizens (Law on Local Self-Government, Official Gazette of the Republic of Serbia, no. 129/2007 and 83/2014).

4.1.2 *Financing of Local Self-Government Units*

The Law on Financing of Local Self-Government Units regulates the financial issue of governmental activities of counties, municipalities and cities (Law on Financing of Local and Regional Self-Government Units, Official Gazette of the Republic of Serbia, no. 62/2006, 47/2011, 93/2012, 99/2013, 125/2014 and 95/2015). The Law defines that local government revenues belong to the source in its territory on different bases. The source income earned on the territory of the local government, according to the Law, is classified as property taxes, except for the tax on transfer of absolute rights and taxes on inheritance and gifts, local administrative fees, local municipal taxes, local taxes, fees for the use of public goods, concession fees, revenues from leasing, revenues from the sale of services to users of the budget of the local government, revenue from fines imposed in misdemeanour proceedings for misdemeanours prescribed by an act of the assembly of the local government, interest income on funds from the budget of the local government, revenue from donations to the local governments and income from contributions (Law on Financing of Local and Regional Self-Government Units, Official Gazette of the Republic of Serbia, no. 62/2006, 47/2011, 93/2012, 99/2013, 125/2014 and 95/2015).

The adoption of the Law on Amendments to the Law on Local Government Finance (Official Gazette of the Republic of Serbia, no. 83/2014) was an impetus in the process of the decentralisation of public finances.

The Republic of Serbia is implementing reform measures directed towards decentralisation. The measures have been implemented by the Government of the Republic of Serbia on certain issues and in some areas assessed as a priority. In order to establish an effective mechanism for the coordination of the decentralisation process, the Government established the National Council for Decentralisation of the Republic of Serbia. In October 2013, the role of the Council was redefined.

In November 2015, the Government of the Republic of Serbia adopted the Programme of Reform of Public Financial Management for the period from 2016 to 2020. The Programme was created as a result of significant effort invested in the reform of public finances in the Republic of Serbia which were not mutually coordinated and appropriate. The Programme was adopted to achieve a comprehensive and integrated approach to public finance reform. The Programme aims to provide a comprehensive and integrated framework for planning, coordination, implementation and monitoring of progress in the implementation of activities of public financial management and to increase transparency and meet the conditions for EU accession (Ministry of Finance of the Republic of Serbia 2015).

4.1.3 Scope of the Public Sector in Serbia

The scope of the public sector in the Republic of Serbia is primarily prescribed by the Law on the Budget System (Official Gazette of the Republic of Serbia, no. 54/2009, 73/2010, 101/2010, 101/2011, 93/2012, 62/2013, 63/2013, 108/2013, 142/2014, 68/2015, 103/2015 and 99/2016). The public sector consists of general government and non-financial enterprises controlled by the state engaged in commercial activities (public enterprises). General government includes the budget of the Republic of Serbia, local government budgets, extra-budgetary funds, social security funds at all levels of government, non-profit and non-market institutions financed and controlled by the state at all levels.

In accordance with the Law on Public Enterprises (Official Gazette of the Republic of Serbia, no. 15/2016), a public enterprise performs activities of general interest and is established by the Republic of Serbia, an autonomous province or local self-government unit. Activities of public interest are activities in the field of electronic communications, mining and energy, nuclear facilities, the issuing of official gazettes and books, weapons and military equipment, the protection, development and promotion of goods of general interest such as water, roads, navigable rivers, lakes, spas, protected areas and others.

In the Republic of Serbia there is a list of users of public resources. The list of users of public resources in the Republic of Serbia is regulated by the Regulations. This list is updated annually. In accordance with the Law of the Budget System, users of public resources are divided into groups:

- the Republic of Serbia (ministries, bodies within ministries, special organisations, cultural institutions, agencies, etc.);
- autonomous provinces;
- cities;
- municipalities;
- mandatory social insurance;
- other users of public resources (agencies, commissions, institutes, institutions);
- other users of public resources which are not included in the consolidated treasury account.

Users of public resource are direct and indirect budget users, resource users of organisations for mandatory social insurance and public enterprises established by the Republic of Serbia or by local government, legal entities founded by such public enterprises, legal entities over which the Republic of Serbia or local government has direct or indirect control of more than 50% of the capital or more than 50% of votes on the board, other legal entities in which public resources comprise more than 50% of total revenues realised in the previous fiscal year, as well as public agencies and organisations to which the regulations concerning public agencies apply.

Budget users (direct and indirect) and resource users of organisations for mandatory social insurance apply the Decree on Budget Accounting. Other users of public resources apply the Law on Accounting and other acts regulating the area of accounting.

4.2 Formulation and Execution of Central Government and Local and Regional Self-Government Budgets

4.2.1 Regulatory and Institutional Framework of the Budget System

In defining the budget and budgetary relations in Serbia, the starting points are determined by the Law on the Budget System. The budget processes of budget planning and preparation, approval, budget execution and supervision of the budget are prescribed for the central budget and the budgets of local self-government (Jones and Pendlebury 2010).

The Law regulates "the planning, preparation, adoption and implementation of the budget of the Republic of Serbia; the planning, preparation, adoption and implementation of the budget of the autonomous province and local self-government; the preparation and adoption of the financial plans of the Pension and Disability Insurance Fund of the Republic of Serbia, the National Health Insurance Fund, the Social Insurance Fund, the Social Insurance Fund for Military Personnel, and the National Employment Service; budget accounting and reporting, financial management, control and audit of public funds and the budget of the Republic of Serbia, the local government budget and the financial plans of organisations for mandatory social insurance; the competence and organisation of the Treasury as an administrative body within the Ministry of Finance and the local government treasury; and other issues of importance for the functioning of the budget system" (Law on the Budget System, Official Gazette of the Republic of Serbia, no. 54/2009, 73/2010, 101/2010, 101/2011, 93/2012, 62/2013, 63/2013, 108/2013, 142/2014, 68/2015, 103/2015 and 99/2016).

The Ministry of Finance performs public administration tasks related to[4]:

- the state budget;
- determination of consolidated balance of public revenues and public expenditures;
- accounting and audit system of accounting statements, bookkeeping;
- the system and policy of taxes, fees and other public revenues; the policy of public expenditures;
- management of available public finances of the Republic of Serbia;
- public debt and financial assets of the Republic of Serbia;
- public procurement;
- macroeconomic and fiscal analysis, quantification of measures of economic policy;
- foreign currency exchange system and foreign loan relations;
- monitoring the implementation of regulations;

[4]http://www.mfin.gov.rs/?change_lang=en. Accessed 14 September 2016.

- system of financial relations with other countries and international financing organisations;
- basics of the system of social insurance contributions;
- securing financing for mandatory social insurance;
- the financial effects of the system of determining and computing salaries which are financed from the budget of the Republic of Serbia, territorial autonomy and local self-governments and funds of mandatory social insurance organisation;
- credit and monetary system;
- banking system;
- aligning activities in the area of planning, obtaining and using donations, EU funds and other foreign development assistance;
- system of payments and payment operations;
- budget control and auditing of direct and indirect users of the Republic of Serbia budget, territorial autonomy and local self-governments and mandatory social insurance organisations and public enterprises, etc.

Within its scope of activities, the Ministry also establishes and promotes international cooperation and provides for the alignment of regulations with the European Union acquis.

4.2.2 *Formulation of Central Government and Local Government Budgets*

The budget is the most important financial instrument of the central and local government. The budget projects revenues, receipts, expenses and expenditures which have the function of priorities, objectives and tasks of central and local governments and their bodies.

The formal structure of the budget at all levels is based on the same legislation and implementation documents, with the mentioned budget documents being comparable and suitable for consolidation. In accordance with legal obligations, the Ministry of Finance consolidates the budgets of local units and publishes data on the general budget of the Republic of Serbia. In the preparation and acceptance of the budget, the Government has the legal obligation to apply budgetary principles, classifications, programming and strategic planning, as well as ensuring the publication of the budget.

The budget is accepted for a fiscal year, which in Serbia corresponds to the calendar year. The budget consists of a general and special part. The general part of the budget is the profit and loss account, the budget surplus or deficit, the total surplus (deficit) and the account for financing. The special part of the budget can be expressed by a system of classification displayed as objectives, expected results, and the activities and resources necessary to achieve these goals. In accordance with the Law, the special part of the budget shows the financial plans of the direct users, according to the principle of separation of powers into the legislative, executive and judicial branches. During the budget preparation and execution, the principles of efficiency, economy, effectiveness, transparency, completeness, accuracy and unique budget classification must be respected (Shah 2007a).

The integrity of the budget system is provided by the common legal basis, single budget classification, the use of uniform budget documentation for drafting budgets, medium-term and financial plans, a unique system of budget accounting, uniform criteria for budget control and audit, transfer of statistical reports and data from one budget level to another and the principles underlying the budgetary procedure, in accordance with the Law on the Budget System.

The budget is prepared and executed on the basis of the single budget classification system (Allen and Tommasi 2001). Budget classification includes economic classification of revenue and benefits, economic classification of expenditure and expenses, organisational classification, a functional classification, program classification and classification according to sources of financing. "The Ministry of Finance Treasury Administration is in charge of the execution of the state budget, budget accounting and reporting, operations related to public payments, as well as other issues related to government finances.

Through its responsible operation, top professional capacity and innovative solutions, the Treasury Administration ensures stable and transparent budget policy, maintains the cutting-edge system of public finances, and promotes efficiency in the utilisation of taxpayers' money.

The Treasury operations are organised into territorial units across the state territory. Apart from the Head Office, the Treasury units are organised into 34 regional offices and 110 local offices which are set up within regional offices. The Head Office consists of main units (departments) and subordinate units (divisions, subdivisions, centres, units). Regional offices consist of internal units (divisions, subdivisions and units). Certain activities are performed by standalone officers who work outside the internal units."[5]

4.2.3 Budget Execution and Budget Execution Reporting

Execution of the budget implies the realisation of revenues and the execution of expenditures in the reporting period of one year. Dynamics of revenue generation determines the dynamics of spending the resources. The Treasury which forms a part of the Ministry of Finance is responsible for the budget execution process in the Republic of Serbia. The Treasury Directorate is responsible for:

- the management of monetary funds of the Republic,
- control of expenditures,
- approval of all budget payments,
- budget accounting and reporting,
- establishment and management of the information system which includes direct and indirect budget beneficiaries, as well as the system of public revenues and public expenditures (permanent information system),
- activities referring to payments, but also those referring to recording and carrying out other activities within the system of consolidated treasury account,
- managing national fund resources referring to the European Union funds,
- recording and monitoring of state aid,
- allocating revenues generated in the privatisation processes.

All budget beneficiaries are required to compile a Budget Execution Report and to submit it to the Treasury Department. The budget execution report stands as an integral part of the set of financial statements in accordance with the provisions of The Decree of Budgetary Accounting (Official Gazette of the Republic of Serbia, no. 125/2003 and 12/2006).

[5] https://www.trezor.gov.rs/index.php?language=en. Accessed 25 September 2018.

The budget execution report is compiled periodically, on a quarterly basis, whereas indirect budget users deliver their report to the direct budget users so that the report is matched to Treasury General Ledger data, so that the Consolidated Budget Execution Report is compiled and submitted by the 20th of the following month.

4.3 Accounting and Financial Reporting

4.3.1 Budget Accounting

Budget accounting in the Republic of Serbia includes bookkeeping, preparation, submission and disclosure of financial reports of budgetary users and organisations of mandatory social insurance.

The Decree of Budgetary Accounting regulates:

- The basis for budget accounting;
- The method of bookkeeping and keeping of accounting records;
- Financial statements and financial reporting;
- Method and deadlines for reporting;
- Treasury General Ledger system.

Budget accounting is based on a cash basis. The application of a cash basis implies the recognition of transactions and business events at the time of receipt or payment of cash assets (Josipović Rodić 2016). The financial result is determined by the change in the balance of cash and cash equivalents. Therefore, the basis for measuring the results is the balance of cash assets (Chan 2003). However, for the purposes of internal reporting, budget users may apply the accrual basis of accounting.

The financial statements on a cash basis are:

1. Cash flow statement;
2. Statement of capital expenditure and financing.

In addition to these reports, budget users produce reports in accordance with the adopted accounting policies. Statements made in accordance with the adopted accounting policies are the balance sheet, the profit and loss account, the budget execution report, the report on the use of funds from the current and permanent budgetary reserves, and the report on guarantees issued during the fiscal year.

4.3.2 Financial Reporting

Financial reporting is mandatory, with the Ordinance on the Method of Preparation, Drafting and Submission of Financial Statements prescribing the form and content of financial reports, the periods covered by the reports, as well as liabilities and deadlines for their submission. The mentioned legislation defines a universal analytical financial reporting framework. The prescribed form and content of financial reports enable the consolidation of financial reports, with the use of uniform accounting policies for all similar transactions and events.

Financial reports are drafted on the following forms:

- Balance sheet;
- Income statement;
- Report on capital expenditures and income;
- Statement of cash flows;
- Report on budget execution.

The balance sheet is a fundamental financial statement of the financial position. The income statement presents the types of revenues and expenses, both from operations and transactions in non-financial assets (revenues from the sale of non-financial assets, expenditure for the purchase of non-financial assets). The report on capital expenditures and income presents all types of receipts and expenditures from the transactions of financial assets and receipts, expenditures from transactions in non-financial assets and shortfalls (surplus) of receipts. The statement of cash flows presents all types of revenues and expenses, both from operations and transactions in non-financial assets and receipts and expenditures from transactions of financial assets and liabilities. The statement of cash flows presents information on surplus (deficit) cash flow, the cash balance at the beginning of the year and the cash balance at the end of the year. The report on budget execution presents total expenses and expenditure, total revenues and receipts and the budget surplus (deficit).

The financial statements are submitted to the Treasury. The financial statements are compiled periodically and annually. The periodic preparation of financial statements actually includes quarterly reporting on budget execution. Therefore, on a quarterly basis, users of budget funds and social security organisations prepare and submit reports on budget execution.

4.4 Audit and Other Oversight (Supervision) in the Public Sector

Oversight of the budget and budget entities in the Republic of Serbia is organised in the following forms: state audit, budget oversight, internal audit and internal control systems (financial management and control).

Implementation of oversight puts an emphasis on monitoring the execution of the budget in relation to the planned amount. Ministers are responsible for the internal oversight of transactions of revenues/receipts and expenses/expenditures of ministries and budget users who are under their jurisdiction, and the Ministry of Finance is responsible for, in addition to the above, internal oversight of borrowings.

Oversight of the execution of the budget is based on the accounting data presented in the form of financial statements. The obligation to present and the presentation of financial statements is a form of oversight and is based on accounting procedures and accounting data. Results of the oversight and audit of the budget ensure the reliability of data on budget execution and provide valuable data for corrective actions.

4.4.1 State Audit

The State Audit Institution (hereinafter: Institution) is the highest authority for the auditing of public funds in the Republic of Serbia.

It was founded in 2005 by virtue of the Law on the State Audit Institution. The State Audit Institution is an independent state authority. The Institution is accountable to the National Assembly of the Republic of Serbia for the conduct of activities stemming from its competence.

The Institution performs these activities pursuant to the Constitution of the Republic of Serbia and the Law on the State Audit Institution and the Rules of Procedure of the State Audit Institution, which defines in detail the manner and procedure of performing activities under the competence of the Institution, the manner of ensuring transparent operation, the decision-making process and other matters significant for the work of the Institution pursuant to the Law. The Institution has a President, Vice-President, the Council, audit departments and support services departments.

The scope and manner of performing activities within the Institution's departments, internal organisation and job classification are defined in more detail by the enactment of the Institution—Rules on Internal

Organisation and Job Classification, enacted by the Council at the proposal of the President of the Institution.

The Code of Ethics for state auditors and other employees of the State Audit Institution define in more detail ethical principles, generally accepted rules of behaviour and professional standards that the state officials, state auditors and other employees of the State Audit Institution must adhere to. The rules of the Code also apply to external experts engaged in the State Audit Institution when performing activities stemming from its competence.

State auditors and other employees are obliged to observe and strictly implement the Law on the State Audit Institution, INTOSAI (International Organisation of Supreme Audit Institutions) audit standards, the INTOSAI Code of Ethics, and the Institution's Code.

The State Audit Institution, as the highest authority in charge of auditing public funds, performs the following activities within its competence[6]:

- plans and performs audit, in compliance with the Law on the State Audit Institution;
- enacts bylaws and other regulations for the purposes of implementing the Law on the State Audit Institution;
- submits reports to the National Assembly of the Republic of Serbia and assemblies of local authorities;
- formulates attitudes and opinions, as well as other forms of public disclosures regarding the application and implementation of specific provisions of the Law on the State Audit Institution;
- on an as-needed basis and in compliance with its capacities, provides expert assistance to the Assembly, the Government of the Republic of Serbia (hereinafter: the Government) and other state authorities on certain significant measures and important projects, in such a manner that does not diminish the independence of the Institution;
- may provide advice to beneficiaries of public funds;
- may give suggestions on the draft proposals of laws and other regulations and may give opinions on issues in the area of public finances;
- may issue recommendations for amendments to applicable laws, based on information received over the course of audit, which produce or may produce negative consequences or lead to unplanned results;

[6] http://www.dri.rs/. Accessed 23 May 2015.

- adopts and publishes audit standards relating to public funds, regarding the exercise of the Institution's audit competence, audit manuals and other expert documents significant for the development of the audit profession;
- determines the education and examination programmes for acquiring the title of state auditor and certified state auditor, organises exams for the acquisition of the titles of state auditor and certified state auditor and keeps the Register of persons that acquired such titles;
- defines the criteria and performs the recognition of expert titles under the competence of the Institution which were acquired abroad;
- cooperates with international auditing and accounting organisations in the area pertaining to accounting and auditing of the public sector;
- performs other matters stipulated by the Law on the State Audit Institution.

The State Audit Institution is the supreme, independent state body in charge of auditing public funds in the Republic of Serbia, providing professional assurance to the National Assembly and the citizens of the Republic of Serbia that the public funds are spent effectively, efficiently and economically.

The State Audit Institution has been a fully fledged member of the International Organisation of Supreme Audit Institutions (INTOSAI) since November 2008, of the European Organisation of Supreme Audit Institutions (EUROSAI) since June 2009 and of the Network of Supreme Audit Institutions of the EU Candidate and Potential Candidate Countries and the European Court of Auditors since August 2010. The Institution has the status of active observer in meetings of the Contact Committee of the Heads of the EU SAIs until the date of accession to the EU, after which the Institution will become a fully fledged member.

4.4.2 Budget Oversight

Budget oversight is inspectorial supervision carried out by the Ministry of Finance. Budget oversight inspectors of the Ministry of Finance are those authorised to perform this form of budgetary oversight.

Budget inspection performs supervision of:

- Direct and indirect budget users;
- Organisations of compulsory social insurance;
- Public enterprises founded by the Republic of Serbia;
- Autonomous provinces and local self-government;
- Other users who receive allocations from budget funds.

Budget oversight involves inspectorial supervision of the legality, expediency and timeliness of the use of budget funds, the timely and comprehensive collection of revenues and receipts under the purview of budget users and bodies of local and regional governments, and inspectorial supervision of adherence to and enforcement of the laws and other regulations pertaining to budget funds and funds from other sources, regardless of whether they concern revenues/receipts, expenses/expenditures, refunds, assets or liabilities. Budget oversight encompasses oversight of accounting, financial and other operating documents.

Budget oversight has an important role in checking the purpose and legality of spending budget-approved and allocated funds. In Serbia, reports on the work of budget inspections are published on the website of the Ministry of Finance.

4.4.3 *Internal Audit and Internal Control Systems*

In the Republic of Serbia, users of budgetary resources have the obligation to establish internal audit. In accordance with the Ordinance on Common Criteria for Organisation and Standards and Methodological Guidelines for the Activities and Reporting of Public Internal Audits (the Official Gazette of the Republic of Serbia, no. 99/2011), internal audit may be established in one of the following ways:

- By organising a special functional independent organisational internal audit unit within the users of public funds, reporting directly to the head of users of public funds;
- By organising joint internal audit units of two or more users of public funds, with the prior consent of the Central Harmonisation Unit (CHU);
- Conducting internal audit by the internal audit unit of another user of public funds, with the prior consent of the CHU.

A special functionally independent organisational unit is established when the user of public funds has more than 250 employees. The organisational unit of internal audit is not allowed to have fewer than three internal auditors, one of whom is the manager. CHU is responsible for the monitoring and reception of applications for training to acquire the title of certified internal auditor in the public sector. The work of internal audit is conducted in accordance with clearly defined plans and in accordance with the plans of individual audit, the annual audit plan and the strategic plan for a period of three years.

The Ministry of Finance is responsible for the coordination, establishment and development of control systems in the public sector.

Even though there is an obligation to establish internal audit in the Republic of Serbia, not all budget beneficiaries have established internal audit. Besides, in certain budget beneficiaries, systematised positions of internal auditors have not been filled due to a lack of competent staff, an inadequate wage system, etc.

Financial management and control are defined as a set of policies, procedures and activities that are established, maintained and regularly updated by the managers. Financial management and control enable goals to be achieved in an economical, efficient and effective way (Shah 2007b). Responsibility for the establishment, maintenance and alignment of financial management and the control system lies with the manager of public fund users. Public fund users prepare and submit to the Ministry a report of financial management, control and internal audit. Based on individual reports, the Central Unit for harmonisation compiles the Consolidated Annual Report on the state of internal financial control in the public sector in the Republic of Serbia.

Conclusions on the state of the financial management system and the control of public fund users according to the last Consolidated Annual Report on the state of internal financial control in the public sector of the Republic of Serbia can be drawn as follows:

- A certain number of public fund users do not have a specific manager for financial management and control;
- A number of public fund users have no plans to implement and develop a system of financial management and control;
- A certain number of public fund users did not attend training on financial management and control;

- Public fund users are gradually developing risk management methodologies;
- The established control systems ensure legality, but are not sufficiently focused on risk management.

The Government of the Republic of Serbia has adopted a Strategy of Development of Internal Financial Control in the Public Sector (Official Gazette of RS, no. 61/2009 and no. 23/2013), with clearly defined activities related to the development of the subject area and the specified deadlines for the accomplishment of the defined activities.

4.5 Challenges in Further Development of Public Sector Accounting and Auditing

The Republic of Serbia has to make efforts to improve the area of accounting and audit in the public sector. Therefore, the Republic of Serbia needs to identify areas which will improve the current state. In this regard, it is deemed necessary to:

- Initiate a process of standardisation and harmonisation in the essential use of the International Public Sector Accounting Standards. In the Republic of Serbia, the International Public Sector Accounting Standards have been declaratively accepted through the adoption of the Rules of Application of the International Public Sector Accounting Standards. It is necessary to make additional efforts to continue the already started process of harmonisation. In the Republic of Serbia, efforts are being made to strengthen the role of a public sector accountant in order to ease the process of implementing IPSAS. The reform of public sector accounting in the Republic of Serbia aims to harmonize the national accounting framework with the International Public Sector Accounting Standards, enable quality reporting and strengthen a comprehensive public financial management;
- Clearly define the application of accounting bases in the financial reporting processes of the public funds' users, as well as in the processes of budget planning and budget execution monitoring. Though in the Republic of Serbia the application of the cash basis is prescribed, it has been established that the modified cash basis in

the financial reporting system is mainly applied, while the cash basis is applied for the needs of the budget preparation. The reform of the public sector accounting must be directed towards the transition to the application of the accrual basis. Accrual accounting is expected to provide with information that are crucial to the effective management of assets and liabilities of the country. Accountants working in the public sector are to be key drivers of the reform, so that the goal is to improve the level of their knowledge and skills;

- Improve all components of financial management and control by emphasising the improvement of control activities and risk management of public funds users by defining the risk management methodology. The analyses of the Consolidated Report on the financial control of the public sector of the Republic of Serbia, Ministry of Finance implies that there is the need for the improvement of the financial management and control processes in accordance with the identified critical areas of functioning;
- Improve and develop internal audit by raising awareness of its' relevance and ensure adequate functioning of the internal audit at the level of each beneficiary of public funds;
- Encourage and develop audits of efficiency, effectiveness and economy with the aim of improving the public sector and economic stability;
- Increase the transparency of reporting to the extent that transparency reflects the level of responsibility of holders of public functions. Individual reports of public sector entities are not sufficiently transparent. A number of public sector entities do not disclose the financial statements of the interested parties, which affects the (non) confidence public in the work of public office holders;
- Strive to introduce a management driven approach through the development of cost accounting to improve the business decision-making process of users of public funds of the Republic of Serbia that would further improve the performance of the public sector.

Since the Republic of Serbia is striving to join the European Union, it is necessary to adjust public sector accounting reporting practices with the member states. Thus, the Republic of Serbia needs to start the process of standardisation and harmonisation of the application of International Public Sector Accounting Standards. Additionally, it is necessary to make further efforts to improve the public sector accounting and auditing in the Republic of Serbia, and to strengthen the implementation process of harmonisation and alignment with the rules of the EU acquis. Lastly, since the accounting reform requires a systematic approach respecting cost benefit analysis, it is very important that the above-mentioned guidelines are implemented, taking into account the personnel, technical and financial potentials in the Republic of Serbia.

References

Allen, R., & Tommasi, D. (2001). *Managing Public Expenditure: A Reference Book for Transition Countries, Organisation for Economic Cooperation and Development*. Paris: OECD.

Chan, J. L. (2003). Government Accounting: An Assessment of Theory, Purposes and Standards. *Public Money & Management, 23*(1), 13–20.

Jones, R., & Pendlebury, M. (2010). *Public Sector Accounting*. Borough, NJ: Financial Times Prentice Hall.

Josipović Rodić, B. (2016). Budžetsko računovodstvo u funkciji zaštite javnog interesa, 47. Simpozijum Saveza računovođa i revizora Srbije, Računovodstvo 1.

Ministry of Finance. (2015). *Program Reform of Public Financial Management for the Period from 2016–2020*. Ministry of Finance of the Republic of Serbia, Belgrade. http://www.mfin.gov.rs/pages/article.php?id=12054. Accessed 1 December 2015.

Shah, A. (2007a). *Budgeting and Budgetary Institutions, Public Sector Governance and Accountability Series*. Washington, DC: The World Bank.

Shah, A. (2007b). *Local Public Financial Management, Public Sector Governance and Accountability Series*. Washington, DC: The World Bank.

Statistical Office of the Republic of Serbia. (2015). *Demographic Yearbook in the Republic of Serbia 2014*. Belgrade: Statistical Office of the Republic of Serbia.

Useful Sites

http://webrzs.stat.gov.rs/WebSite/repository/documents/00/02/07/26/Statisticki_kalendar_2016.pdf.

http://www.dri.rs/.

https://www.trezor.gov.rs/.

http://www.mfin.gov.rs/pages/article.php?id=12054.

http://www.slglasnik.com/.

CHAPTER 5

Public Sector Accounting, Auditing and Control in Slovenia

Tatjana Jovanović

5.1 Territorial Organisation, Scope of the Public Sector and Distribution of Public Revenues

5.1.1 Territorial Organisation

The Republic of Slovenia has been an independent state since 1991 after the referendum on independence and on separation from the former Socialist Federal Republic of Yugoslavia. Slovenia became a full Member State of the European Union on 1 July 2004. Today, Slovenia is considered one of the most economically developed countries of southeastern Europe.

Based on the 2015 census, the Republic of Slovenia covers 20,273 square kilometres and has a population of 2,064,632 living in 6036 settlements. The country is subdivided into 212 municipalities. The Constitution of the Republic of Slovenia (The Official Gazette

T. Jovanović (✉)
University of Ljubljana, Ljubljana, Slovenia
e-mail: Tatjana.Jovanovic@fu.uni-lj.si

V. Vašiček and G. Roje (eds.), *Public Sector Accounting, Auditing and Control in South Eastern Europe*, Public Sector Financial Management, https://doi.org/10.1007/978-3-030-03353-8_5

of the Republic of Slovenia, no. 33/91-1, 42/97 – UZ68, 66/00 – UZ80, 24/03 – UZ3a, 47, 68, 69/04 – UZ14, 69/04 – UZ43, 69/04 – UZ50, 68/06 – UZ121,140,143, 47/13 – UZ148 and 47/13 – UZ90,97,99, hereinafter: the Constitution)[1] is the fundamental law of the independent state which was ratified by the National Assembly of the Republic of Slovenia on 23 December 1991. Along with important issues concerning human rights, economic and social relations, public finance, the Constitutional Court, etc., the Constitution of the Republic of Slovenia also determines local self-government. It guarantees the right to local self-government in municipalities and other local entities. According to the Constitution, the state is organised at two levels: the central level (central government) and local level (municipalities).

The Local Self-Government Act (The Official Gazette of the Republic of Slovenia, no. 94/07, 76/08, 79/09, 51/10, 40/12 – ZUJF in 14/15 – ZUUJFO) is the central legal act which stipulates that the establishment of a municipality is based on the Act on the Establishment of Municipalities and on Determining their Territory (The Official Gazette of the Republic of Slovenia, no. 108/06 and 9/11). The Local Self-Government Act prescribes that a local community may organise lower organisational forms: village, locality or quarter communities if this division is explained by geographical, historical, administrative, economic or cultural reasons or if this is in the interest of a part of the local population. Currently, there are 212 municipalities. Out of this number, the majority do not have the legally determined minimum number of inhabitants (5000), and eleven have the status of an urban municipality. The same Act stipulates the scope and structure of municipalities and other smaller local units, their bodies, control over their acts and work, as well as other important issues.

The scope of the activity of municipalities includes the following duties: managing municipality assets, facilitating conditions for economic development, planning spatial development, building dwellings and social housing, managing local public services, improving social welfare (preschool and primary education, child care and families, socially

[1] Official Gazette of the Republic of Slovenia stands for a public record titled Uradni list Republike Slovenije in which all laws, regulations, decrees, appointments and official decisions passed in the Parliament or adopted by the Government are published in Slovenian language and released in the public domain: https://www.uradni-list.si/.

underprivileged people, people with disabilities, the elderly, etc.). Moreover, the duties involve natural environment protection, and management and maintenance of water and energy utility plants. In addition to the already mentioned tasks, a municipality must provide conditions for adult education, telecommunication centres, libraries, specialised information documentation centres, cultural activities such as theatres, museums and archives, radio and television stations, press, sport and recreational facilities, scientific and research activities, a network of public services, construction and maintenance of public roads, supervision of public events, etc.

5.1.2 Central and Local Government Financing

The Constitution of the Republic of Slovenia stipulates that municipalities must raise their own revenue. However, financially disadvantaged municipalities, unable to fully perform their duties, are entitled to receive additional financial assistance from the state in accordance with the principles and criteria prescribed by law. Municipality financing is more precisely determined by the Act on the Financing of Municipalities (The Official Gazette of the Republic of Slovenia, no. 32/06, 123/06 – ZFO-1 and 57/08 – ZFO-1A), which provides for a balanced model of financing to satisfy the needs and interests of the local population irrespective of the citizens' financial status, contribution to public finance or place of residence. Moreover, the objective of this model of financing is to ensure proportionality between the municipality's functions and its sources of funds. The Act on the Financing of Municipalities also provides municipalities with more financial autonomy in obtaining funds and the spending thereof.

Slovenia's system of public finance is relatively centralised. Therefore, according to data on the state's and local entities' budget execution for 2014, financing at the level of municipalities as local entities accounted for only 19.14% of total public spending. Pursuant to the Act on the Financing of Municipalities, municipalities finance their activities from the following sources (Cvikl and Zemljič 2005):

- compensation fees for the use of municipal land;
- inheritance and gift taxes;
- tax on gambling;
- real property transaction tax;

- municipal taxes;
- contributions and self-contributions;
- environmental duties;
- penalties;
- concession duties;
- municipal communal rates.

Furthermore, one of the most important revenue sources is a share of 54% of personal income tax paid by residents of the municipality two years previously, namely the share that appertains to a municipality to the amount of its appropriate expenditure for the financing of local activities of public significance for the current year.

Pursuant to Article 13 of the Act on the Financing of Municipalities, the appropriate volume of funds to finance appropriate expenditure is ensured by a system to calculate the revenue from the personal income tax appertaining to each municipality in the current fiscal year. Firstly, in accordance with Article 12 of the Act on the Financing of Municipalities, in order to calculate the amount of the appropriate expenditure it is necessary to determine the average per capita amount of funds necessary to finance activities of public significance in an average municipality in Slovenia. Each fiscal year, the municipality revenue from personal income tax intended to finance appropriate expenditure is calculated as the total sum of determined tax collected from taxpayers with permanent residence in an individual municipality, in accordance with Article 14 of the Act on the Financing of Municipalities. If 70% of the amount of municipal revenue from personal income tax imposed on taxpayers in a municipality is not equal to or if it does not exceed the appropriate volume of funds to finance the appropriate expenditure, the municipality will be allocated additional funds of the remaining amount of 30% derived from personal income tax, as well as the surplus revenue derived from personal income tax which in some municipalities exceeds the appropriate volume of funds for financing the appropriate expenditure. Government grants are allocated through the solidarity equalisation fund whose principal source of financing is a share of personal income tax, which, pursuant to the law, belongs to all the municipalities (Brezovnik et al. 2014).

Since financing appropriate expenditure implies financing duties and functions imposed by the law, in accordance with the Act on the Financing of Municipalities, a local entity which cannot ensure the financing of appropriate expenditure by using revenue from personal income tax is entitled to receive grants from the government budget through financial equalisation.

The Act on the Financing of Municipalities provides for municipal independence in financing those functions, tasks, programmes and projects which the municipal legislation regulates autonomously outside the system of financing appropriate expenditure. In order to finance the above-mentioned duties and business operations, the municipality uses revenues from all sources of finance, where the revenue from personal income tax may be used only if the necessary legal functions and tasks of the municipality are assured. Furthermore, the Act on the Financing of Municipalities stipulates that municipalities may be granted additional funds from the state budget for the co-financing of individual investments outlined in the municipal development plans.

Regulating the system of co-financing investments, the Act on the Financing of Municipalities guarantees the realisation of one of the fundamental principles of proportionality, ensuring equal conditions to meet the common needs of all inhabitants regardless of their municipality of residence. In line with this goal and pursuant to Article 23 of the Act on the Financing of Municipalities, each year government grants are allocated to local entities according to legal criteria and measures.

A municipality may use a scope of resources intended for co-financing municipal investments, within the fiscal year determined for the execution of the investment. For multiannual projects, a municipality may use the appropriate scope of resources determined for a maximum of two fiscal years. The appropriate scope of resources or appropriate expenditure for the financing of the previously stated tasks is determined on the basis of a mathematical formula in which the appropriate scope of resources per capita is defined by the Act.

The correction factors taken into consideration are:

- The ratio between the revenues from solidarity equalisation and financial equalisation to finance appropriate expenditure and common earmarked funds (20%);
- The ratio between the per capita length of local roads in an individual municipality and the per capita length of local roads in Slovenia (30%);
- The ratio between the per capita area of a ten-kilometre borderline in a municipality and the per capita area of a ten-kilometre borderline in the state (10%);

- The ratio between per capita farming land in use in the area limited by natural factors in a municipality and per capita farming land in use in the area limited by natural factors in the state (20%);
- The ratio between the per capita land area of "Nature 2000" in a municipality and the per capita land area of "Nature 2000" in the state (10%);
- The factor of the surface area, the number of inhabitants and low density of the population in each municipality (10%).

5.1.3 Scope of the Public Sector in Slovenia

According to the system of national accounts of the national statistics, the economy of Slovenia is divided into institutional sectors determined by the Standard Classification of the Institutional Sector (SKIS). The sectors include: Public Administration and Defence, Mandatory Social Security (O), Education (P), Health and Social Care (Q), and Culture, Entertainment and Recreational activities (R). The Standard Classification of Institutional Sectors (hereinafter SKIS) is the obligatory national standard for recording, collecting, processing and disseminating statistical data relevant for the statistical monitoring of economic conditions and trends. The SKIS is based on the provisions of the European System of Accounts (ESA 2010), which is the obligatory statistical standard of the European Union.

The Statistical Office of the Republic of Slovenia classifies the Slovenian economy into five institutional sectors: Non-financial corporations (S.11), Financial corporations (S.12), General government (S.13), Households (S.14) and Non-profit institutions serving households—(NPISG, S.15). In the system of national accounts, the public sector is determined based on the SKIS subsectors and includes:

- Government (S.13)
- Non-financial state-owned enterprises (S.11001)
- The Central Bank (S.121)
- Other public financial corporations (S.12201)
- Other public financial intermediaries except insurance corporations and pension funds (S.12301)
- Public financing auxiliaries (S.12401)
- Public insurance corporations and the pension fund (S.12501).

The general government sector consists of all institutional units under public control known as non-market producers since less than 50% of their operational costs are covered by the sale of goods on the market. Primarily, this group is made up of the treasuries of public finance—the state budget, local government budgets, the Health Insurance Institute, the Institute for Pension and Disability Insurance, and the majority of public institutions, public agencies, public funds and some other units. The general government sector consists of more than 2600 units, which are included in the calculation of the government budget deficit and debt (Šoltes et al. 2010).

State-owned enterprises are entities controlled by the state or local government. The government-controlled enterprises in Slovenia have to comply with one of the following conditions: (a) government's control of more than 50% capital share, (b) government's control of the management board or other company's body, (c) the authorization for the appointment and replacement of board members and sub-board members, as well as (d) the legal possibility to purchase a controlling interest of shares. There are still just over 600 state-owned enterprises in the Republic of Slovenia (Janc 2009).

In line with the Public Finance Act (Z The Official Gazette of the Republic of Slovenia, no. 11/11, 14/13, 101/13, 55/15 and 96/15 – ZIPRS1617) and related to the scope of public sector accounting, the public sector consists of direct and indirect budgetary users, the Health Insurance Institute (ZZZS) and the Institute for Pension and Disability Insurance (ZPIZ) (both in primary healthcare), public commercial institutions, public corporations and other legal entities in which the central and/or local government has a decisive influence on their management. Direct budget spending units are bodies and organisations of central and/or local government, whereas indirect spending units are state funds, public institutions and agencies founded by central and/or local government, in accordance with Article 3 of the Public Finance Act. Since government grants are allocated to units defined by the law as natural persons and legal entities, they receive government grants based on a contract signed or a decision made by a direct budget user. Consequently, the grants are allocated directly to the ministries and municipalities as direct budget users, whereas indirect budget users receive the grants through direct budget users (Cvikl and Korpič-Horvat 2007).

A more precise definition of direct and indirect users of the state or municipal budget is stipulated in the Ordinance on Defining Direct and

Indirect State and Local Government Budgetary Users (The Official Gazette of the Republic of Slovenia, no. 46/03).

In accordance with the Ordinance, indirect budget users are defined as:

- Those organised as legal entities such as public institutions, public agencies or public funds;
- Those founded and owned by the central government or local government;
- Those which provide public goods and services and whose function is of public interest;
- Those financed from the central government or local government budget, the Health Insurance Institute, the Institute for Pension and Disability Insurance and from other sources.

Indirect budgetary users are as follows:

- The Health Insurance Institute and the Institute for Pension and Disability Insurance;
- Public institutions, public agencies and public funds which are founded by indirect budgetary users;
- Self-governing local communities;
- The Chamber of Agriculture and Forestry and public institutions founded by the Chamber of Agriculture and Forestry.

5.2 Formulation and Execution of Central and Local Government Budgets

The Constitution of the Republic of Slovenia lays down important provisions on public finance. In line with the Constitution's provisions, the state and local communities raise funds for the performance of their duties by means of taxes and other compulsory charges, as well as from revenues from their own assets. The state imposes taxes, customs duties, and other charges by law, whereas local communities impose taxes and other charges under conditions provided by the Constitution and law. Moreover, the provisions prescribe the budget system and its main principles, state borrowings and guarantees by the state for loans, which are only permitted on the basis of law, and oversight of public finance.

However, in defining the budget and budgetary relations in Slovenia, the main act is the Public Finance Act, which came into force on 1 January 2000. The Public Finance Act fully regulates the management of public finance (with regard to revenues and expenditures) of all public finance entities at the central and local level and, as already mentioned in the previous section, it is the main finance Act for direct and indirect budgetary users.

5.2.1 Formulation of Central Government and Local Government Budgets

The budget preparation procedure is done in accordance with a number of legal procedures every year. The procedure starts with macroeconomic forecasts and a medium-term framework which both constitute the budgetary memorandum. In Slovenia, the budget is planned in line with the principle known as a "top-down" mechanism, according to which first the general budgetary framework is defined and only then can budgetary users make their financial plans. In the preparation and acceptance of the central government budget, a two-stage budgetary preparation approach is applied. The first stage begins with the announcement by the Office for Macroeconomic Trends and Development of the economic trends and the most important macroeconomic aggregates and finishes with the approval of budgetary expenditures, namely the nominal expenditure ceilings. Since 2015, the Act on Fiscal Rule has been in force (The Official Gazette of the Republic of Slovenia, no. 55/15), which ensures the medium-term balance of revenue and expenditure of the central government budget without borrowing, as well as the criteria for determining exceptional circumstances of deviation from the medium-term fiscal balance and the manner of their occurrence. The first stage continues with the introduction of the budgetary memorandum along with the determination of the priority tasks and the targeted proportion of the surplus and deficit for the next four years. The procedure of the preparation of the central government budget in the first phase is over with the approval of the budget expenditures, namely the nominal expenditure ceiling.

In the second stage, the guidelines for supplementing or elaborating and adjusting the budget memorandum are issued, comprising government decisions, basic economic assumptions and guidelines for the preparation of the proposed central government budget, an estimate regarding the accounts of revenues and expenditures, the financial assets and liabilities account, the financing account of the central government budget, as well as the procedures and schedules for completing the preparation of the central government budget.

The Ministry of Finance has a key role in both stages of the budget preparation. Following the guidelines related to the budget memorandum, direct budgetary users draw up their proposed financial plans which, along with the detailed, supporting explanations, must be approved by the Ministry of Finance. The Ministry of Finance tables the plan to be approved by the government. Next, the budget plan is submitted to the National Assembly to be adopted.

The system of the preparation of the local government budget is slightly different from that of the central government budget. At the level of the central government, the Slovenian National Assembly must approve the final version of the budget. However, regarding the local, municipal level, the municipal council is responsible for adopting the budget. The main legal document for the preparation of both the local and central government budget is the Public Finance Act. Furthermore, each year the Ministry of Finance provides guidelines for the preparation of the local government budget due to the fact that considerable differences and deficiencies are often discovered between the municipalities in spite of the clear provisions of the Public Finance Act. In 2005, the IT application APPrA-O was implemented to support the municipalities (Ministrstvo za javno upravo 2012).

In all the periods of the budget preparation, execution, monitoring and implementation, different budget classifications with specific purposes are applied. The classifications ensure transparency of the budget and answer questions related to who uses the public budgetary funds and how and why they do so. The classifications determined by the Public Finance Act, the Ordinance on the Functional Classification of the Budget (The Official Gazette of the Republic of Slovenia, no. 43/00) and the Ordinance on the Programme Classification of Budget Expenditure (The Official Gazette of the Republic of Slovenia, no. 112/03, 56/05, 141/06 in 58/09) are the following:

- Institutional classification—who uses the public money;
- Economic classification—how public money is spent and for which economic purposes;

- Programme and functional—what public money is spent on and for which functions.

Both the state budget and municipal budget consist of a general part, a special part and a development programmes part.

5.2.2 *Budget Execution and Budget Execution Reports*

The main tasks of the budget execution are determined in compliance with the budgetary objectives and the principles stipulated in the Public Finance Act. The process of budget execution is determined by the legal framework containing all predefined objectives on one hand, and the flexibility to adjust to changed fiscal circumstances on the other. The precise and operating procedures of budget execution are determined by the Public Finance Act and the annual or biannual Budget Execution Act of the Republic of Slovenia as well as the Ordinance on the Procedures of Budget Execution in the Republic of Slovenia (The Official Gazette of the Republic of Slovenia, no. 50/07, 61/08, 99/09 - ZIPRS1011 and 3/13), which prescribes the necessary documentation for budget execution.

Successful budget execution is carried out in three mutually connected processes:

- Planning and ensuring liquidity during budget execution;
- Spending budget appropriations;
- Redistributing budgetary appropriations.

In the process of budget execution, the process of planning and ensuring liquidity should assure sufficient funds for direct budget users to make payments from the budget. It requires competent authority to cooperate well with direct budget users. The process consists of two procedures: determining quotas and the preparation of monthly plans. The objective of the implementation of quotas is to ensure the optimisation of the budget liquidity management by the budget users' financial services. In order to further improve the management of the funds, monthly liquidity drafts are prepared containing a monthly plan of the budget cash flow on the basis of which the direct budget user's commitments are paid.

The budget spending process consists of a stage of entering into commitments and signing a contract, reporting on the commitments entered into, obtaining verification for the payment from the budget, preparing of the bookkeeping documents and methods of payment, and finally actual payment for the commitment entered into.

The process of entering into commitments refers to all those operations of budget users which result in the committed expenditure of the budget. Budget users may enter into a commitment on the basis of a previously signed contract or some other document which has the same legal consequences as a contract, determined by laws and other regulations, unless otherwise provided by the Public Finance Act. Budget users may only make payments up to the amount of the planned expenditures taking into consideration the purpose of the intended expenditure as determined in the budget financial plan. In particular situations, prior to the commitment, written consent is required by the Ministry of Finance.

A budget user should examine whether the vendor fulfilled the obligations in the purchase order before actual payment is made. Each outgoing from the budget must be based on an authentic bookkeeping document issued by the vendor where the commitment to a payment is established. The authorising officer examines if the documents conform to the purchased goods and/or services, the contract requirements and to the purchase order. The document is initialled to acknowledge that the products or services received are acceptable and conform to the terms and conditions of the purchase order. The authorising officer examines the content of the invoice and whether it conforms to the purchase order and, before the actual payment is made, the officer checks if there are sufficient funds to make the payment.

The payment order from the budget is based on complete and correct invoices. The verifying officer conducts verification of the payment transaction. The authorising officer is a staff member with budget responsibility and, in the context of the payment process, is responsible for authorising legal and reasonable expenditure.

Based on appropriate and complete documentation, the accounting department uses the accounting application to prepare the specification of the payment order from the budget for each individual budget user. The specification contains individual invoices itemised for each transaction individually.

The last stage of the budget execution involves payment. Once checks are made to ensure that all the previously stipulated controls have been performed and documented, a payment order is issued. The payment order brief contains the code and name of the budget user, the budget item, the expenditure incurred until the estimated payment day, as well as the residual available funds. Unless the payment order exceeds the available funds for that day, the finance department makes payment of the verified and approved commitment.

Budget appropriations may not be reallocated unless stipulated differently in the Public Finance Act (ZIF) and the Budget Execution Act. The reallocation of appropriations may be carried out only under the certain predefined conditions and taking into consideration the structure of the proposed budget.

5.3 Accounting and Financial Reporting

5.3.1 Budgetary Accounting

In the field of public accounting, the Accounting Act (The Official Gazette of the Republic of Slovenia, no. 23/99 and 30/02-1253) which entered into force on 1 January 2000 and the aforementioned Public Finance Act are the fundamental regulations based on law. In budgetary accounting in Slovenia, there are numerous other pieces of subordinate legislation which are used on the grounds of the Accounting Act and the Public Finance Act.

Budgetary accounting is conducted on the principle of double-entry bookkeeping and according to the schedule of accounts in a uniform chart of accounts, which is different from the one applied in the private sector. The chart of accounts is further organised into classes, groups and analytic accounts. The account books are public documents, which are divided into fundamental and subsidiary ones. The fundamental account books are the journal and general ledger, while the subsidiary ledgers are analytic records and other sub-ledger records which complement the accounts of the general ledger. It is mandatory to keep fundamental account books, while sub-ledger records are kept only if there is no other way to provide the authentic data. However, it is compulsory to keep a cashbook, general ledger, and sales and purchase ledger.

It is legally prescribed that a budget user must keep account books and financial records in order to enable the monitoring of business operations and of operating results financed from the budget and other public sector financial sources on one side, and business operations and operating results financed from the sales of goods and services on the market on the other side. The account books and financial records should provide an evaluation of purpose-specific, economical and effective consumption of budgetary appropriations. According to the Accounting Act, the financial sources for the provision of public facilities, goods and services are not only received from the central government or local authority budget but also from the prices the central and local government charge for the use of specific public facilities or for public goods and services.

In budgetary accounting in Slovenia, revenues and expenditures are recognised on a cash-flow basis (cash received or paid—paid realisations). Pursuant to Article 15 paragraph 3 of the Accounting Act and Article 3 of the Ordinance on the Measuring and Breakdown of Revenues and Expenditures of Users of the Uniform Chart of Accounts, revenues or expenditures are recognised when the following two conditions are fulfilled:

- A business event resulting in the recognition of a revenue or expense has occurred;
- Cash or its equivalent has been received or paid or if receivables or liabilities relating to revenues or expenses have been settled in another way without actual cash flow.

State entities, municipal entities, smaller local entities, the Health Insurance Institute and the Institute for Pension and Disability Insurance and public funds (other users of the uniform chart of accounts), whose founder is the government or a municipality, exclusively use the cash accounting basis in recognising revenues and expenditures. All other legal entities under public law (public institutions, agencies, institutes, chambers, etc.) which are users of the uniform chart of accounts have revenues and expenditures recognised on the accrual accounting basis, recognising revenues and expenses when a business event occurs (invoiced realisation). Nevertheless, this group of users, for the sake of financial records, also keeps account books based on the cash flow principle, according to Article 15 of the Accounting Act. Regarding the above-mentioned classification of budgetary users into direct and indirect users, as well as the accounting division of these users into defined and other users of the uniform chart of accounts, it is important to emphasise that the divisions of these two users are not equal. In other words, all indirect users are not necessarily defined as users of the uniform chart of accounts.

Fixed assets are recognised at their purchase value or estimated value if the purchase value is not known. The purchase value, in addition to the purchase price, includes all the costs which can be directly attributed to the activation of the fixed assets for the planned application (e.g. costs of assembling, installation, transport, etc.), while the costs of interests on loans obtained and the costs of the purchase of capital goods are not included in the direct costs of the purchase of assets. Fixed assets whose purchase value does not exceed EUR 500 such as small inventory can be written-off as a lump sum at the moment of the purchase. In the account books, the written-off value is either recognised as the cost of materials and, after the write-off, the fixed assets are no longer recognised in the account books or are recognised in a manner such that the written-off value is recognised as a decrease in the purchase value.

The depreciation of fixed assets is recorded in compliance with the Slovenian Accounting Standards (SRS). In budgetary accounting, the manner of application and the rates of the write-offs are prescribed by the Ordinance on the Manner and Rates of Tangible and Intangible Fixed Asset Write-offs. Extraordinary write-offs are recorded in the event of the elimination or destruction of an asset, its permanent removal from use, a drop in its market value or a reduction in the predicted period of its use, etc. If stipulated in the Memorandum of Association, the budgetary user must have the consent of the founder in the case of the disposal of a fixed asset.

Investments in real estate concern real estate owned for the purpose of earning revenue from leasing, or in order to increase the value of long-term investments.

The following examples illustrate such real estate:

- Plots of land owned in order to increase the value of a long-term investment;
- Plots of land without a determined purpose of use;
- Properties owned or under a finance lease which are leased;
- Empty, privately owned property for the purpose of leasing.

Financial investments concern investments in company, state or municipality capital and loans. The initial value is recognised at the acquisition cost, while the value may increase later if the company makes a profit, or may decrease if it incurs a loss.

Revenue and expenses are classified in accordance with the provisions of the Accounting Act and legal regulations, primarily the Ordinance on the Breakdown and Measurement of Revenues and Expenses of Legal Entities under Public Law and the Slovenian Accounting Standards (SRS).

Revenues are classified as tax revenues, non-tax revenues, investing revenues, received donations, transfer revenue and funds received from the EU. Tax revenues are all the paid contributions collected pursuant to the law. Non-tax revenues result from operating activities, financing activities, administrative fees and charges, as well as all the other revenues. Investing revenues pertain to the sale of fixed and current assets, stocks and financial assets. Received donations are revenues from received funds, while transfer revenues are realised through transfers of funds from other public finance institutions. Funds received from the EU pertain to appropriations allocated from the EU budget and other EU institutions.

Expenses are classified as current expenses, current transfer expenses, operating expenses, operating transfer expenses and payments to the EU budget. Current expenses include labour expenses, costs of material and other costs for goods and services, as well as funds redirected to budgetary funds. Current transfer expenses relate to payments made without goods or services being received in return and for a purpose other than that of purchasing goods or services, such as for welfare benefit.

Operating expenses involve all payments for the purchase of fixed assets (e.g. real estate and the maintenance and renovation of buildings and other property). Operating transfer expenses relate to transferred government grants provided for paying the operating expenses of the beneficiaries. They also relate to expenses intended for paying the operating expenses of beneficiaries, which are recognised as soon as they result in liabilities for the benefits received. Payments of funds to the EU budget are classified in accordance with the source of these funds.

The financial result is the positive difference between revenues and expenses (surplus) or the negative difference between revenues and expenses (deficit). The surplus is allocated pursuant to the law and by the order of the founder of the legal entity, while the deficit is covered pursuant to the law and by the order of the founder of the legal entity.

The revaluation of fixed assets is an adjustment made to the recorded value of an asset to accurately reflect its current market value affected by general and specific economic and social causes. If the book value does not exceed the fair value, it is possible to estimate the asset at the fair value. However, if the book value exceeds the fair value, it is possible to reduce the recognised value of the asset to the fair value.

The Slovenian public accounting system is specific in that it is a modified version of an accounting system where the main accounting basis is the cash basis and where an accrual accounting basis is applied in the case of particular budget users. Even though the cash basis is the main principle in use, the bookkeeping system and the uniform chart of accounts enable the preparation of a balance sheet where all assets, receivables and liabilities are recognised. Eventually, a consolidated balance sheet is prepared at the government level.

Obviously, there is a difference between the bookkeeping system for the defined group of budget users of the uniform chart of accounts (primarily using an accrual accounting basis but also a cash basis) and the bookkeeping system for the budget group of other users (exclusively using a cash accounting basis), particularly when recording a business event at its occurrence or at the moment of paying liabilities and collecting receivables. The group of other budget users recognises expenses which have not yet been paid in the account of liabilities, while the group of defined budget users recognises them in completely different accounts of liabilities. A similar situation occurs with revenues which have not yet been paid and which are, in the case of the group of other budget users, recognised as short-term receivables, and, in the case of the group of defined budget users, as revenues. This system of budget accounting enables the cash basis to be the single principle for the financial statements.

5.3.2 Financial Reporting

There are three types of financial reports:

- Report on the budget execution and financial plans;
- Statement of accounts;
- Accounting reports.

In July, the Prime Minister reports to the government on the Report on the Budget Execution and Financial Plans and the government forwards this report to the Slovenian National Assembly. As for the municipalities, the mayor reports to the local council. The Health Insurance Institute and the Institute for Pension and Disability Insurance (ZZZS, ZPIZ) report to the Ministry of Finance on the execution of the financial plans.

The statement of accounts of the government budget is a government act which presents the structure of the budget for the last year, a forecast, and realised revenues and other income by the government, as well as expenditures and other expenses by the government. The statement of accounts consists of a general part, a special part, and explanations and specifications which are defined in the Instructions for the preparation of the government or municipal budget's statement of accounts and the methodology on the preparation of the report on achieved objectives and direct and indirect budgetary users' results (The Official Gazette of the Republic of Slovenia, no. 12/01, 10/06, 8/07 in 102/10).

The statement of accounts primarily consists of:

- A business report with a report on the achieved objectives and results, along with a report by the Accounting Court, which the government proposes to the Slovenian National Assembly, and the mayor to the municipality council;
- Data from the balance sheet; and
- Disclosures for deviations.

The general part of the statement of accounts consists of:

1. A statement of revenues and expenditures (Bilanca prihodkov in odhodkov);
2. A statement of financial receivables and investments (Račun finančnih terjatev in naložb);
3. A statement of financing (Račun financiranja).

The special part of the statement of accounts consists of direct budgetary users' realised financial plans. Direct budgetary users prepare statements of accounts of their financial plans which comprise the Report on the Achieved Objectives and Results, as well as the Accounting Report, while indirect budgetary users prepare only the Accounting Report.

Disclosures to the budget's statement of accounts consists of disclosures to the general part of the budget's statement of accounts, disclosures to the special part of the budget's statement of accounts, disclosures to the execution of the developmental plans and disclosures to the data in the balance sheet.

The accounting report is prepared in accordance with the Ordinance on Drawing up the Annual Budgetary Accounting Reports, Budgetary Users and Other Entities under Public Law. The accounting report consists of an accounting and operating part. The accounting part consists of a balance sheet, an income and expense statement, and disclosures to the statement.

The operating part of the report presents detailed information on the business activities of the budgetary user, namely a legal person under public law. The Report on the Achieved Objectives and Results is an integral part of the business report.

The balance sheet is a financial statement which consists of data on the state of assets and liabilities and the sources of obligations at the end of the fiscal period. The mandatory enclosures to the balance sheet are:

- Report on the state and movement of tangible and intangible fixed assets;
- Report on the state and movement of long-term investments and loans;
- Disclosure statements determined by the Ordinance.

The income and expense statement is an accounting statement which contains data on incomes and expenses realised during the fiscal year. The mandatory enclosures are:

- Statement of financial receivables and investments;
- Statement of the funding account;
- Disclosure statements determined by the Ordinance.

Since the defined users of the unified chart of accounts apply the accrual accounting basis when recording incomes, expenses and financial reports, the mandatory enclosures include:

- Income and expense statement by type of activity;
- Income and expense statement on a cash basis;
- Statement of financial receivables and investments on a cash basis;
- Statement of the funding account on a cash basis.

The third main component of the accounting part of the report is the disclosure statements which provide data on the accounting statements and explanations of each statement.

The operating part of the accounting report consists of information on the budgetary users' business operations. The budgetary user determines the content, while the Ordinance on Drawing up the Annual Budgetary Accounting Reports, Budgetary Users and Other Persons under Public Law defines the main contents whose objectives are to report on the problems and achievements in the business operation within the period observed.

According to Article 93 of the Public Finance Act, the Consolidated Balance Sheet of the Government and Municipality is prepared at the government level concerning the consolidated balance sheet at the level of the government and municipalities on 31 December every year. The Ordinance on the Preparation of the Consolidated Balance Sheet of the Government and Municipality determines the preparation of the consolidated balance sheet and defines its main components:

- Balance Sheet of indirect budgetary users;
- Balance Sheet of direct budgetary users;
- Balance Sheet of the Institute for Pension and Disability Insurance (ZPIZ);
- Balance Sheet of the Health Insurance Institute (ZZZS);
- Balance Sheet of the Municipality;
- Balance Sheet of the Government; and
- Consolidated Balance Sheet of the Government and Municipality.

Direct and indirect budgetary users of municipalities and other smaller municipal entities are the first to draft the balance sheet on the basis of the balance sheet and data from the budget users' books of accounts because data on the assets and liabilities of the balance sheet, and the receivables and liabilities between all the direct and indirect budget users of the municipality and the municipal budget, are offset, and the appropriations received increase or decrease by the difference from the offset. Next, the municipalities, the direct and indirect government budget users, the Institute for Pension and Disability Insurance, and the Health Insurance Institute prepare their consolidated reports and submit them to the Ministry of Finance.

The Ministry of Finance prepares the balance sheet of the government budget based on the data from the balance sheet and the accounts of the government budget. Next, based on the balance sheet of the government budget, the direct and indirect budgetary users' balance sheet as well as the balance sheet of the Institute for Pension and Disability Insurance and the Health Insurance Institute, the Ministry of Finance prepares the government balance sheet in accordance with the previously offset receivables and liabilities of all the participants involved except for the receivables for the appropriations allocated to state-owned enterprises, while the general fund decreases or increases by the difference from the offset. Every second year the Ministry of Finance proposes the consolidated balance sheet to the government by 31 May, and the government proposes it for a reading in the National Assembly, along with the revised statement of accounts for the previous year.

5.4 Audit and Other Oversight (Supervision) in the Public Sector

Oversight of public finances in the Republic of Slovenia is organised at several levels. The National Assembly is the highest supervisory body in the state, whose supervisory function is political due to the function of oversight of the executive power in the state, but it is also social as it has the possibility of parliamentary investigation. The Court of Audit, accountable to the National Assembly, is the highest auditing institution of the state, which independently carries out external audits of all users of public funds.

The Budget Supervision Office of the Republic of Slovenia and the government represent the second level of oversight. The Budget Supervision Office of the Republic of Slovenia is a central body of the public internal financial control system responsible for the development, harmonisation and supervision of the financial management and internal control system as well as internal audit of users of direct and indirect budget spending at the central and local level. The government carries out oversight of public finances through its services.

Elementary oversight of budgetary users is carried out in the form of internal audit. Internal audit is a procedure of examination, monitoring and analysis of the organisation's operations with the aim of improving the organisation's business performance.

Along with internal audit, internal accounting controls, although not considered a part of public finance oversight, are considered very important. The management of direct and indirect budget users is responsible for setting up an adequate system of procedures and responsibilities of internal controls and internal audit pursuant to Article 100 of the Public Finance Act.

5.4.1 *State Audit*

The Court of Audit is the highest body for supervising government accounts, the government budget and all public spending in Slovenia pursuant to Articles 151 and 152 of the Constitution of the Republic of Slovenia. It is in charge of auditing the following budgetary users:

- A public law entity;
- A private law entity if it has received aid from the budget of the European Union, the government budget or the budget of a local authority; if it is a concession-holder; if it is a company, bank or insurance company in which the state or a local authority has a majority stake;
- A natural person who has received aid from the budget of the European Union, the state budget, or the budget of a local authority; is carrying out a public service or securing public goods on the basis of a concession.

The Court of Audit has a president and two deputy presidents who form the Senate of the Court of Audit. On the proposal of the President of the Republic, they are appointed for a term of nine years by the National Assembly by a majority vote of all the deputies in a secret ballot.

In addition to its members, the Court of Audit also has a maximum of six supreme state auditors who head the audit departments, and a secretary of the Court of Audit, who heads the support services. They all have the status of public officials. They are appointed by the president of the Court of Audit for a term of nine years.

The Court of Audit may carry out regularity and performance audits or it may audit any act on past operations as well as any act on the planned business operation of any user of public funds where the act may be any act prescribed by law or any special financial statement or report which the user of public funds is obliged to prepare at the request of the Court of Audit.

Regularity audits provide relevant and sufficient data to enable an opinion to be expressed on the compliance of operation with the regulations and guidelines that any user of public funds is required to observe in the conduct of business operations, while performance audits provide relevant and sufficient data to enable an opinion to be expressed on the economy, efficiency and effectiveness of business operations. The opinion issued by the Court of Audit on the business operation of the auditee must be respected by every state body, local community body and the relevant user of public funds. The business operation of a user of public funds includes all actions by the user of public funds which have an impact on the user's receipts and expenses, revenues and expenses or assets and liabilities, respectively, and which are therefore considered business operations in the restricted sense. All actions by the user of public funds which have an impact on the state of public assets, public debt, the provision of public goods or the state of the environment are considered business operations in the broader sense. In addition to the audits carried out as described above, the Court of Audit may conduct other audits, if so provided by a specific law.

The Court of Audit also provides recommendations to the users of public funds at the time of performing the audit, and it may make comments on working drafts of laws and other regulations. Moreover, it may participate in meetings and seminars on public finance issues, put forward proposals in the report on its work which is submitted to the National Assembly once a year, and, finally, may express opinions on public finance issues.

The Court of Audit must conduct audits in accordance with generally accepted auditing principles and rules and in accordance with international standards of auditing. In the Instructions on Auditing Execution (The Official Gazette of the Republic of Slovenia, no. 43/12) as a subordinate act of the Court of Audit Act (The Official Gazette of the Republic of Slovenia, no. 11/01 in 109/12) the following standards and guidelines are mentioned:

- International standards of the supreme auditing institutions, published by INTOSAI—International Organisation of Supreme Auditing Institutions;

- European guidelines for the execution of international auditing standards published by INTOSAI;
- International standards of auditing published by IFAC—International Association of Experts.

The Court of Audit starts the process of audit by issuing a decision on the undertaking of audit. The Court of Audit may, prior to the commencement of audit, demand the user of public funds to provide all information which it considers relevant to its audit, including bookkeeping documents, data and other documentation, and make other enquiries necessary for the planning or conducting of the audit. The user of public funds should enable the authorised staff of the Court of Audit to carry out the examinations necessary for achieving the objectives of the audit. The audit comprises the following:

- An examination of the system or of certain sub-systems of the business operations and accounting;
- An examination of bookkeeping and other documents related to the business operations;
- An examination of the premises, facilities and equipment used by the auditee in its business operations;
- Any other audit actions necessary to achieve the audit objectives.

The process of audit is completed when an audit report is issued. In the audit report, the Court of Audit provides an opinion on the business operations of the auditee. Before the audit report is issued, the auditee is invited to a clearance meeting. The auditee receives a draft audit report to serve as the basis for discussion. If the audit is carried out on several auditees (a cross-sectional audit), the draft audit report is provided to individual auditees in the sections that are relevant to them.

After the clearance meetings, an auditor authorised by the Court of Audit submits the draft audit report, including the auditee's comments, if any, to the competent member or to the Supreme State Auditor of the Court of Audit. Having evaluated the comments to and the findings of the audit, the competent Member or the Supreme State Auditor issues a proposed audit report and delivers it, within 15 days of the final clearance meeting, to the auditee and to the officers of the auditee who were responsible in the period covered by the audit performed.

The competent member or supreme state auditor of the Court of Audit reviews the audit report and the auditee's comments, and establishes whether the comments are justified, whether the findings are based on documentary evidence and whether the audit procedures have been carried out in accordance with auditing standards. Having evaluated the comments to and the findings of the audit, the competent member or the supreme state auditor issues a proposed audit report and delivers it, within 15 days of the final clearance meeting, to the auditee and to the officers of the auditee who were responsible in the period covered by the audit performed. In cases where no clearance meeting is necessary, the competent member of the Court of Audit issues the proposed audit report within 10 days after having received the auditee's notification that no disclosure in the draft audit report is challenged. The auditee and the auditee's officer who was responsible in the period covered by the audit may file an objection against any audit disclosure in the proposed audit report within eight days.

If an audit disclosure in the proposed audit report is challenged or some doubt has been expressed in the opinion referred to in the preceding paragraph about the professional correctness of a disclosure, such a disclosure is considered to be disputable. The user of public funds in whose business operation the irregularities or inefficiencies have been disclosed must submit to the Court of Audit a report on the irregularities and inefficiencies, known as a response report (a response/complaint), within a time limit from between thirty and ninety days.

5.4.2 Budgetary Oversight

The Budget Supervision Office of the Republic of Slovenia, as part of the Ministry of Finance, is a central body of the public internal financial control system responsible for the oversight of the spending of budgetary funds, and the preparation of common methods of internal auditing in public. Furthermore, the Budget Supervision Office provides instructions and guidelines for the execution of the internal audit of direct budgetary users at the central and local level. Along with responsibility for the development of internal auditing services within the whole system of financial supervision in the public sector, the Office organises training for internal auditors in the public sector.

The Budget Supervision Office consists of four different sectors:

- Sector for the auditing of European agricultural funds;
- Sector for the auditing of European structural funds;
- Sector for budgetary inspection;
- Sector for internal financial control.

In the spending of EU funds, the Budget Supervision Office performs pre-accreditation reviews, conducts the independent control of expenditures, certifies declarations of expenditures and issues winding-up declarations. It regularly reports to the European Commission on irregularities regarding the use of EU funds, acts as the contact point of the European Anti-Fraud Office (OLAF), and coordinates activities relating to the protection of EU financial interests. The office performs budgetary inspection and the development, harmonisation and supervision of the financial management and internal audit of direct and indirect budgetary users at the central and local level.

Budgetary inspection involves the inspection and supervision of the execution of the Public Finance Act and other regulations important for the regulation of business operations carried out with budgetary funds. The parties in the inspection and supervision are indirect and direct budgetary users of the central or local budget. Along with the above, the task of the inspection is to supervise the execution of the Act on the Transparency of Financial Relations and Maintenance of Separate Accounts for Different Activities (ZPFOLERED-1) and the supervision of the spending of earmarked funds received by municipalities from the central budget according to Article 29 of the Financing of Municipalities Act—ZFO-1. Based on the reports, including the anonymous ones, budgetary inspection considers whether to carry out inspection oversight, which is conducted if there is reasonable suspicion of violations of the regulations under the Budget Supervision Office jurisdiction.

5.4.3 Internal Audit and Internal Control System

The Budget Supervision Office of the Republic of Slovenia, besides oversight of the spending of EU funds and budgetary inspection, plays an important part in the coordination of the work and training of internal auditors. Internal auditors are not employees of the Office but are either organised as independent auditors from the private sector or are employees of budget users. In order to provide an efficient auditing service, internal auditors may be employed in the Common Affairs Service providing audit for several organisations.

The internal supervision of public finance, which comprises the complete system based on financial management, internal controls and internal audit, is established by a budget user in order to manage business operations and ensure lawful, economical and efficient spending of public funds.

The internal supervision of public finance refers not only to internal audit but also to a complete system of financial management and internal control. In 2004 the Budget Supervision Office of the Republic of Slovenia issued Guidelines for Internal Audit, defining precisely the functions, objectives and procedures of internal controls. Pursuant to Article 100 of the Public Finance Act, the management of direct and indirect budget users is responsible for the efficient execution of internal controls. Internal controls are necessary on account of internal and external factors such as financial, legal and commercial risks, which may endanger the objectives, set by budget users.

The main objectives of internal controls are:

- Efficient execution of the budgetary user's tasks;
- Appropriate use of funds and their protection against loss due to negligence, misuse, bad management, mistakes, fraud and other irregularities;
- Business operations in accordance with laws, legal regulations and management directions;
- To ensure timely, complete and reliable accounting information and data as well as a true and fair view of financial statements;
- To ensure equal opportunities and environmental protection.

Although management bears responsibility, the execution of internal control as an organised system of procedures and responsibilities may be delegated to members of staff. Internal auditors perform control within the framework of internal audit services to provide efficient internal audit and avoid the irregular and unplanned spending of public funds. Internal auditors may be the budget user's employees or they may, as the staff of the Common Affairs Service, conduct audit for several budget users. Nevertheless, most often, internal audit is conducted by chartering an external auditor.

The performance of internal auditors is prescribed by the Ordinance on the Guidelines for the Harmonious Performance of Internal Oversight of Public Finance (The Official Gazette of the Republic of Slovenia, no. 79/99, 124/00, 79/01, 30/02) and the Guidelines for State Internal Auditing. Internal audits examine, monitor and analyse all the operational procedures and functions of the organisation for the purpose of improving its business operations. The internal auditor is accountable to the head of the institution. One of the important tasks of the internal auditor is to consult the auditors of the Court of Audit and participate in cases of external audits. The internal auditors' reports are considered by the head of either indirect or direct budgetary users, the Office for Budget Oversight of the Republic of Slovenia and the Court of Audit. Management is expected to adequately respond to the internal auditor's report and to accept measures to eliminate the irregularities, shortcomings and weaknesses discovered by the auditor. If there is reasonable suspicion of fraud or another criminal act or offence, the auditor should inform the competent authorities (e.g. the government, the National Assembly, etc.).

5.5 Challenges in Further Development of Public Sector Accounting and Auditing

The Public Finance Act and the Accounting Act are the fundamental legal documents in the field of public finance and public sector accounting in the Republic of Slovenia, coming into force in 2000 and since then have not been changed substantially. Some minor modifications have been introduced to provide solutions for specific problems encountered in practice, while the systemic legislation in this field has not been altered.

The instability of public finance in the Euro zone required a policy of tighter public finance discipline and transparency in budgetary planning. Thus, in November 2011 a set of legislative measures for five regulations and directives was introduced at the EU level with the aim of strengthening fiscal responsibility and economic management of the Member States. Therefore, Slovenia published the Constitutional Act on the amended Article 148 of the Constitution of the Republic of Slovenia (The Official Gazette of the Republic of Slovenia, no. 47/13) committing itself at the Constitutional level to having revenues and expenditures of the state budget balanced in the medium-term without borrowing, or to having revenues that exceed expenditures. A temporary deviation from this principle is only allowed in exceptional circumstances. Along with the amendment of the Constitution of the Republic of Slovenia, in 2015 the Act on Fiscal Rule was adopted relating to the precise content and implementation of Article 148 of the Constitution of the Republic of Slovenia. This Act allowed for the implementation of the majority of Directives of the EU Council in 2011 (2011/85/EU, 8 November 2011) related to the requirements on budgetary frameworks of the Member States. Since there are still certain measures that need to be implemented in the Slovenian legal system, amendments to the Public Finance Act and the Accounting Act are being considered.

The professional community has suggested that certain changes need to be introduced since the Republic of Slovenia is an EU Member State and is consequently required to report on the public finance deficit and debt, use the ESA 2010 methodology, respect the Maastricht rules, etc. The main problems concerning immediate solutions derive from the fact that the public accounting system is based on the cash basis, while at the EU level the accrual accounting basis is applied. In February 2016 both of the above-mentioned proposals of laws were scheduled for a public hearing and in spring 2017 they were forwarded to the government of the Republic of Slovenia.

Exposure drafts of the amendments to the Public Finance Act and the Accounting Act in 2016 included proposals for several changes in the public accounting system, as well as further improvements of public sector financial management. One of the major proposed changes was the implementation of the accrual accounting basis and EPSAS to commence as of 1 January 2022. However, the proposed amendments from 2016 were not enacted in Slovenian legislation, so there no major changes of the accounting system rules and principles were made.

In addition, in March 2018 minor changes in the Public Finance Act were passed. These changes were the result of the Council Directive 2011/85/EU (dated from the 8th November 2011) implementation. The Directive and consequently the changes of the Public Finance Act (2018) did not refer to public sector accounting matter but they influenced the medium-term fiscal policy planning due to public finance sustainability establishment, so that the medium-term fiscal planning started being regulated through two important government documents; the State program development programme and the Medium-Term Fiscal strategy. Additionally, the supplemented provisions of the Public Finance

Act committed the government to prepare the budget, which was in line with the framework of National Assembly but also enhanced the change of some documents supporting the budget memorandum. Finally, the obligation of public debt and tax expenditures reporting was enacted according to the Directive provisions.

Slovenian public financial management's problems remain unresolved for the near future. Currently, there are several challenges in public sector financial management area that exceed the topic of the accounting system and accounting techniques. The financial control mechanisms and the Slovenian Parliament as well, are handling and discussing basic business models including processes, obligations and responsibilities in public sector entities individually and for the public sector as a whole and a more complex structure. Prior to focusing on accounting system's solutions, there are several organisational and technical problems of 2.500 public sector entities (i.e. schools, hospitals) to be solved such as the problem of disintegration of IT applications for accounting and budgetary execution, the problem of bottom-up financial management of those entities, as well as the problem of politically chosen management boards of those entities.

Bearing in mind the accounting practice in other SEE countries and the trend of moving towards the adoption of accrual accounting and the implementation of IPSAS or EPSAS, as well as the Slovenian practice (i.e. suggestions from the supreme body for public sector financial control—the Court of Audit), the future development path of the Slovenian national accounting system should be set towards implementing accrual accounting basis for the public sector entities financial reporting, but keeping the cash flow basis for budgetary purpose is the option that should represent. Following both basis, the financial management system and control system could use accounting information for both, management and budgetary purposes.

References

Brezovnik, B., Finžgar, M., & Oplotmik, Ž. J. (2014). *Financiranje slovenskih občin*. Maribor: Lex Localis.

Cvikl, M. M., & Korpič-Horvat, E. (2007). *Proračunsko pravo: Priprava, izvrševanje in nadzor proračunov*. Ljubljana: GV Založba.

Cvikl, M. M., & Zemljič, P. (2005). *Zakon o javnih financah (ZIF): s komentarjem*. Ljubljana: Bonex.

Janc, M. (2009). *Ureditev sredstev v državni lasti in v lasti lokalnih skupnosti v Sloveniji*. Ljubljana: CEF.
Ministrstvo za javno upravo. (2012). *Sisitem javnih finance*. Ljubljana: Upravna akademija.
Šoltes, I., Bilbija, M., Jeršič, N., & Cerar, M. (2010). *Pojmovnik javnih financ*. Ljubljana: Nebra.

Useful Sites

https://www.uradni-list.si/.
www.intosai.org.
www.ifac.org.

CHAPTER 6

Public Sector Accounting, Auditing and Control in the Federation of Bosnia and Herzegovina

Jelena Jurić and Maja Letica

6.1 Territorial Organisation, Financing and Scope of the Public Sector

6.1.1 Territorial Organisation

Bosnia and Herzegovina (hereinafter: BiH) is a country in South Eastern Europe that gained its independence after the separation and disintegration of the Federal Republic of Yugoslavia in the 1990s.

According to the preliminary data of the Census of 2013,[1] there are in total 3,791,622 persons registered in BiH, of whom 2,371,603 in the Federation of BiH, 1,326,991 in the Republic of Srpska and 93,028

[1] The last census was conducted in 2013 but due to methodological disagreements in data processing, the official data have not yet been published.

J. Jurić · M. Letica (✉)
University of Mostar, Mostar, Bosnia and Herzegovina
e-mail: maja.letica@ef.sum.ba

V. Vašiček and G. Roje (eds.), *Public Sector Accounting, Auditing and Control in South Eastern Europe*, Public Sector Financial Management, https://doi.org/10.1007/978-3-030-03353-8_6

in the Brčko District.[2] BiH has a total area of 51,209.20 km^2, most of which is mainland (51,197 km^2) and 12.20 km^2 is water.[3]

At the end of the war in BiH, the Dayton Agreement was signed,[4] and Annex IV of the Dayton Agreement is considered to be the Constitution of BiH. The Constitution of BiH is the base for the administrative-territorial organisation of BiH and it defines BiH as a democratic state with a complex territorial organisation. BiH is a complex federal state with elements of confederation, administratively divided into two entities: the Federation of Bosnia and Herzegovina, and the Republic of Srpska and Brčko District (hereinafter: BD). The Federation of Bosnia and Herzegovina (hereinafter: FBiH) is administratively divided into cantons that are further divided into municipalities and cities. Republic of Srpska (hereinafter: RS) is administratively divided into 62 municipalities. The city Town of Brčko is a separate administrative unit—District. Pursuant to Article 3 of the Constitution of BiH, the responsibilities of the institutions of BiH are as follows: foreign affairs, foreign trade policy, customs policy, monetary policy (in particular, organisation of the Central Bank of BiH according to the Currency Board arrangement), financing of institutions and international obligations of BiH, implementation of international and inter-entity criminal regulations, including relations with Interpol, establishment and functioning of common and international communication devices, adoption of regulations on transport between entities, and air traffic control.[5]

The Constitution of FBiH (Official Gazette of FBiH, 1/94, 13/97, 16/02, 22/02, 52/02, 63/03, 9/04, 20/04, 33/04, 71/05, 72/05, and 88/08)[6] was adopted at the session of the Constitutive Assembly of FBiH on 30 March 1994, shortly after the signing of the Washington

[2] Agencija za statistiku BiH.

[3] http://www.bhas.ba/obavjestenja/Preliminarni_hr.pdf (November 2013).

[4] Started in Dayton on 21 November 1995, and signed in Paris on 14 December 1995.

[5] http://www.ads.gov.ba/v2/attachments/1951_USTAV_BOSNE_I_HERCEGOVINE_hrv.pdf.

[6] Official Gazette of FBiH stands for a public record titled Službeni novine Federacije BiH, in which all laws, regulations, decrees, appointments and official decisions passed in the Parliament or adopted by the Government are published in native language and released in the public domain: http://www.sluzbenilist.ba/Docs/index/fbih.

Agreement.[7] According to the Constitution of FBiH, the Federation of BiH consists of 10 cantons—federal units with a wide range of responsibilities handed down by the Constitution of FBiH. Cantons are further divided into 79 municipalities and 9 cities. The Constitution of FBiH also defines the responsibilities of certain government levels. According to the Constitution, the exclusive responsibilities of the entities are: citizenship of FBiH, economic policy, including planning and reconstruction and land use policy at the federal level, the adoption of regulations on finance and financial institutions of the Federation and fiscal policy of the Federation, prevention of terrorism, intercantonal crime, unauthorised drug trafficking and organised crime, allocation of electronic frequencies for radio, TV and for other purposes, energy policy, including distribution between cantons, and providing and maintaining the necessary infrastructure, and financing federal authority activities, institutions and institutions established by the federal authorities through taxation, borrowing or other means. Shared responsibilities of the Federation of BiH and the cantons relate to the following: ensuring human rights, healthcare, environmental care, the communication and transport infrastructure, social policy, implementation of laws and other regulations on citizenship and travel documents of BiH citizens from the territory of the FBiH and the stay and movement of foreigners, tourism, and the use of natural resources. The cantons have exclusive responsibility for the following issues: establishment and monitoring of police forces, the development of educational policy, including the regulation of education, the establishment and implementation of cultural policy, the development of housing policy, including regulations on the design and construction of housing facilities, the development of policy on the regulation and provision of public services, the regulation of local land use, improvement of local business and charity activities, local plants for

[7] The Washington Agreement is an agreement signed between Croats from Bosnia and Herzegovina (represented by the Republic of Croatia) and Bosniaks, i.e. belonging to the Republic of Bosnia and Herzegovina (Bosnians were dominant then in the government) on 18 March 1994 in Washington. A truce was agreed between the Croatian Defence Council and the Army of the Republic of Bosnia and Herzegovina. The internal organisation of the territory with the Bosnian and Croatian population in the Republic of Bosnia and Herzegovina has been transformed into the Federation of Bosnia and Herzegovina constitued by federal units, or cantons, that have equal rights and responsibilities.

the generation of electricity, providing a radio and television transmission service, implementation of social policy and the establishment of social services, the creation and application of a cantonal tourism policy, the development of tourism resources, financing the activities of cantonal authorities or their agencies through taxation, borrowing or other means.

According to the Law on the Principles of Local Self-government in the Federation of BiH (Official Gazette of FBiH, 49/06, 51/09), local self-government units (hereinafter: LSUs) have the following responsibilities: guaranteeing and protecting human rights and fundamental freedoms in accordance with the Constitution of BiH; adopting the LSU budget; adopting LSU development programmes and creating conditions for economic development and employment; the development and implementation of spatial planning and environmental care, the adoption of spatial, urban and implementation plans including zoning; developing and implementing housing policy and adopting housing and other construction programmes; developing and implementing a policy of use and setting levels of reimbursements for the use of public goods; developing and implementing a policy on the use and management of construction land; developing a policy on the management and use of LSU assets; developing a policy on the natural resources management of the LSUs and the allocation of funds generated from their use; management, financing and improvement of the activities and facilities of local communal infrastructure (water supply, waste water disposal and its processing, solid waste collection and disposal, public hygiene, cemeteries, local roads, bridges, public lightening, public parking); the organisation and improvement of local public transport; the development of preschool education policy; improvement of the network of institutions and the management and financing of institutions and the construction of cultural and sports facilities; evaluating the work of institutions and service quality in the field of healthcare, social welfare, education, culture and sports, and providing funds for the improvement of their work and quality in accordance with people's needs and the possibilities of the local self-government unit; analysing the state of public order and peace, and the safety of people and property; organising, implementing and taking responsibility for the protection and rescue of people and material goods in the event of natural disasters; adopting regulations on taxes, contributions, remunerations and fees within the scope of responsibilities of LSUs, and other activities in accordance with the Constitution and laws.

6.1.2 *Financing of Central State, Entities and Local Government Units*

6.1.2.1 Financing of Central State

Due to the complex organisation of Bosnia and Herzegovina, the financing of certain levels of government is in accordance with that organisation. The financing of central state, entities and local government units is determined by the following laws: the Law on the Treasury of Institutions of BiH (Official Gazette of BiH,[8] 27/00), Law on the Budgets of Institutions of the Federation BiH (Official Gazette of FBiH, 102/13, 13/14, 8/15, 91/15 and 102/15), and other related laws.[9]

According to the Law on the Treasury of Institutions of BiH, the budget represents the budget of the institutions of BiH that provide an annual estimation of revenues and other receipts as well as expenses. According to the same Law, the Treasury is a central element in the financial management of the funds of the institutions of BiH and other budget beneficiaries and a body that has the leading role when formulating budgetary procedures: the estimation of revenues and other receipts; money management through a single account, planning and supervision of budget execution, development and maintenance of the information system; planning and debt management; financial property management; regulation and implementation of internal control. The Treasury Single Account (hereinafter: TSA) was established by the same Law as a comprehensive account where all operations are registered and which contains all the budget funds of the institutions of BiH. In accordance with Article VIII of the Constitution of BiH, the FBiH provides 2/3 and the Republic of Srpska 1/3 of revenues for the budget of institutions of BiH that are transferred monthly from the entities to the account opened in the Central Bank of BiH. Around 75 budget beneficiaries in BiH are funded from the budget of institutions of BiH.[10] Revenues collected at the level of BiH are paid into the budget of the institutions of

[8] Official Gazette of BiH stands for a public record for Bosnia and Herzegovina titled Službeni glasnik BiH, in which all laws, regulations, decrees, appointments and official decisions passed in the Parliament or adopted by the Government are published in native language and released in the public domain: http://www.sluzbenilist.ba/Docs/index/bih.

[9] Such as the Law on the Indirect Taxation System in BiH, the Law on the Distribution of Public Revenues in the FBiH.

[10] Institutions of BiH, different agencies, ministries, administrations, offices.

BiH and to the TSA. The Law on Payments into the Single Account and Distribution of Revenues (Official Gazette of BiH, 55/04) regulates the method of payment of indirect taxes, import and export duties, excise duties, value added tax (VAT) and all other taxes charged on goods and services, including tax on transportation and tolls according to the Law on the Indirect Taxation System in BiH, and other revenues and fees in the TSA. Amounts from the TSA are allocated to beneficiaries in accordance with the Law on the Indirect Taxation System in BiH, and the shares of the entities and the District are determined based on single coefficients of allocation.

6.1.2.2 Financing of Entities and Local Self-Government Units

The complex territorial organisation of BiH due to its division into two entities and further into cantons and municipalities has given great responsibilities to the aforementioned levels of government when collecting revenues and financing its functions. As can be seen in the previous sub-chapter, the institutions of Bosnia and Herzegovina are financed from the budget at the level of Bosnia and Herzegovina only. The financing of other levels of government is defined based on other laws, as presented below.

The Law on Budgets of the Institutions of the FBiH (Official Gazette of the FBiH, 102/13, 13/14, 8/15, 91/15, 102/15) provides for the planning, formulation, adoption and execution of the budget of the FBiH, cantons, cities and municipalities.

According to the Law on the Distribution of Public Revenues in the FBiH (Official Gazette of the FBiH, 22/06, 43/08, 22/09), public revenues are allocated from the single account of the FBiH to the cantons and local self-government units. Part of the revenues belonging to the FBiH relate to the financing of functions of the Federation, and this part amounts to 36.10% of the revenues. The part for financing the functions of the cantons is 51.48%. This part is then allocated to each canton according to certain parameters[11] based on formulae containing a corrective coefficient for certain cantons using a different basis. An allocation of 8.42% of public revenues goes to local self-government units and 3.90% to the Direction for Roads.

[11] The population of the canton (57%), the surface area of the canton (6%), the number of pupils in primary education (24%), and the number of pupils in secondary education (13%).

6.1.3 *Scope of the Public Sector in FBiH*

In the Federation of Bosnia and Herzegovina, the scope of the public sector is defined by the Law of the Budgets of Institutions of the FBiH. According to this Law, the scope of the FBiH is the budget of the FBiH, the budgets of cantons, the budgets of local self-government units and extra-budgetary beneficiaries. Based on this Law, budget beneficiaries are ministries and other administrative bodies and others that are included in the budget as budget beneficiaries. Extra-budgetary beneficiaries are business companies, organisations and institutions involved in providing public services or doing public service and are established by special regulations, and other legal entities where the Federation, cantons, cities and municipalities have a decisive influence based on equity structure. Extra-budgetary beneficiaries are legal entities established by law that are financed from dedicated taxes and tax revenue or contributions. In accordance with of the Law on the Budgets of Institutions of the FBiH, the Pension and Disability Fund, the Health Fund, the Employment Fund as well as other funds established by law are deemed extra-budgetary funds.

Entities that receive continuous or occasional grants payable are not classified as budgetary beneficiaries, and are not classified as headings, chapters, nor budget units in the organisational classification of the budget, regardless of the percentage of funding received from grants, such as current or capital transfers to non-profit organisations, citizens' associations, subventions for public companies, or grants to other levels of government that are not classified in the budget as budgetary beneficiary (Salkić and Salkić 2011: 10).

The Ministry of Finance or the Finance Service keeps a record of budget beneficiaries by prescribed budget classification.

6.2 Formulation and Execution of Central Government and Local and Regional Self-Government Budgets

6.2.1 *Legislative and Institutional Framework of the Budget*

The bases for determining the budget and budgetary relations in the FBiH are provided by the Law on the Budgets of Institutions of the FBiH (Official Gazette of the Federation of BiH, 102/13, 13/14,

8/15, 91/15, 102/15): "This Law regulates the planning, preparation, approval and execution of the budget of the Federation of Bosnia and Herzegovina, the budgets of cantons, cities and municipalities and the financial plans of extra-budgetary funds, budget principles, borrowing, guarantees and debt management, the programme of public investments, fiscal responsibility rules, accounting, reporting, supervision and audit of the budget and other budgetary beneficiaries."

The Law on the Budgets of Institutions of the FBiH is applied equally on entity, cantonal and local self-government budgets and on their budget and extra-budgetary beneficiaries. Differences that exist arise from differences between the responsibilities of certain levels of government.

6.2.2 *Preparation and Adoption of the Budget in the FBiH*

The budget is the most important financial act that determines the budget beneficiaries' financial activities plan and includes a projection of revenues and receipts and the expenses and expenditures of the FBiH, cantons, cities and municipalities for a period of one fiscal year (Law on the Budgets of Institutions of the FBiH (Official Gazette of the FBiH, 19/06, 76/08, 5/09, 32/09, 9/10, 36/10, 45/10, 25/12).

The formal structure of the budgets of all levels is based on the same legal basis and implementation documents, so the budgets are mutually comparable. When formulating and adopting budgets, the responsible levels of government need to apply budget principles, budget classifications, programme and strategic planning, and ensure the publication of the budget in the Official Gazette of FBiH.[12]

According to the Law on the Budgets of Institutions of the FBiH, the budget of the FBiH is adopted by the Parliament of the Federation of BiH, and the cantonal budgets by legislative authorities (cantonal assemblies) or city and municipal councils for the budgetary year. In the FBiH, the budgetary year corresponds to the calendar year and starts on 1 January and ends on 31 December. Revenues, receipts, expenses and expenditures of the budget and financial plan are presented according to the budget classifications:

[12]Official Gazette of FBiH stands for a public record titled Službeni novine Federacije BiH, in which all laws, regulations, decrees, appointments and official decisions passed in the Parliament or adopted by the Government are published in native language and released in the public domain: http://www.sluzbenilist.ba/Docs/index/fbih.

- Organisational classification—which contains associated and mutually adjusted parts of budgets and budget beneficiaries that achieve the set goals by appropriate means.
- Economic classification—which contains revenues and receipts by natural types and expenses and expenditures by their economic purpose.
- Functional classification—a set of tasks, functions and programmes of the Federation, cantons, municipalities, cities and extra-budgetary funds classified by their purpose.
- Programme classification—which contains expenses and expenditures reported through activities and projects associated in programmes on the basis of mutual goals.
- Funding/funding resources—which contains revenues and receipts that are used to settle expenses and expenditures of a certain type and purpose (Official Gazette of FBiH, 10/13).

These classifications should be mandatorily applied at all levels of government in order to successfully adopt and supervise the budget of different levels of government.

The budget consists of a general and specific part and a capital budget. The general part of the budget includes the revenues and expenses account, the capital receipts account, and the financing account. The revenues and expenses account of the budget of the FBiH and cantons, municipalities and cities reports on revenues and expenses. The capital receipts account reports on receipts from non-financial assets and expenses for non-financial assets. The financing account includes receipts from financial assets, received loans and expenditures for financial assets and repayments of loans and leases. The special part of the budget consists of beneficiaries' plan of expenses and expenditures, reported by using economic classification and allocated in current expenditures and capital investments.

The capital budget consists of expenses for capital investments, by years and sources of funding. The financial plan of extra-budgetary funds consists of a general part comprising the revenues and expenses account and the financing account, and a special part where revenues and receipts as well as expenses and expenditures allocated in programmes are reported, both consisting of activities and projects. The budgets of cantons, cities and municipalities and the financial plans of their extra-budgetary funds are aggregated at the cantonal level and are then submitted to the Ministry of Finance within 15 days following their submission for consolidation.

6.2.3 *Budget Execution and the Report on Budget Execution*

Execution of the budget during one year is the continuous realisation of revenue and execution of expenses determined by the budget. The adopted budget represents the framework of consumption of all beneficiaries spending. Budgetary expenses can vary from the level determined by the budget by certain purposes. The dynamic of the realisation of budgetary revenues determines the framework and dynamics of budget spending.

The formulation and execution of the budget of the FBiH is based on the principles of unity, accuracy, equilibrium and legality of the budget, the annuality principle, the principle of universality, efficiency, cost-effectiveness, transparency, and participation. All revenues and receipts, expenses and expenditures are reported in the budget using the gross principle. The budget must be balanced so that total revenues and receipts cover total expenses and expenditures. Revenues and receipts are used for the settlement of expenses and expenditures, unless otherwise provided for in the Law on the Budgets of Institutions of the Federation BiH (The Official Gazette of FBiH, 102/13, 13/14, 8/15, 91/15,102/15) and in the Law on Budget Execution for a particular year. Budget beneficiaries may take over liabilities reported under expenses of the budget of the current year only for the purposes and to the extent determined in the special part of the budget if all conditions determined by the law and other regulations are met.

Within the Federal Ministry of Finance, the Treasury is established for the purpose of budget execution and for reporting on budget execution, budget execution supervision, money management and TSA keeping and bookkeeping. More precisely, "The treasury shall be the basic organisational unit within the Federal Ministry of Finance and cantonal ministries of finance where in accordance with this Law and other regulations activities shall be performed related to planning budget execution and implementation of the budget of the Federation and cantonal budgets, bookkeeping and accounting policies, cash management and maintaining the Treasury Single Account, repayments of debt, issuing guarantees, issuance of new debt and management of unused funds and property" (Law on the Treasury of the FBiH, Official Gazette of FBiH, 58/05, 19/03,79/07).

Budget and extra-budgetary beneficiaries are obligated to prepare financial reports on budget execution during the period. More precisely,

"Financial reports of budget and extra-budgetary beneficiaries shall be reports on the balance and structure and changes of assets, liabilities, own resources, revenues, expenditures or cash flows" (Law on the Budgets of Institutions of the FBiH, Official Gazette of FBiH, 102/13). In addition, the Federal Ministry of Finance mandatorily submits to the Government quarterly, semi-annual and nine-monthly financial reports and an annual financial report. While municipal and city finance services submit quarterly reports to the municipal and city council and cantonal ministries of finance, extra-budgetary funds submit their quarterly reports on the execution of financial plans to the responsible ministries, cantonal ministries of finance and the Federal Ministry of Finance. Cantonal ministries of finance are obligated to submit consolidated reports for the budgets of municipalities and cities, and reports for the cantonal budget to the Federal Ministry of Finance. This Ministry then submits a budget execution report to the Government. This report must comply with the contents and classification of the budget accounts.

The Rulebook on Financial Reporting and Annual Accounting of the Budget in the Federation of Bosnia and Herzegovina (Official Gazette of FBiH, 69/14) is to provide for the form and content of financial reports, guidelines for periodical reports and annual accounting preparation, periods for which the same are prepared and the obligations and terms of their submission. All this refers to the budget of the Federation of Bosnia and Herzegovina, the budgets of the cantons, cities, municipalities and the financial plans of extra-budgetary funds.

6.3 Accounting and Financial Reporting

6.3.1 Budgetary Accounting

Given that the Federation of Bosnia and Herzegovina is itself complex and consists of 10 cantons, 21 municipalities and 6 cities (Sarajevo, Mostar and recently Zenica, Tuzla, Bihać, and Široki Brijeg), financial reporting on budgets is complex as well because each canton has its own Ministry of Finance. In addition, there are 23 extra-budgetary funds that submit reports to the Ministry of Finance of the FBiH. Every canton has its own health insurance fund and employment fund, but pension and disability funds are organised at the federal level. The Ministry of Finance of the FBiH has no responsibilities over cantons in terms of financial reporting. The Budget of the FBiH has 46 beneficiaries.

Due to the complex structure of the FBiH, financial and budgetary reporting is regulated by a series of laws and by-laws. The Law on the Budgets of Institutions of the FBiH is an umbrella law from which all other laws and by-laws relating to financial and budgetary reporting derive.

The Law on the Budgets of Institutions of the FBiH defines specific categories as follows: the budget refers to the act that is used for revenues and receipts planning, and expenses and expenditures of the FBiH, cantons, cities and municipalities for the period of one fiscal year; budget expenditures refer to expenditures for financial and non-financial assets and repayments of loans and leases; budget revenues refer to tax and non-tax revenues, received transfers and donations, and other revenues; budget receipts refer to cash inflows from financial and non-financial assets and borrowing; budget expenses refer to expenses specified in the law and implementing legislation for the functions and programmes planned in the budget and financial plans of budget beneficiaries. Budget expenses also include employees' wages and allowances, employers' contributions and other contributions, costs for material, small inventory and services, current transfers and other current expenses, capital transfers and interest payments. Budget accounting refers to an accounting system that regulates planning, recording, analysing, supervision and reporting on business events of budget beneficiaries and extra-budgetary funds; public revenues represent all cash funds collected from revenues, fees and revenues from public services and activities, receipts from issued securities, credits, transfers and donations that must be deposited in the TSA; consolidation refers to the presentation of financial data of various mutually connected budgets and/or budget beneficiaries and extra-budgetary funds as if they were a single entity; modified accrual accounting basis refers to the accounting basis that records and recognises revenues and receipts in the period when they are measurable and available, or paid in the TSA, while expenses and expenditures are recognised when the obligation (liability) is created and in the reporting period it relates to regardless of when payment is made; net financing refers to the difference between the acquisition of receipts from financial assets and the borrowing and expenditures for the purchase of financial assets and debt repayment; current balance refers to the difference between budget revenues and budget expenses. A positive difference between revenues and expenses is called current surplus, and a negative difference is current deficit; total surplus/deficit refers to the difference between the current surplus/deficit and net acquisition of non-financial assets; total financial result refers to the sum of the total surplus/deficit and net financing.

The budget represented at the level of the analytical account must contain the following:

- A detailed presentation of all public revenues and receipts of the budget;
- Expenses and expenditures of each budget beneficiary reported by categories, sub-categories, main groups, projects and funding sources;
- A proposal of a budget surplus schedule or resources for budget deficit funding.

Budget accounting regulates the book of accounts, accounting records and data processing, the content of the accounts of the analytical chart of accounts, recognition of revenues and receipts and expenses and expenditures, an estimation of the balance sheet position, revaluation, financial reporting and other issues related to budget accounting for all budget beneficiaries and extra-budgetary funds. The application of the *International Public Sector Accounting Standards* (IPSAS) is not obligatory but is optional and recommended.

The Government adopts a decree on accounting for the budget of the Federation, cantonal, city and municipal budgets and extra-budgetary funds. The Ministry also provides for the implementation of unique accounting procedures and adopts regulations on bookkeeping and on the content and method of financial reporting for all budget beneficiaries and extra-budgetary funds. In this way, the Ministry ensures uniform business events recording as one of the basic presumptions of reliable consolidated financial reports.

According to the Decree on Accounting of the Budgets in the Federation of BiH (Official Gazette of FBiH 34/14), a modified accrual accounting basis is the accounting basis that records and recognises revenues in the period when they are available and measurable, and expenses are recognised in the period when the liability is incurred.

The Decree on Accounting of the Budget of the Federation of BiH regulates fund accounting, accounting books, accounting records and data processing, internal accounting supervision, reporting of revenues and receipts, expenses and expenditures, estimation of balance sheet positions, revaluation, financial and budget reporting, presentation of financial reports and assets, and the recording of the indebtedness and liabilities of budget and extra-budgetary beneficiaries. In accordance with the Decree, accounting of the budget is based on the accounting principles of accuracy, truthfulness, reliability, comprehensiveness, timeliness and individual presentation of business events. Budget beneficiaries are obliged to record the budget using the double-entry bookkeeping principle, according to the account schedule from the Analytical Chart of Accounts for the budget and for budget beneficiaries, using the fund bookkeeping principle and accounting groups, complying with the provision of Article 33 paragraph 2 of the Law on Accounting and Audit in the Federation BiH (Official Gazette of F BiH, 83/09) or using the IPSAS once they are officially published in the Bosnian/Croatian/Serbian language. Budget beneficiaries are also to provide data individually by types of revenues and receipts, expenses and expenditures in the bookkeeping of the budget as well as data on the state of assets, liabilities and ownership sources.

The Rulebook on Financial Reporting and Annual Accounting for the Budget in the Federation BiH (Official Gazette of F BiH, 69/14 and 14/15) regulates standards of budget classification, fund accounting, the analytical chart of accounts for the budget and budget beneficiaries, business books and accounting records, the estimation of balance sheet positions and list of assets, liabilities and receivables. The provisions of this Rulebook relate to the budget of the Federation of BiH, the budgets of cantons, cities and municipalities, and budget beneficiaries and extra-budgetary funds must implement them. The Rulebook provides for budget classification standards such as the organisational, economic, and functional and fund classification.

Organisational classification is to ensure identification of financial responsibility at the level of primary, secondary and tertiary budget beneficiaries. Budget beneficiaries classify activities and services of the Government of the FBiH and the governments of cantons, cities and municipalities by categories of synthetic classification of the Government's functions as an integral part of this Rulebook.

Fund classification represents a systematic framework that enables the planning and recording of budget transactions by segments to ensure control of dedicated spending of the budget funds. Budget beneficiaries enter data in the accounting books based on the following fund classification where the principle of fund bookkeeping is used:

1. the general fund is used for reporting all sources and funds, revenues and expenses of the budget and budget beneficiaries except those that are reported in another fund by special legal requirements;
2. the fund of revenues by special regulations is used for recording all activities financed from revenue sources used only for special purposes based on regulations, excluding capital projects, debt servicing and trust funds;
3. the dedicated revenues fund is used for revenues arising from regular activities of budget beneficiaries or are realised by free exchange of goods and services in the market by budget beneficiaries whose purpose is prescribed in accordance with Article 15 of the Law;
4. the domestic donations fund is used for accounting purposes to report domestic donations and to record all activities financed from domestic donations;
5. the foreign donations fund is used for accounting purposes to report foreign donations and to record all activities financed from foreign donations;
6. the domestic debt servicing fund is used for accounting purposes to report revenues and receipts collected for the settlement of a part or for the whole of domestic debt, as well as interest payments and repayments of outstanding principle due in the coming years;
7. the foreign debt servicing fund is used for accounting purposes to report revenues and receipts collected for the settlement of a part or for the whole of foreign debt as well as interests payments and repayments of outstanding principle due in the coming years;
8. the capital investments fund is used for accounting purposes to report investment activities of the budget and budget beneficiaries, as well as revenues and receipts sources used for the purchase or construction of fixed assets. Since, in the budget documents, capital projects are reported separately from the current budget, they are reported for accounting purposes separately through the capital projects fund.

However, although funds are prescribed, accounting is not based on fund classification but all transactions and events are recorded in the general fund.

The Rulebook prescribes the structure of the chart of accounts by classes:

- Class 0: Fixed assets
- Class 1: Cash, short-term receivables and deferrals (prepayments and deferred expenses)
- Class 2: Inventories
- Class 3: Short-term liabilities, accruals and deferred income
- Class 4: Long-term liabilities, accruals and deferred income
- Class 5: Fixed assets sources
- Class 6: Expenses
- Class 7: Revenues
- Class 8: Capital transactions
- Class 9: Off-balance sheet records

In the accounts of Class 0: Fixed assets, all goods, rights and accruals that individually remain in whole or partially in the same form for at least one year are recorded. Fixed assets are depreciated (written-off) under the expense of sources (Class 5) and not under expenses as prescribed by IPSAS. When purchasing, cost purchases are not capitalised but are reported under expenses at the time of purchase.

Material and small inventory is recorded just within Class 2 to control its use, given that the purchase of these values is placed directly under expenses. This material is not classified under material used further in production or under material used by budget beneficiaries for use. Placing the entire material directly under expenditures at the moment of purchase does not comply with IPSAS.

Liabilities due in a period longer than one year are recorded in Class 4, as are liabilities whose remaining term is shorter than one year and that are initially formed with an agreed term longer than one year. No matter how they are initially formed, all liabilities due within one year are classified as short-term liabilities.

According to this Rulebook and in accordance with the Law on the Budgets of Institutions of the FBiH, expenses are incurred in the period in which the payment liability arises, no matter when the payment is made. Expenses are related to payments, although there is a set of revenues that do not require payments, such as depreciation, shortages, impairment, provisions, etc.

Revenues and receipts are recognised in the accounting period when they are measurable and available, or on a cash basis. When recognising revenues, it is necessary to differentiate between recognition of revenues arising from exchange transactions and which can be recognised on an accrual basis and revenues from non-exchange transactions and which can be based on a cash basis.

Re-evaluation is defined as a subsequent procedure of evaluation of fixed assets. It is specified in the Rulebook that the revaluation of fixed assets should be made so that cumulative indices of the price-rise of producers of industrial products apply on purchase and allowance or on earlier revaluated values. Revaluation of receivables and payables is carried out in accordance with the contract. The effects of revaluation are recorded under sources. Revaluation is carried out using the price change index published by the Institute of Statistics of the FBiH. In this context, revaluation is not deemed to be a procedure in compliance with IPSAS.

6.3.2 Financial Reporting

Financial reports of budget beneficiaries and extra-budgetary funds represent reports on the state and structure and modifications of assets, liabilities, own sources, revenues, expenses, receipts, expenditures or cash flows.

As for budget execution reporting, the Law on the Budgets of institutions of FBiH determines the following deadlines:

1. The Ministry of Finance submits to the Government quarterly, semi-annual and nine-monthly financial reports within 30 days following the expiration of the accounting period, and an annual report by 15 April of the current year for the previous year. Budget beneficiaries submit quarterly financial reports to the Ministry of Finance within 20 days following the expiration of the accounting period, and for the fourth quarter of the previous year by 28 February of the current year.
2. Municipal and city finance services submit quarterly reports to the municipal and city council and cantonal ministries of finance within 20 days following the expiration of the accounting period, and for the fourth quarter by 5 March of the current year.
3. Extra-budgetary funds submit quarterly reports on the execution of financial plans to the responsible ministries, cantonal ministries of finance and the Federal Ministry of Finance within 20 days following the expiration of the accounting period, and for the fourth quarter of the previous year by 5 March of the current year.

4. Cantonal ministries of finance submit consolidated quarterly reports on the execution of the budgets of cantons, municipalities and cities to the Ministry of Finance within 30 days following the expiration of the accounting period, and for the fourth quarter of the previous year by 15 March of the current year.
5. The Ministry of Finance submits a report on budget execution for the previous year to the Government and the Government submits it for adoption to the Parliament within six months following the end of the fiscal year.

Public companies and institutions financed from public revenues as well as public companies for which the Ministry of Finance issues guarantees for borrowing shall submit quarterly financial data to the responsible ministry. The type, method and deadlines for the submission of financial data are prescribed by the Minister of Finance.

The Law regulates that financial reporting is a set of data on the financial position, business performance and cash flows of the budget and budget beneficiaries, extra-budgetary funds and extra-budgetary beneficiaries determining that the preparation and presentation of financial reports (balance sheet, income statement, cash flow statement) in the manner set out in the IPSAS according to the Accounting and Audit Act is deemed financial reporting.

The Law on the Budget of Institutions of FBiH prescribes that the Report on the Execution of the Budget shall contain the following:

1. Revenues and receipts, expenses and expenditures for the fiscal year approved by the Parliament or subsequently modified;
2. Realised revenues and receipts, expenses and expenditures during the year reported so that the difference between the approved budget and its execution can be clearly seen;
3. The initial and final balance of TSA;
4. The initial and final balance of assets, liabilities and ownership sources;
5. An explanation of significant deviations;
6. Data on all modifications based on borrowing and debt management and on guarantees given during the fiscal year;
7. Data on the use of the budget reserve.

According to the Rulebook on the Financial Reporting and Annual Accounting for the Budget of the Federation BiH (Official Gazette of FBiH, 69/14 and 14/15), periodical reports are as follows:

- Review of revenues, receipts and financing by economic categories;
- Expenses and expenditures by economic categories;
- Special data on salaries and number of employees;
- Special data on current and capital transfers;
- Cross-classification of expenses and expenditures of the budget by economic and functional classification;
- Record of remittances from the current budget reserve;
- Record of outstanding liabilities;
- Review of revenues, receipts, expenses and expenditures by economic categories;
- Expenses, expenditures and allocated funds by sources of financing for development and investment projects;
- Report on intended transfer costs.

According to the Rulebook, annual reports contain the following:

- accounting reports of budget beneficiaries;
- statement (analysis, textual part).

The basic financial reports of budget beneficiaries in the FBiH for the budget year are as follows:

1. Revenues and expenditures account;
2. Balance sheet;
3. Cash flow statement;
4. Capital Expenditures and Financing Report,

and on an annual basis the following are prepared and submitted:

- The Form on Special Data on Salaries and Number of Employees;
- The Annual Budget Execution Report;
- The Annual Investment Report;
- The Report on the Calculated and Paid Fees for Protection from Natural and Other Disasters.

Budget beneficiaries review and adjust annual calculations of the budget beneficiaries they are responsible for (in the form of separate reports), and then consolidate these calculations and prepare consolidated annual calculations in the form of financial statements. Based on individual annual calculations, a consolidated annual budget calculation is prepared.

The Rulebook specifies consolidation as a process of the formulation of a unique report for all budget beneficiaries that is to eliminate transactions between participants in consolidation. Consolidated financial reports are prepared by cantonal ministries of finance and the Federation. Consolidation of all annual financial reports for the level of the Federation is performed by the Federal Ministry of Finance. Consolidation is carried out on the following forms: Revenues and Expenses Account, Balance Sheet, Cash Flow Statement, Capital Expenditures and Financing Report, Annual Budget Execution Report.

Additional forms are as follows:

1. Other financial data—fixed assets in the form of goods and rights as of 31 December;
2. Other financial data—other non-current assets as of 31 December;
3. Other financial data—contingent liabilities as of 31 December.

Along with annual accounting reports, budget beneficiaries are to submit a textual report discussing budget execution with special reference to the deviations of realised revenues from planned revenues and expenses by economic and functional classification, or a statement analysis, so the textual part of the report is to consist of the following:

- general economic situation in the reporting period processed by ministries of finance and finance services at all levels of authority;
- budget execution and analysis of deviation of realised revenues from planned revenues, receipts, financing, expenses and expenditures;
- analysis of employee costs;
- analysis of receivables;
- analysis of liabilities;
- analysis of fixed assets in the form of goods and services;
- explanation of any significant post-balance events;
- conclusion.

The financial reporting of budget beneficiaries provides relevant and reliable data to the beneficiaries, and represents a key element of the responsibilities of budget beneficiaries, ensuring public analysis of decision-making related to public expenditure.

6.4 Audit and Other Oversight (Supervision) in the Public Sector

Supervision of budget and budget entities in the Federation of Bosnia and Herzegovina is organised through the following forms: state audit, budget supervision, internal audit and financial planning and control.

The accounting system of the budget should have a high level of organisational arrangement and formality and be set up to ensure efficient budget execution and to enable control over budget execution. Internal supervision and state audit are established as control mechanisms in the functioning of the budget system. The purpose of internal supervision and state audit is to serve the public because the public needs reliable and objective data not only on the accuracy of financial documentation and financial operations but also on the purposefulness and effectiveness of all state units that spend taxpayers' money in any way (Vašiček et al. 2001: 491–492).

Executives of budget beneficiaries are responsible for accounting, internal control and transaction supervision in the relevant entity. The Minister of Finance is responsible on behalf of the Government for accounting and internal supervision of borrowing transactions and debt repayment.

Supervision of the budget not only includes supervision of accounting and financial activities but extends to all fields of activity of state units and as such represents a management tool for ensuring reasonable belief that the stated goals have been achieved.

State audit represents an activity of state importance that is one of the key elements in the functioning of the budget system (adapted according to Vašiček et al. 2001: 493–494).

6.4.1 State Audit

The role of state audit is to confirm the mutual trust of the public and in its findings to provide taxpayers with objective and reliable data on how their funds are spent. With increasing public awareness, there is a growing need to control the work of persons or units managing public goods and different systems of data, so control and reporting systems are being developed to facilitate accountability. As the number of functions of the modern state increases, so does the importance of protecting public interest and consequently of auditing public expenses. Government auditing is therefore being developed. State audit is developed as an efficient, objective and professional supervision model of the state bureaucratic structure and of all public officials deriving from the people and their representatives—parliament (Vašiček et al. 2001: 478–479).

The audit of annual reports of the institutions of the Federation of BiH, i.e. budget beneficiaries, is performed by the Office for the Audit of Institutions in the Federation of BiH (hereinafter: Office) representing a supreme audit institution (Law on the Audit of Institutions in the Federation of BiH, Official Gazette of FBiH, 22/06).

The main goal of the Office is to ensure, by means of auditing, independent opinions on budget execution and financial reports, on the use of resources and on the management of state property by the Government, budget institutions and public institutions in the Federation of BiH. In this way, the Office will contribute to reliable reporting on the use of budget funds, and on the transparent and high-quality management of public revenues, costs and assets in the Federation of BiH.

The Office informs responsible institutions and the public on its findings and provides recommendations by the timely and public publishing of audit reports. In accordance with the provisions of the Law on the Budget in the FBiH, the Office prepares a draft of its annual budget and submits it for approval to the parliamentary commission responsible for auditing, and then, based on the deadlines prescribed in the Law on the Budgets in the FBiH, it submits the draft budget to the Ministry of Finance of the FBiH to include it in the draft budget of the FBiH for the next fiscal year.

The Office is responsible for a financial audit, a performance audit and other specific audits of budget beneficiaries in the FBiH. The Office applies the INTOSAI standards of audit and ensures that the Office staff and other persons involved in any audit duties according to this Law work in accordance with these standards. The audit standards of the International Accounting Federation (IFAC) are used when auditing public companies if applicable.

The responsibility of the Office includes, in accordance with the provisions of the Law on the Audit of Institutions in the FBiH, all public institutions in the Federation of BiH, including:

- The Parliament of the Federation of BiH;
- The President of the Federation of BiH;
- The Government of the Federation of BiH and ministries of the Government of the Federation of BiH;
- Extra-budgetary funds established by law;
- Public funds, institutes and agencies.

The responsibility also encompasses:

- Assemblies and cantonal governments in the Federation of BiH;
- Municipalities in the Federation of BiH;
- All budget institutions directly financed from the budgets adopted by Parliament, cantonal assemblies and municipal councils;
- Extra-budgetary funds that can be established by law;
- Funds that represent a loan or grant for BiH provided to some institution or project in the Federation of BiH from international bodies and organisations;
- Funds provided from the budget to any other institutions, organisation or body.

The responsibility of the Office also includes companies in which the state holds 50% plus one or more shares of ownership.

6.4.2 *Budget Supervision, Internal Audit and Internal Control*

Budget supervision is the inspection supervision of legality, timeliness and intended use of budget resources requiring measures for removing detected illegalities and irregularities, and includes supervision of the accounting, financial and other business documents of the supervised entities.

Budget supervision is performed in budget beneficiaries and extra-budgetary funds, legal and natural entity beneficiaries of the budget funds and financial plans of extra-budgetary beneficiaries, as is supervision of credit funds used on the basis of guarantees.

According to the provisions of the Decree on Accounting of the Budget of FBiH (Official Gazette of FBiH, 34/14), budget beneficiaries ensure a system of constant *internal accounting supervision* by establishing an internal control system. The internal control system ensures the establishment of the organisation, policies and procedures used to achieve the intended results in the government programmes.

Internal accounting supervision checks whether business transactions are performed in accordance with the legal regulations, whether there is adequate accounting documentation and whether financial reports provide complete, reliable and relevant information on the results of the financial operations and financial positions.

Budget beneficiaries organise an internal control system in accordance with international standards of internal control to ensure the performance of activities within the main operation.

The Ministry of Finance is responsible for issuing instructions for the establishment and maintenance of the internal control system, and budget beneficiaries issue a Rulebook on internal controls. The internal control system ensures the establishment of the organisation, policies and procedures used to achieve the intended results in the government programmes. The monitoring and evaluation of the system is the responsibility of the internal audit. The provisions of the Law on the Internal Audit in the Public Sector in the FBiH (Official Gazette of FBiH, 47/08) refer to beneficiaries of public funds of the budget of the Federation of BiH, cantons, cities and municipalities and extra-budgetary funds.

In the context of the same Law, *internal audit* is an independent, objective assurance and consultative activity created to add value and improve the business of the organisation, which implies all public fund beneficiaries, while *internal control* implies different mechanisms used to ensure the correct implementation of decisions related to budget policy and other policy, especially in the following fields: financial reporting, the efficiency of the communication system among executives and their personnel, accounting control, process control and public procurement control.

According to the Law on Internal Audit in the Public Sector in the FBiH, internal auditors are authorised to perform a systematic review and evaluate risk management and internal controls. Internal auditors assess the adequacy and efficiency of financial management and the control system in the sense of:

- risk identification, risk evaluation and risk management by the organisation management (public fund beneficiaries);
- fulfilment of tasks and achievement of defined objectives of the organisation (public fund beneficiaries);
- economical, efficient and effective use of resources;
- adjustment with established policies, procedures, laws and regulations;
- protecting organisational funds from losses due to all kinds of irregularities;
- integrity and credibility of information, accounts and data, including internal and external processes of reporting.

The function of internal audit is based on the principles of independence and objectivity, competence and professional attentiveness, integrity and confidentiality. It is carried out in accordance with the Methodology and Guidance on Internal Audit in the Public Sector issued by the Central Harmonisation Unit in the Federation (CHU) with the approval of the Coordinating Committee of Central Harmonisation Units in BiH, and International Standards for the Professional Practice of Internal Audit issued by the Institute of Internal Auditors (IIA) and adopted by Coordinating Committee with the application of the Professional Code of Ethics for internal audit issued by IIA and adopted by the Coordinating Committee. The CHU, established in the Federal Ministry of Finance, is authorised to ensure development in the field of internal audit, supervision of the implementation of all relevant regulations on internal audit by internal audit units (established either at the beneficiary level or at the level of the Ministry of Finance for multiple beneficiaries) and coordination of the activities of internal audit units for public fund beneficiaries. The CHU prepares an annual consolidated internal audit report based on the annual reports of internal audit units and submits it to the minister. The minister submits the consolidated report to the Government of the Federation of BiH for consideration and adoption. The consolidated internal audit report contains summary information on the implementation status of the recommendations incorporated in the internal audit reports that are submitted during the year by the internal audit units. The Annual Consolidated Internal Audit Report contains an analysis of the activities of the CHU, including recommendations for the improvement of activities adopted by the Coordinating Committee.

Not later than six months after the report on audit is issued, an executive of the internal audit unit monitors the implementation of the internal audit recommendations given in the previous internal audit report to evaluate whether the revised organisation has conducted corrective activities and whether the intended results have been achieved, and informs the executive of the organisation about this. The executive of the internal audit unit prepares an annual internal audit report that must contain the issued auditor reports and data on other activities completed by or in progress on 31 December of the previous year not later than 60 days following the end of the year. A copy of the report is submitted to the executive of the organisation and to the CHU.

6.5 Challenges in Further Development of Public Sector Accounting and Auditing

Over the past two decades, a growing number of governments have begun moving away from pure cash accounting towards accrual accounting (OECD 2016). The recent spread of accrual accounting to the public sector can be attributed to a number of related factors, including: (a) a growing recognition of the limits of pure cash accounting, (b) the development of accrual-based international standards for government fiscal and financial reporting including Government Finance Statistics Manual (GFSM) and IPSAS, (c) the professionalisation of the government accounting cadre and resulting introduction of private sector techniques into the public sector, and (d) the advent of computerised financial management information systems (FMISs) which greatly reduce the transaction costs of collecting and consolidating accrual-based information (Cavanagh et al. 2016: 1).

The research of the legislative framework and the characteristics of the current system indicate that the development of national accounting in the Federation of BIH moves towards the application of the full accrual basis. However, there are no clear guidelines and paths defined for further development of public sector accounting in the FBiH. Although, budget users in the FBiH have used a modified accrual basis and the State has normatively declared the intention of the transition to full accrual basis and full implementation of IPSAS, no concrete actions have been taken, nor has the strategy and an implementation plan for the application of full accruals and IPSAS been developed.

Financial statements of the government should reflect full economic impact of political decisions and with the implementation of the accrual accounting, the State demonstrates its willingness to achieve greater transparency and accountability, with the final aim to produce better accounting information for better decision-making, in order to contribute to a better use of public funds.

Reforms of public accounting witness that introducing accrual accounting is a necessary step that enables gathering the information that reflects the true and long-term economic impact of political decisions. Federation of BiH is facing similar challenges like all SEE countries in the region. FBiH, as well as any other country in a process of considering implementing accrual accounting in the public sector, will in the near future face the task which assumes the complete commitment of the necessary resources to implement the reform.

In other words, there is the perception and the awareness that implementing international accounting standards, such as IPSAS, is a necessity for improving transparency and accountability and for building trust. However, it is important to acknowledge that implementing IPSAS is not the end or the goal by itself, but a step further on a path of providing high-quality financial statements and improving operational performance, therefore enabling sound public financial management.

Nevertheless, the successful implementation of IPSAS is not without challenges. These challenges and their effects must be taken into account. FBiH, with the accrual accounting adoption aim on mind, needs to develop a framework for implementation and must invest in building capacity among the personnel that will be responsible for driving the implementation process, build strong institutions and systems to facilitate the process, and be ready for the change of management initiative and the change of public management strategic policy planning.

With the above mentioned in mind and taking into account Bosnia and Herzegovina membership application to the EU, the Federation of Bosnia and Herzegovina needs to interpret its competitive position in international (European) contexts and take into consideration the ongoing international (European) TSA trends and reforms, in order to achieve the harmonisation of financial reporting, budget monitoring and control process, and in order to develop a strategy and annual implementation plan for the gradual application of full accruals and IPSAS implementation.

When referring to the state audit, represented by the Office for the Audit of Institutions in the Federation of BiH (hereinafter: Office), the Strategy of development for 2017–2020, sets the following strategic goals for the period 2017–2020. These are: preserving and strengthening the independence of the Office, enhancing the quality of auditing in line with the ISSAI standards, strengthening Office Capacity as well as strengthening auditing impact on society through active contribution to achieving efficiency and effectiveness of public administration, and strengthening cooperation with domestic and international audit institutions and associations. Achieving the aforementioned goals is a challenge by itself. In the audit practice of both public and business sector, there is a need for quality control, public supervision and better understanding of independence in every sense. This requires people ready to take this challenge and such people will be the key resource of the future financial and accounting reform of the public sector in Federation of Bosnia and Herzegovina, embracing the implementation of IPSAS.

References

Cavanagh, J., Flynn, S., Moretti, D. (Eds.). (2016). *Implementing Accrual Accounting in the Public Sector*. International Monetary Fund. Fiscal Affairs Department.

OECD. (2016). Accrual Practices and Reform Experiences in OECD Countries Results of the 2016 OECD Accruals Survey. *Journal on Budgeting, 16*(1), 9–28.

Salkić, M., & Salkić, A. (2011). *Računovodstvo proračuna i proračunskih korisnika*. Sarajevo: FIN PROFI d.o.o.

Vašiček, V., et al. (2001). *Proračun – Budžet*. Sarajevo: Revicon.

Useful Sites

https://www.accaglobal.com/content/dam/ACCA_Global/Technical/pub-sect/pi-IPSAS-implementation-current-status-and-challenges.pdf.

http://www.ads.gov.ba/v2/attachments/1951_USTAV_BOSNE_I_HERCEGOVINE_hrv.pdf.

www.ba.undp.org/…/bosnia…/SNCBiH2013/BiH_SNCBiH_BHS-L.pdf.

www.bhas.ba/obavjestenja/Preliminarni_hr.pdf.

http://ijsser.org/uploads/ijsser_01__42.pdf.

https://www.pwc.com/rw/en/assets/pdf/second-edition-global-survey-government.pdf.

http://www.sluzbenilist.ba/Docs/index/fbih.

http://www.sluzbenilist.ba/Docs/index/bih.

CHAPTER 7

Public Sector Accounting, Auditing and Control in the Former Yugoslav Republic of Macedonia

Atanasko Atanasovski and Zoran Minovski

7.1 Territorial Organisation, Scope of the Public Sector and Distribution of Public Revenues

7.1.1 Territorial Organisation

The former Yugoslav Republic of Macedonia is a small landlocked south-eastern European country covering 25,713 km^2 with a population of 2m according to the last census in 2002. The country gained its independence from Yugoslavia in September 1991. The former Yugoslav Republic of Macedonia is an upper middle income country with GDP per capita of USD 5232 in 2016 (World Bank 2017). The country was granted the status of

Former Yugoslav Republic of Macedonia (abbreviated as FYR Macedonia) officially changed its name to the Republic of North Macedonia in February 2019.

A. Atanasovski (✉) · Z. Minovski
University Ss. Cyril and Methodius, Skopje, Macedonia
e-mail: atanasko@eccf.ukim.edu.mk

V. Vašiček and G. Roje (eds.), *Public Sector Accounting, Auditing and Control in South Eastern Europe*, Public Sector Financial Management, https://doi.org/10.1007/978-3-030-03353-8_7

EU candidate country in 2005, and in 2009 the EU Commission proposed to start negotiations on full EU membership. However, further progress has been blocked as a consequence of a dispute over its name with Greece.

In 2004 the parliament adopted the new Law on the Territorial Organisation of Local Self-Government (Official Gazette 55/2004–149/2014[1]), so today there are 80 municipalities, 33 of which are considered cities with more than 3000 citizens. The City of Skopje is considered an additional and separate unit of local self-government and county. Although the municipalities are the prime units of territorial organisation and local government, in 2009 the parliament adopted eight planning regions (counties) for statistical, economic and administrative purposes.

Local government is responsible for urban planning, development and landscaping, including permits for construction works. All utility services for the quality of life and local economic development through local economic policy are of high priority as well. The local government is also responsible for support to local cultural institutions and organisations, sport and recreation, education and social welfare of children, health protection through involvement in local hospital governance bodies, preservation of the natural environment, fire protection, etc.

The eight counties (planning regions) were established in 2009 in order to promote more balanced and sustainable economic development among counties with significant differences in population density, capital investments, GDP and the living standards of residents. Although established according to EU NUTS requirements, counties have councils which are expected to engage in developing five-year programmes for regional development, to increase the competitiveness of the local economy, to foster innovation capacities, to ensure optimal exploitation of mineral resources, human resources, the revitalisation of rural areas and villages, to support inter-municipality and cross-border cooperation, etc.

7.1.2 Scope of the Public Sector

The public sector in the former Yugoslav Republic of Macedonia consists of all public institutions that are established by the central or local

[1]The main activity of the Public Enterprise Official Gazette of the Republic of Macedonia is publishing of laws, other regulations and acts in the Official Gazette of the Republic of Macedonia, as well as issuing of official newspaper "The Official Gazette of the Republic of Macedonia," as an activity of public interest. The publishing of the laws, other regulations and acts is conducted in written and electronic form, available at: http://www.slvesnik.com.mk/doma.nspx.

government and fulfil administrative and public functions or perform public activities, and are financed generally through the state or local budgets. Private entities that provide services of public interest are not considered as an integral part of the public sector (private hospitals, private schools and universities, private kindergartens, etc.). Public enterprises (usually public utility companies) that are established by parliament or by central and local governments and which perform services of public interest are also considered part of the public sector.

The financing of the public sector goes through the state budget and local budgets. The state budget incorporates the central budget and the budgets of funds (Law on Budgets, 2005). The central budget relates to budget users of central government and incorporates the principal budget, the donations budget, the budget on loans and the budget on self-financing activities. The pension insurance fund, the fund for health insurance and the fund of the agency for employment are incorporated in the state budget. Local governments have their own budgets with a financing structure similar to the state budget. The Ministry of Finance is responsible for proposing the state budget to the Government before the budget is presented to the parliament for enactment. The mayors are responsible for proposing local budgets for enactment by the local councils.

Budget users are considered the first line of users of the funds of the state and local budget, and this includes institutions that are part of the legislative, executive and judicial branch. These are the parliament, the central government, the President of the Republic and other executive organs and the judicial system, including the Constitutional Court. Unit users of the budget are the second line of budget users. Institutions in the area of education, science, culture, child protection, social welfare, the judicial system and public prosecution are financed through the respective budget user, and as such they are considered as unit users of the budget.

7.2 Formulation and Execution of Central Government and Local and Regional Self-Government Budgets

The process of budget formulation, approval, execution, reporting and monitoring is defined in the Law on Budgets as the budgetary process. The main purpose of budget formulation and execution is macroeconomic stability and stable and sustainable economic development

(Law on Budgets, Official Gazette of the Republic of Macedonia, 64/2005–167/2016). The budgetary process for central and local governments and the execution and reporting on the budget are based on the same principles of completeness, balance, specific identification, economy, efficiency, effectiveness, transparency and sound financial management. Besides, the budgetary process is essentially the same for central government and for local governments, including the majority of budget components. Differences can be observed in respect of the bodies responsible for approving the budget and reports on budget execution. For the central government, this role is played by the parliament, and for local budgets the city or municipality council.

7.2.1 Formulation of Central Government and Local Government Budgets

The budget of the Republic projects revenues or receipts and expenses or expenditures, where the maximum amount of available funds for spending is determined according to projected revenues and receipts. The budget relates to the period of one fiscal year which corresponds to the calendar year up to 31 December of each year.

Projected revenues and other receipts in the budget can be observed is several sub-budgets such as the revenues and receipts of the basic budget, revenues of the budget from self-financing activities, revenues of the donations budget, revenues of the loan budget and revenues and other receipts of the funds and municipalities budget.[2]

Several types of budget classifications are used to identify the specific use of budget funds, to monitor and control the execution of the budget and the appropriateness of spending budget funds, and for reporting on the budget and budget execution analysis. The classifications are prescribed by the Minister of Finance and could be analysed as organisational, economic, functional and programme classifications.

The documents used as a basis for budget preparation are:

- Strategic priorities of the government of the former Yugoslav Republic of Macedonia;

[2]When loans are originated, cash received in exchange of recognised debt to lenders is considered as revenues in a special sub-budget in the year of loan origination/receipt of cash.

- Fiscal strategy;
- Proposed strategic plans of the budget users and budget policy;
- Priorities of municipalities.

Based on an analysis of the execution of strategic priorities from the previous year, the government determines by 15 April the strategic priorities for the following years and these need to be incorporated by all budget users of the central budget and funds in their budget through government programmes and sub-programmes.

The Ministry of Finance prepares a fiscal strategy that should be adopted by the government by the end of May. The fiscal strategy relates to the directions and the objectives of the fiscal policy for the following three years and it determines the major categories of projected revenues and allowed expenditures. It contains the basic economic assumptions and guidance for budget preparation, an estimate of the amount of revenues, expenditures and financing for the following year and the medium term of the following three years. Along with the strategy, the Ministry of Finance proposes the maximum amount of allowed expenditures for the following three years per budget user or fund.

The Ministry of Finance prepares a budget instruction letter to invite budget users of central government and funds to prepare budget requests. The budget instruction letter contains projections of macroeconomic indicators found in the fiscal strategy, the determined strategic priorities with proposed programmes and sub-programmes, the maximum amounts of allowed fund as per budget user, and guidance on the preparation of draft budget requests, a plan on programmes of development, and a plan on job places.

Budget users prepare strategic plans that cover a period of three years and contain programmes and activities planned to fulfil strategic priorities of the government. Programmes and activities are described and expressed in financial terms in the framework of maximum allowed expenditures by the government. Budget users' strategic plans are important supportive documents once they file budget requests for the budget of the forthcoming year.

The Ministry of Finance distributes a budget circular to all budget users by 15 June and to all mayors by 30 September. These are instructional documents that should be used by budget users to develop budget requests by 1 September. They contain information on projections on macroeconomic indicators, the strategic priorities of the government, the maximum allowed amounts for the budget user and guidance on the preparation of budget requests. The budget circular is distributed to municipalities with different information content that includes an assessment of revenues redistributed from the central to the local governments' budget, criteria for the redistribution of VAT revenues to local governments, information on specific budget allocations, and block and other allocations for municipalities.

The Ministry of Finance is responsible for preparing the state budget and for submitting the proposed budget to the government by 1 November. The proposed budget document has three components: a general part (which shows the total revenues and expenditures for the fiscal year and projections for the following two years); a special part (which contains allowed amounts of budget users and funds by programmes, sub-programmes and items) and a development part (which contains budget users' plans for development). The government proposes the budget to the parliament by 15 November, and the budget needs to be adopted by the parliament by 31 December at the latest.

7.2.2 Budget Execution and Budget Execution Reporting

The continuous execution of the budget throughout the fiscal year is performed according to the Law on Budgets 2005–2016 and separate laws on budget execution adopted for each fiscal year. The execution means the collection of revenues and other receipts and settlement of expenditures according to the maximum allowed amounts and per designated purpose. The management of the budget and unit users is responsible for the collection of revenues and receipts, which are deposited in a single treasury account and recorded in the Treasury Ledger on appropriate accounts. The Treasury operates (functions) as a single and unique cash account, through which all transactions of the state budget are executed. The Treasury is a complex system of administration of activities related to the collection and spending of state (public) money through the Treasury Single Account that covers all budget users of the central government and local governments.[3] Public enterprises established by the central or local governments are not budget users and they are

[3]There are two separate laws for formulation and execution of the central government budget and local government, although the budgetary process is very similar.

excluded. This complex system of administration activities covers (Law on Budgets, 2005–2016):

- Managing the treasury cash account and other accounts established by the Ministry of Finance;
- Maintaining a register of budget users and unit users;
- Maintaining a Treasury Ledger;
- Budget accounting for the basic part of the central budget;
- Recording revenue collection and allocation for all budget users;
- Maintaining records on all budget payments and expenditures;
- Maintaining records on all payables and other obligations borne by all budget users;
- Proposing and monitoring compliance with treasury procedures by all budget users;
- Opening and closing cash accounts and other accounts within the Treasury Ledger for all budget users;
- Approving the breakdown of annual financial plans by quarters and months;
- Preparing daily and periodically reports on budget execution for central government and municipality budgets, etc.

The Law on Budget Execution[4] determines the manner of spending budget funds according to budget programmes, sub-programmes, and items. A transparent procedure should be followed when the budget funds are spent in order to achieve effectively and efficiently the objectives of the programme. Effectiveness means that the objectives are fulfilled within the accepted deadlines, while efficiency means that this is done with the minimum use of funds.

After the budget is adopted in the parliament, budget and unit users draft an annual financial plan presenting spending dynamics per quarter and month. These are analysed in the Treasury department and, upon their approval, budget and unit users can effectively start payments and the execution of the budgets (Law on Budget Execution, 2016).

[4] A separate law is adopted each year using the same title. Each time when adopted, the year of issuance is added. This is why when refering to laws in this chapter, authors refer to the set of laws refering to a few years period.

The Treasury decides on the allocation of allowed expenditures per quarter in a procedure that considers the financial plans submitted by budget users, the dynamics of revenue and receipt collections, and the seasonal nature of expenditures, including the specifics of capital expenditures and investment projects.

Budget users can only execute payments of expenditures through formal request payments submitted to the Treasury where control is performed. The execution of the local government budget is the responsibility of the mayor, who can execute payments from the cash account of the municipality. Banks are not allowed to open transaction accounts for budget and unit users. If budget users take on a debt, they are obliged to report it to the Treasury for the purpose of recording the debt in the single database on total debt. If the payment of the debt is planned for the following fiscal years, the bearing of such a debt by budget users is only possible if ex ante approval by the Treasury is requested. The budget users of the central government budget request approval from the government, while budget users of municipalities request approval from their respective administration. Municipalities could decide to raise a loan or issue interest-bearing securities, but approval is needed from the Ministry of Finance and a decision needs to be taken by municipality councils (Law on Financing of Units of Local Self-Government, Official Gazette of the Republic of Macedonia, 134/2008–126/2016).

The Ministry of Finance is responsible for preparing the annual account for the Budget of the Republic and for submitting it to the government by 31 May. Together with the central budget annual account, the Ministry submits municipality annual accounts and the report of the auditor general on the main budget together with commentaries by the Ministry. The Government submits the annual account for the approval of parliament by the end of June.

Reporting on budget execution should be transparent and timely, and therefore monthly reports on budget execution are disclosed on the website of the Ministry of Finance. The Ministry also has semi-annual reporting responsibility, where the semi-annual report on budget execution is submitted for approval to the government by 31 July. The report is accompanied with updated information on macroeconomic indicators and projected revenues, expenditures and debt for the fiscal year (Law on Budgets, 2005–2016).

At the local government level, budget users of the municipality budget prepare monthly reports on the execution of their financial plans and report to the mayor. The mayor is responsible for preparing quarterly reports on budget execution and these are submitted with explanatory commentaries to the municipality council and the Ministry of Finance. Upon approval of these reports, the mayor will transparently report to the general public. The mayor prepares and the municipality council approves the annual account of the budget, a report that shows the planned and actual revenues and expenditures for all budget users of the local budget. The council should approve the annual account by 15 March at the latest and submit it to the Ministry of Finance by 31 March.

The council also approves an annual report with the following contents (Law on Financing of Units of Local Self-Government, 2008–2016):

- Annual account;
- Report on assets, accounts receivables, liabilities and sources of assets;
- Report on the execution of investment programmes, specific purpose allocations, capital and block allocations and allocations for delegated duties;
- Report of the chief accountant confirming the accuracy and reliability of the annual account.

7.3 Accounting and Financial Reporting

7.3.1 Budgetary Accounting

Budget users are obliged to maintain accounting records in accordance with the requirements of the Law on Accounting of Budgets and Budget Users (Official Gazette of the Republic of Macedonia, 61/2002–145/2015) and related by-laws, including accepted accounting principles and standards. The objective should be to measure financial statements items accurately, truthfully, securely, completely, on time, and regularly. The accounting standards to be used by budgets and budget users in the former Yugoslav Republic of Macedonia are the International Accounting Standards for the Public Sector (IPSAS). However, so far, only IPSAS related to the cash flow basis has been translated and used in the public sector.

Accounting for budgets and budget users is based on the double-entry bookkeeping system, and it should be made uniform through the use of accounts from the prescribed chart of accounts for budgets and budget users. It should be detailed enough for analysis to be performed based on information for all kinds of revenues, receipts, expenses and expenditures, as well as the condition of assets and liabilities. Data on assets are not required concerning the budget of the Republic and budgets of local municipalities.

When budgets, budget users and unit users realise revenues from other sources, beside the central budget, separate accounting is required for these revenues charged by state agencies, revenues from self-financing activities, revenues from donations, revenues from loans and other revenues.

Accounting records of budgets and budget users are: the Journal, General Ledger, Cashbook, Fixed Assets Ledger and analytic records that contain books on suppliers' and own invoices, the Purchases Ledger, inventory and fixed asset registers, and books on receivables and payables. The Journal is used to chronologically record transactions that result in revenues, expenditures, assets and liabilities and can be established as a single journal or a system of journals where each is used for recording similar transactions. Optionally, the separate books for analytic records do not need to be maintained if the General Ledger allows the breakdown of transactions on analytic accounts.

The legal requirements for accurate, regular and reliable accounting records are strong and the law recognises the responsibility of the budgets and budget user key manager and chief accountant who are liable for the accuracy and compliance of accounting records with legal requirements. The Ministry of Finance is responsible for developing all by-laws and instructional guidance related to budgetary accounting.

The cash basis is used for recognising revenues and expenses in the General Ledger, which means that revenues and expenses are recognised in the period when the corresponding cash is received or payments are made. Revenues are not recognised when gifts are received in the form of material and non-material assets, surpluses during inventory counts, or any other material assets received for which payments have not been made. Similarly, material and non-material assets that are disposed of without consideration, shortages of inventory counts, and write-offs of assets and receivables are not considered expenses. If revenues are not collected as cash, they are recognised as deferred income. If expenses are not paid, they are recognised as accrual items. Loans taken are considered as revenues, while payments regarding installments of loans and borrowings in total are considered as expenses.

Long-term and short-term assets are initially measured at cost, being the purchase price increase for import tariffs, transport and other related expenses, including VAT. Assets with a purchase price of a single item below EUR 300 are regarded as inventory and are charged as expenses upon purchase regardless of their useful life. However, if these kinds of assets need to be considered as a group (pieces of furniture, equipment, pieces of art, telecommunication and IT equipment, etc.), then they are recognised as long-term assets regardless of the single item's cost.

Depreciation of fixed assets is recognised on a straight-line basis with depreciation rates prescribed by the Decision of the Ministry of Finance. Depreciation is calculated based on cost or revaluated cost. Depreciation is charged even if the use of the asset has stopped or the functionality and used capacity of the asset has declined significantly. The depreciation should not be calculated for assets damaged as a result of *vis major* or if use is stopped following a decision by a state agency. Assets that are considered historical heritage, or used in the line of defence of the country, are not depreciated. Revaluation is obligatory for all budget users and unit users, and is calculated through the application of the price index for manufacturers of industrial products.

Budgets and budget users should once a year at least, preferably on 31 December, undertake a reconciliation (count) procedure and compare actual assets and liabilities with balances carried forward in the accounting records. This procedure relates to all assets and liabilities, not only inventories and non-current material assets.

7.3.2 Financial Reporting

In terms of disposing of annual financial reporting responsibility, budgets and budget users need to prepare the following basic financial statements: the balance sheet, income statement (statement on revenues and expenses) and consolidated statement. The consolidated statement is prepared by budget users that operate through unit users and represents a full overview of revenues and expenditures of the unit users. The balance sheet and the statement on revenues and expenses should provide a true, faithful and comprehensive overview of revenues, receipts, expenses and expenditures, as well as the financial condition of assets, liabilities and sources of funding.

Financial statements are prepared for the period of a fiscal year, as of 31 December, in a format prescribed the Ministry of Finance and should be maintained as a permanent document. Together with explanatory commentaries by the management, financial statements represent the annual account document.

Unit users have responsibility to prepare and present the annual report to their respective budget user by 1 March. Budget users and funds prepare and present consolidated statements to the Ministry of Finance by 31 March for the previous fiscal year. Based on the consolidated statements of all budget users and funds, the Ministry of Finance prepares the annual report for the planned and executed revenues and expenses of the central budget and presents the annual report to the government by 31 May.

The procedure of budget formulation and execution for central government users and local government, although very similar, is defined in two separate laws: the Law on Budgets and the Law on Accounting of Budgets and Budget Users.

The annual account of the budget of the Republic contains the following appendices (Law on Accounting of Budgets and Budget Users, 2002–2015):

- Statement of collected revenues and paid expenses on all budget accounts from the budget of the Republic, compared with planned budget revenues and approved spending followed by explanations of variance;
- Detailed overviews of reserve spending and guarantees executed for loans raised during the fiscal year.

The Single Treasury Cash Account and the Treasury Ledger record all spending by central government and local government users. However, the central budget and the respective Annual Account (annual report) are approved by the parliament. The local budget and the respective annual report are approved by municipality councils. The interaction points are as follows:

- Local municipalities share their budgets with the Ministry of Finance in the process of annual budget formulation;
- Municipalities may not raise loans or debt instruments without MoF approval;
- Approved annual reports of local budgets are accompanying documents of the annual report of the Republic (report of the central government budget) submitted to the parliament for approval.

The annual reports of municipalities are prepared according to the same rules and they accompany the annual account of the budget of the Republic. The municipality council approves the annual report by 15 March and presents it to the Ministry of Finance by 31 March at the latest.

The government is responsible for reviewing and submitting all annual report documents (the budget of the Republic, funds and local budget annual reports) to the parliament by 30 June. In addition, budget users have the obligation to submit an annual report to the Central Registry and the State Audit Office by the end of February.

7.4 Audit and Other Oversight (Supervision) in the Public Sector

Oversight of the budget and budget entities in the former Yugoslav Republic of Macedonia is organised in the following forms: budgetary oversight, state audit, internal audit and internal control systems (financial management and control).

Implementation of oversight puts the emphasis on monitoring the execution of the budget in relation to the planned amount, as stated in the budget planning process. The ministers are responsible for internal oversight of transactions of revenues/receipts and expenses/expenditures of ministries and budgetary users who are under their jurisdiction, and the Ministry of Finance is responsible for, in addition to the above, internal oversight of borrowings.

Oversight of the execution of the budget is based on the accounting data presented in the form of financial statements, whose content is legally prescribed. The obligation and presentation of financial statements is a form of oversight and is based on accounting procedures and accounting data.

Oversight of the execution of the budget and audit of the budget represent the end of the budget cycle. The results of oversight and audit of the budget ensure the reliability of data on budget execution and provide valuable data for corrective actions.

7.4.1 State Audit

The State Audit Office is the supreme audit institution in the former Yugoslav Republic of Macedonia, whose objective is to inform the parliament, the government and other public authorities and the general public in a timely manner and objectively on the outcome of the audits performed. The State Audit Office supports parliament by presenting the irregularities and non-compliance with laws and regulations of audited entities identified during the audits.

The main principles of the operations of the State Audit Office are: independence, objectivity, competence, professionalism, team work, transparency and integrity (State Audit Office 2012).

The State Audit Office is managed by the Auditor General, elected together with his or her deputy by the parliament for a mandate of nine years. The Auditor General has considerable duties and ultimate authority according to the Law on State Audit concerning the annual audit programme in the public sector and professional education and capacity building of the office. The budget of the State Audit Office is secured within the budget of the Republic and parliament approves this budget with a separate decision when the budget of the Republic is subjected to approval.

The state audit is performed in accordance with the auditing standards and code of ethics of INTOSAI. These are adopted by the Ministry of Finance through their publication in the Official Gazette. The State Audit Office performs financial audit, compliance audit and performance audit engagements. While performing these engagements, the state audit executes:

- Inspection of the accounting records and reports, accounting and finance procedures and information systems in order to arrive at a conclusion on whether the financial statements give a true and fair view of the financial condition and results in accordance with accepted accounting principles and standards;
- Review and assessment of internal control reports and public internal financial control, and a review and assessment of the system of financial management and control;
- Evaluation of transactions connected with public revenues and expenses for the purposes of assessing the legality and appropriateness of spending in accordance with approved budgets;
- Assessment of the quality of public expenditure in terms of economy, efficiency and effectiveness;
- Assessment of measures taken by the subjects of audit following recommendations issued by the State Audit Office.

The independence and objectivity of the state audit is secured through additional mechanisms that are established through the law, such as reliance on team work, banned political activities and membership of political parties for state auditors, safeguards against self-review threats when the audit is performed on subjects where auditors had prior employment, etc. Further, the annual programme for audit engagements of the state audit is submitted to the Parliament of the Republic for information purposes only.

The following lie under the scope of the state audit: the Parliament of the Republic, the President's Office, central and local government budgets, budget users and unit users, public enterprises established by parliament or local municipalities, commercial entities under dominant state ownership, agencies and other institutions established by law, other institutions financed through the state budget, the National Bank, political parties which obtain funds from the budget, and users of EU funds and funds from other international institutions (Law on State Audit, Official Gazette of the Republic of Macedonia, 66/2010–27/2016).

All these institutions and entities which are subject to state audit are engaged in audit assignments in cycles. However, the budget of the Republic and the budget of funds are audited each fiscal year. The state audit has guaranteed access to the subjects of the audit, their documentation and records, and the scope of the audit cannot be impaired by the subject of the audit.

The state audit reports transparently on the outcomes and results of each audit. This means that the draft audit report is sent to the subject of the audit for commentaries. In 30 days, the state audit writes the final report, distributes it to the subject of the audit and the authorities responsible for monitoring and oversight of the work of the audited entity. The final reports of the audit along with the commentaries of the audited entities are published on the website of the State Audit Office.

The State Audit Office prepares an annual report that documents all performed audits during the year and submits it together with individual final reports for audited entities to the Parliament of the Republic by 30 June. The parliament needs to formally review and conclude on the report.

Since the establishment of the State Audit Office in 1999, the office has increased its capacity to perform quality audit in the public sector and its reports have been appreciated by the general public when multiple cases of poor public financial management and governance were highlighted. However, experts are continuously calling for additional legal and institutional capacity-building changes in order to arrange appropriate institutional responsiveness and follow-up for state audit reports. There is a need to introduce execution orders for the state audit in cases where subjects of the audit make no improvements following recommendations in the state audit reports. A legal framework is needed for the Parliament of the Republic to be more ready to act upon state audit reports and recommendations in respect of all audited entities. As good practice, the parliament should establish an audit sub-committee within the Committee on Financing and Budget (Nikolov and Dimovska 2017).

7.4.2 Public Internal Financial Control and Internal Audit

Since its independence, one of the primary strategic objectives of the former Yugoslav Republic of Macedonia was to join and integrate with the European Union in order to develop its economy and provide better living standards for its citizens. In 2005 the former Yugoslav Republic of Macedonia received EU candidate country status, and since then has implemented continuous reforms to align the regulatory framework and institutional capacity with the requirements of the EU acquis.

The area of financial control in the public sector requires a common and harmonised approach for the development of modern systems for internal control in the public sector, a combination of management responsibility and functionally independent internal audit. The goal is to build a system to guarantee the reasonable use of public funds, as well as stop irregularities and doubts regarding fraud and corruption. The prospects of using EU funds in the process of the country's accession to the EU require efficient systems for management, monitoring, internal control and audit in order to develop national capacities for decentralised management and the implementation of programmes and to safeguard EU financial interests.

Considering the needs explained above, the Ministry of Finance created in 2006 a "Strategy to develop PIFC in the former Yugoslav Republic of Macedonia" and planned for the steady and continuous development of the PIFC system as part of the overall public administration reform. PIFC represents a consolidated system established by the government for the management, monitoring, control and audit of the use of public funds and EU funds. The basic elements of the system are (Ministry of Finance 2006):

- A financial management and control system (FMC);
- Functionally independent internal audit (IA);
- Central harmonisation of methodologies for FMC and IA.

Following these efforts of the Ministry of Finance, the first Law on PIFC was passed in 2009 and changes were consecutively implemented to build and improve continuously the PIFC system. The Ministry of Finance and the respective Central Harmonisation Unit within the Ministry were given the primary role of implementing and maintaining the PIFC system. The PIFC system should be implemented within all budget users from the executive, legal and judicial branches, and in state funds, municipalities and the City of Skopje.

The main objectives of financial management and control are defined as (Law on Public Internal Financial Control, Official Gazette of the Republic of Macedonia, 90/2009–192/2015):

- Performance of activities in an appropriate, ethical, economical, effective and efficient way;
- Compliance with the requirements of the laws, other regulations, adopted policies, plans and procedures;
- Safeguarding of assets and other resources from losses caused by inappropriate management, unjustified spending and utilisation, irregularities and wrongdoing;
- Increasing accountability for the successful completion of tasks;
- Appropriate treatment and recording of financial transactions;
- Timely financial reporting and monitoring of performance.

The Law identifies the important duty of the manager or director of the public sector entity for financial management and internal control, including internal auditing in all organisation processes, structures, programmes and operations controlled by the manager. The manager is responsible for controlling the accounting and financial reporting processes, the implementation and permanent assessment of financial management and control processes, the financial and control competences of employees, effective risk management and appropriate and efficient internal controls. The public sector manager should establish a financial affairs unit and delegate responsibilities to competent employees, although he or she will always be liable for the effectiveness of the whole PIFC system. The Law also defines the elements of a sound internal control system within the public sector entity, and these correspond to the COSO internal control framework.

Internal audit should be established in each public sector entity, and should be permanently based as a unit of at least two internal auditors for public sector entities with an annual budget of MKD 50 m (EUR 850,000), or an internal auditor should be engaged on a contractual basis from another public sector entity if the entity concerned manages a smaller budget.

The following types of internal audit engagements are recognised by law (Law on Public Internal Financial Control, 2009–2015):

- Financial audit;
- Compliance audit;
- Auditing of internal control systems;
- Performance audit;
- IT audits.

The internal audit should be performed according to international standards for the professional practice of internal auditing and the code of ethics for internal auditors, as developed by the Institute of Internal Auditors. These are translated and adopted by the Ministry of Finance through their publication in the Official Gazette, together with the Act on the Internal Audit Charter that should be adopted by each public sector entity.

An internal audit unit or department is functionally independent in the public sector entity by means of the opportunity to report directly to the manager of the entity. Internal auditors should not have executive responsibilities delegated to them, including responsibilities connected with financial management and control. The manager of the entity cannot dismiss auditors or reallocate other duties and workplace responsibilities to internal auditors without documenting the case for such arrangements to the Central Harmonising Unit.

The Central Harmonising Unit is responsible for:

- Drafting laws and by-laws in the area of financial management, control and internal auditing;
- Developing methodology and professional standards and guidance for FMC and IA;
- Coordinating training for employees engaged in FMC and IA;

- Coordinating the implementation and development of FMC and IA systems in all public sector entities;
- Monitoring the quality of FMC and IA systems, etc.

For the goal of achieving the greater harmonisation and uniform establishment of FMC and IA systems in the public sector and to enable better communication on legal and regulatory issues between public sector entities and the Ministry of Finance, two specialised committees have been established within the Ministry: the Committee on FMC and the Audit Committee.

The manager of a budget user from the executive, legal and judicial branch, managers of funds and mayors of all municipalities are responsible for presenting an annual report to the Central Harmonisation Unit. This report contains:

- A report on budgeted and executed funds per budget item;
- A report on realised programmes, projects and contracts;
- Annual reports or consolidated reports;
- A report on the self-assessment of the FMC system;
- A statement on the quality and condition of internal controls;
- A report on activities for the implementation and development of the FMC system;
- A report on internal audit engagements and activities of the IA department.

7.5 Challenges in Further Development of Public Sector Accounting and Auditing

One of the main challenges for the further development of public sector accounting is the process of transition towards accrual-based accounting and the implementation of IPSAS for the purpose of financial reporting by the general public sector. The Government with the financial support of the World bank in September 2014 began a CIPFA-based training programme for public sector accountants with the help of Slovenian experienced public sector development consultants. The goal was to build initial capacity of trained accountant that can apply IPSAS requirements within public sector institutions and develop localised certification programme that adheres to CIPFA standards in order to increase the overall technical capacity within the public sector. However, the program was not localised successfully and training is not offered on continuous basis for the majority of public sector serving and aspiring accountants.

One could argue that the path toward accrual-based accounting in the public sector of former Yugoslav Republic of Macedonia has not been actively pursued, since there is lack of other ongoing projects at the moment supported by the Government of the former Yugoslav Republic of Macedonia to undertake rather complicated and systematic procedures for the successful implementation of accrual-based accounting. The implementation should result in benefits at the macroeconomic level, since assets and liabilities will be reported and fiscal policy and fiscal stability will be supported. Public debt will be better assessed and the process of managing, holding, and deploying public assets will be improved. The process of full IPSAS implementation should gain political ownership, i.e. its introduction should be supported by the highest levels of government. Large technical capacity should be created within several supporting institutions and key officials with considerable IT, accounting and other skills. A project unit should be established dedicated to phased implementation of IPSAS accrual-based accounting, with specific milestones to be achieved by budget and unit users towards full compliance of financial statements with IPSAS accrual accounting requirements. In addition to the development of more complicated accounting policies, appropriate and continuous training should be provided to accountants working in the public sector in order to consistently implement the reform through the whole public sector.

Concerning state audit in the public sector, the capacity of the State Audit Office needs to be further enhanced through the training of staff and the sharing of international experience and expertise in order to perform performance audit engagements within public sector entities. Further, the general public should become more familiarised with the role of the state audit office and how audit reports should be used for the better monitoring and control of operations of public sector institutions. The State Audit Office could make audit reports and other results of audit work more readily available to the general public through its website. Although other institutions of the judicial system follow up on audit reports and undertake legal measures in response to significant findings of non-compliance with laws and regulations, further recognition of state audit findings, support and follow-up actions by the parliament are needed.

The system of public internal financial control could be further developed through the establishment of continuous training for responsible officers in financial management and control, and through the enhanced scope of entities responsible for establishing financial management and control systems and internal audit. Public sector entities need to establish quality assurance units for financial management and control, and also for internal audit.

References

Ministry of Finance. (2006). *Strategy for the Development of Public Internal Financial Control in the Republic of Macedonia*. Available via http://finance.gov.mk/files/u10/ja_za_PIFC_usvoena_od_Vladata_na_16_02_2006l.pdf. Accessed 14 November 2017.

Minovski, Z., Hughes, J., & Kocevski, A. (2016). Transition to Accrual Accounting in the Public Sector. *Journal of Contemporary Economic and Business Issues, 3*(2), 75–88.

Nikolov, M., & Dimovska, G. (2017). *Assessment of Legal and Regulatory Requirements Related to the Work of the State Audit Office*. Skopje: Westminster Foundation on Democracy.

State Audit Office. (2012). *Strategy for Development of the State Audit Office 2013–2017*. Skopje: State Audit Office. Available via http://www.dzr.mk/Uploads/Strategija_razvoj_2013_2017_001.pdf. Accessed 14 November 2017.

World Bank. (2017). *Overview, Country Context for FYR Macedonia*. Washington, DC: World Bank. Available via http://www.worldbank.org/en/country/macedonia/overview. Accessed 27 May 2017.

Useful Sites

http://www.slvesnik.com.mk/doma.nspx.
http://www.slvesnik.com.mk/id-and-basic-information.nspx.

CHAPTER 8

Public Sector Accounting, Auditing and Control in the Republic of Srpska

Bobana Čegar, Jelena Poljašević and Duško Šnjegota

8.1 Territorial Organisation, Scope of the Public Sector and Distribution of Public Revenues

8.1.1 Territorial Organisation

The Republic of Srpska is one of two entities in Bosnia and Herzegovina. It borders with the Republic of Serbia, Montenegro and the Republic of Croatia and has an inter-entity boundary with the Federation of Bosnia and Herzegovina. The area of the Republic of Srpska is 25,053 km^2 or about 49% of the territory of Bosnia and Herzegovina, and has a population of 1,326,991. The Law on the Territorial Organisation of the Republic of Srpska (Official Gazette of RS, no. 69/09, 70/12

B. Čegar · J. Poljašević (✉) · D. Šnjegota
Faculty of Economics, University of Banja Luka,
Banja Luka, Bosnia and Herzegovina
e-mail: jelena.poljasevic@ef.unibl.org

V. Vašiček and G. Roje (eds.), *Public Sector Accounting, Auditing and Control in South Eastern Europe*, Public Sector Financial Management, https://doi.org/10.1007/978-3-030-03353-8_8

and 83/14)[1] stipulates that the territory of the Republic consists of municipalities and towns comprising seven cities and 57 municipalities.

Local governments, the manner and conditions of their training, jobs, and other questions of authority are governed by the Law on Local Self-Government (Official Gazette of RS, no. 101/04, 42/05, 118/05). The jurisdiction of municipalities includes tasks related to urban planning and construction, housing and communal activities, culture, primary healthcare, social care, childcare, sport and physical culture, tourism, catering, crafts and trade, protection of natural resources and the environment, providing legal assistance, information and public notifications, protection from natural disasters, and more. Cities that consist of several municipalities have responsibilities that are assigned to the municipality.

8.1.2 *Financing of the Central Government and Local Units*

Budget funds belonging to cities and municipalities, which are used for the financing of their activities, are determined by the Law on the Budget System of the Republic of Srpska (Official Gazette of RS, no. 121/12, 103/15).

Funds belonging to the national budget and which are shared between the Republic and the municipalities and cities are paid under the account of public revenues of the Republic, while funds which belong entirely to the municipality and the city are paid directly to the account of public revenues of municipalities or the city.

The most significant tax revenues of the budget are revenues from indirect taxes. These revenues make up about 66% of the budget revenues of the Republic of Srpska. These revenues are divided as follows: 72% to the national budget, 24% to the budgets of municipalities and cities, and 4% to the public company "Roads of the Republic of Srpska".

The second most important revenue is revenue from income tax, accounting for approximately 12% of the budget of the Republic. This income tax is shared in the ratio of 75% to the national budget and 25% to the budgets of municipalities and cities. After the flood of 2014 which devastated BiH, municipalities affected by this natural disaster started receiving 50% of revenues from personal income tax. The individual

[1] Official Gazette of the Republic of Srpska (RS) stands for a public record titled Službeni glasnik Republike Srpske, in which all laws, regulations, decrees, appointments and official decisions passed in the Parliament or adopted by the Government are published in native language and released in the public domain: http://www.slglasnik.org/.

share of municipalities and cities in the distribution of revenue from income tax is performed according to the following criteria: 75% based on the number of inhabitants, 15% based on the area of the municipalities, and 10% based on the number of pupils in secondary school. Revenues from concessions, water fees, fees for agricultural land, revenues from taxes on the use, possession and carrying of goods, and revenues from fees for the use of natural resources for the production of electricity are also shared between the Republic budget and the budgets of municipalities and cities.

Revenues that entirely belong to the national budget are revenues from corporate income tax, taxes, fees, fines, revenues from illegally acquired property and proceeds, revenue from grants that belong to the Republic, revenues generated by general government units through regular and supplemental activities, and other income.

Revenues that belong directly to the budgets of municipalities and cities include property tax, fines imposed in misdemeanour proceedings for violations established by the acts of towns (municipalities), municipal administrative fees, utility fees, special water charges—fees for the protection of water, municipal fees for the use of natural resources and others of general interest, taxes on winnings from gambling, tax, fees for concessions awarded by local governments, and other income, such as income from grants, transfers and revenues that budgetary users earn by performing regular and additional activities, and the like.

All fixed assets necessary for the performance of the mandatory functions of local self-government are granted to local government units. These assets include public infrastructure, business and other property of public companies founded by local governments, property which is financed by the local budget or through volunteers, and other property acquired by a unit of local government as a legal successor and from institutions that have ceased to exist.

Local governments own property, and use and dispose of assets in accordance with regulations and in the interests of the local population

Local governments are divided into developed, medium-developed, underdeveloped and extremely underdeveloped municipalities. The Republic provides special financial support to underdeveloped and extremely underdeveloped municipalities by introducing appropriate procedures of equalisation or equivalents to remedy the consequences of the unequal distribution of potential sources of financing and the financial burden that must be supported. Such procedures do not diminish the discretionary powers of local government carried out within its own jurisdiction.

8.1.3 The Scope of the Public Sector

The public sector and its subsectors are defined by the methodology of the International Monetary Fund, through the Government finance statistics, the System of National Accounts and the European System of National Accounts. The public sector consists of the general government sector, and public financial and nonfinancial corporations and quasi-corporations.[2] In the Republic of Srpska, the general government sector is defined by the Law on the Budget System of the Republic of Srpska (Official Gazette of RS, no. 121/12, 52/14 and 103/15).

According to this law, the budget system of the Republic of Srpska consists of the budget of the Republic, the budgets of municipalities and cities, and the budgets (financial plans) of funds. The same law defines budgetary users as the authorities, organisations and other entities of the public sector (excluding public enterprises) that are financed from the state budget, municipalities, cities and funds under their control. Funds[3] in terms of this Law are the Health Insurance Fund of the Republic of Srpska, the Public Fund for Child Protection of the Republic of Srpska, the Pension and Disability Insurance Fund, and the Employment Agency of the Republic of Srpska.

With the aim of monitoring the purposeful spending of budget funds and determining the exact number of budget users, the Rulebook on Acquiring the Status of Budgetary User (Official Gazette of RS, no. 116/13) was adopted. This Rulebook provides for the establishment of the Register of Users of the Republic Budget, Users of Municipality and City Budgets, and Users of Funds. Budget users of the Republic are those that meet the following criteria: (a) budget users whose founder is the Republic of Srpska; (b) administrative authorities, Republican administrative organisations and institutions of the Republic of Srpska and other users who are fully or partially financed from the budget revenues of the Republic of Srpska; and (c) public institutions established in accordance with the law on governing the system of public services that are fully or partially financed from the revenue budget of the Republic of Srpska. Municipality and city budget users are users that meet the following criteria: (a) budget users founded by the municipality;

[2] GFS 2001, 2.59.

[3] The Pension and Disability Insurance Fund has been part of the Republic budget since 1 January 2016.

(b) organisations and institutions as well as other users that are fully or partially financed from the revenue budget of municipalities and cities; and (c) public institutions established in accordance with the law on governing the system of public services that are fully or partially financed from the proceeds of municipal and city budgets. Budget users' funds in terms of the regulations are:

- Pension and Disability Insurance;
- Health Insurance Fund of the Republic of Srpska;
- Public Fund for Child Protection of the Republic of Srpska;
- The Employment Agency of the Republic of Srpska.

Budget users in terms of this Rulebook are not considered public companies, whose organisation and business fall under the Law on Public Companies. The Register of Republic Budget Users and Funds, as well as the comprehensive Register of Budget Users of the Republic of Srpska, is guided and maintained by the Ministry of Finance, while the Register of Budget Users of Municipalities and Cities is established and maintained by municipality and city departments. The public sector of the Republic of Srpska consists of the general government sector and public companies. The Law on Public Companies (Official Gazette of RS, no. 75/04 and 78/11) defines a public company as a legal entity that is registered in the Courts Register as a company in the form of a joint stock company or a limited liability company to perform activities of general interest and in whose share capital the Republic of Srpska or local government directly or indirectly holds a majority stake. According to the Agency for Intermediaries, IT and financial services in the Republic of Srpska have 128 public companies.

8.2 Formulation and Execution of Central Government and Local and Regional Self-Government Budgets

8.2.1 The Legal and Institutional Framework of the Budget

In BiH, all phases of the budgetary process are conducted at the level of BiH common institutions, at the level of both entities, as well as at the level of the Brcko District. These stages include the preparation, adoption, execution and control of the budget. In the Republic of

Srpska (RS), the legal basis of the budgetary system primarily consists of the Law on the Budget System (Official Gazette of RS, no. 121/12, 52/14, 103/15). This law regulates the budget system of the Republic of Srpska, the preparation, planning, method of drafting, adoption and execution of the entity's budget, the budgets of municipalities, cities and funds, borrowing and debt servicing, financial reporting and control of the budget of the Republic, municipalities, cities and funds (Article 1 of the Law). Accordingly, the RS budgetary system consists of the budget of the Republic, the budget of the municipalities and cities, and the budget of funds.

8.2.2 Budget Preparation and Adoption

The budgetary process encompasses a set of activities and procedures related to the budget. The first step in the budgetary procedure is the preparation of the budget, followed by the adoption, execution and control of the budget. An efficient budget preparation process requires a unique preparation procedure, making decisions on time, setting and respecting limits and focusing on policy changes.

The preparation of the budget or budget drafting includes budget initiatives, revenue planning, expenditure planning and preparation of budget proposals. The initiative for drawing up the budget comes from the highest entity authority that performs public financing which is the Ministry of Finance. The preparation of the entity's budget is based on the Budget Framework, which includes not only projections for the following year, but for two years after that and takes place for an established budget calendar which begins on 15 February and ends on 15 December, Three-year (medium-term) budget planning assumes that the annual budget is planned as a three-year rolling budget plan or an estimate of the annual budget for the next fiscal year and the preliminary budget projections for the next two fiscal years.

The National Assembly adopts a decision to approve the budget for each subsequent fiscal year. If the budget is not adopted before the beginning of the next fiscal year, the National Assembly decides on temporary financing, but for no longer than a semi-annual period, for example from 1 January to 30 June. The approved budget is published in the Official Gazette of RS, and it is in accordance with the principle of balance between budget revenues and expenditures.

Based on the mid-term (rolling) transmission planning principle, budget projections for the coming year become the starting point for the preparation of the budget for the following year. Subsequent changes in policies are added or subtracted from the starting point to reach regularly revised budget estimates. Subsequent changes which include implications for the following fiscal years are also immediately updated in the revised estimates, ensuring that budget estimates are always up-to-date and accurate.

The budget preparation itself, but also other stages in the budget procedure, is carried out based on a single budget classification system which includes economic, functional, organisational and fund classification of the budget funds and budget expenditure.

Functional classification of public expenditures classifies expenditures according to the purpose for which they are incurred, while economic classification classifies them based on the type of expenditure. Organisational classification refers to the place of the transaction and allows for identification of the financial responsibility at the level of relevant institutions, organisational budget units and final budget spending units. Fund classification provides information on the financing sources, classifying them into one of the following five funds: the general fund, the revenues' fund under special regulations, the grant fund, the privatisation and succession fund and the fund for specific projects.

It is noteworthy that in the RS the terms "budgetary revenues" and "budgetary expenditures" are not equivalent in terms of revenue and expenditure defined by the International Accounting Standards for the Public Sector. Budgetary revenues consist of public revenue, current and capital loans from the country and abroad, and transactions received from other budget units, while budgetary expenditures include expenses for personal income (compensation to employees), expenses arising from the use of goods and services, expenditures for financing, and other financial expenses, subsidies, loans, payments for social protection and other transactions for budget users. The difference comes from the application of a different basis in drafting the budget reports on the one hand, and the financial statements of general purpose on the other. The budget reports are made according to modified accrual basis, which implies recognition of expenditures on an accrual basis and revenues on a cash basis, while financial statements of general purpose use the full accrual basis. Finally, drafting the budget does not include items that have the character of expenditure but do not require, or do not lead to, cash flow (e.g., amortisation), based on the IPSAS.

8.2.3 Budget Execution and the Report on Budget Execution

Budget execution is a phase of the budget procedure which involves collecting budget revenues and financing the needs of budget users. Budget execution is entrusted to executive authorities and it is defined how and for which purposes the funds can be spent. Budget users and funds can incur liabilities and use the funds only for the defined purposes and up to the limits determined by the budget. Efficient budget execution requires the following (Poljašević 2014):

- confirmation that the budget will be implemented in accordance with the powers set out in the law and in relation to the financial and political aspect;
- adjustment of budget execution to significant changes in the macroeconomic environment;
- solving problems that arise during implementation;
- purchase management and the efficient use of resources.

Monitoring the dynamics of the collection and spending of public funds in the Republic of Srpska is conducted through the treasury system. The initial development of the treasury system in the Republic of Srpska was associated with cooperation with the United States Government, and the signing the Memorandum of Understanding which defined the activities and deadlines for the establishment of the treasury. The treasury system was introduced at the beginning of 2002 as part of the USAID project "Reform of Public Sector Accounting in the Republic of Srpska" (Čegar 2016). In order to achieve the goal of control over the spending of public funds, the upper limits of available funds for different items (compensation to employees, use of goods and services, etc.) are entered into the treasury system. The limits are defined in the budget and budget users must not exceed those amounts. Subsequently, budget users receive money and pay liabilities through a single treasury account.

Reporting on the budget execution includes budget resources and budget expenditure up to the end of the current fiscal year (which is also the end of the calendar year), but also the resources and expenditures that occur after that date, but no later than the deadline for the preparation and submission of annual financial statements if the legal requirements are fulfilled and the amount of these funds and expenditures can be included in the budget of the current fiscal year. The Ministry of Finance reports quarterly to the Government on the entity's budget execution for the current fiscal year. The government delivers the semi-annual and annual reports on the budget execution to the National Assembly. In line with the Law on the Budget (Article 47), the report on budget execution should contain:

- an overview of budget resources and budget expenditures which were approved by the National Assembly in the previous year;
- an overview of the collected budget resources and executed expenditures during the previous fiscal year, presented in a manner where the difference between the approved and executed budget is clearly visible;
- an explanation concerning greater differences;
- data on borrowing and debt management;
- data on the use of budget reserves;
- data on guarantees approved during the previous fiscal year;
- opening and closing amounts on the single treasury account and on the special purpose account;
- data on reallocations.

Apart from previous data and information, the report of budget execution should show data on the opening and closing value of the assets, liabilities and fund sources.

8.3 Accounting and Financial Reporting

8.3.1 Budget Accounting

The domain of accounting and auditing important to the organisation and functioning of the bookkeeping and accounting system and the preparation and presentation of financial statements is provided for in the Law on Accounting and Auditing of the Republic of Srpska. This Law applies to all forms of joint stock companies, other profit and non-profit associations, entrepreneurs that apply the double-entry bookkeeping system, and the budget. According to this Law, IAS/IFRS, IFRS for SME and IPSAS represent the normative basis for financial reporting. In the

Republic of Srpska, bookkeeping applies to all legal entities regardless of whether they are profit-oriented or not, while entrepreneurs can choose whether to keep their books according to the system of single or double-entry bookkeeping.

In addition to the above-mentioned Law, accounting and financial reporting for budget users is also regulated by the Law on the Budget System of the Republic of Srpska, but also by a set of rules. The Law on the Budget System of the Republic of Srpska in chapter VI provides for budget users to prepare individual and consolidated annual financial reports and for the deadline for their preparation. The Rulebook on Accounting, Accounting Policies and Accounting Estimates for Budget Users in the Republic of Srpska prescribes the organisation of bookkeeping and the accounting system and accounting policies of budget users. This Rulebook, as well as the Law on Accounting and Auditing, prescribes that budget users in the Republic of Srpska use international accounting standards for the public sector as a normative basis.

The aforementioned acts prescribe that these standards be used by budget users which include administrative bodies, organisations and institutions of the Republic of Srpska, municipalities and cities, funds and other users that are financed from the budget of the Republic of Srpska. Public companies are not considered as budget users.

The technical and organisational framework for the establishment and management of the bookkeeping and accounting system of budget users is the treasury system regulated by the Law on the Treasury. The basis for determining the accounting policies is the International Accounting Standards for the Public Sector (hereinafter: IPSAS) published by the Board of International Accounting Standards for the public sector and the Rulebook on Budget Classifications, Account Content and Application of the Chart of Accounts for Users of Budget Revenues of the Republic, Municipalities, Cities and Funds. This Rulebook regulates bookkeeping documents, business records, inventory, budget classification and budget accounting, accounting policies, errors and changes in accounting policies, transactions after the reporting date and consolidated financial statements. For the organisation and functioning of the bookkeeping and accounting system, it is important to divide budget users into those that fully operate in the treasury system, those that partly operate through the treasury and those that are entirely outside this system. The relation of budget users to the Treasury determines the organisation of accounting and the manner of financial reporting.

The recording of business transactions is carried out by applying the prescribed analytical chart of accounts. Budget users are obliged to record changes of assets, liabilities, net assets, the budget and other revenues and receipts, the budget and other expenses and expenditures, and the results on six subsidiary accounts prescribed by the analytical chart of accounts for users of budget revenues.

The structure of the accounts consists of ten classes:

Class 0—Non-financial assets;
Class 1—Financial assets;
Class 2—Liabilities;
Class 3—The sources of and the off-balance registers;
Class 4—Expenses;
Class 5—Expenditure for the acquisition of non-financial assets;
Class 6—Expenditure for financial assets and repayment of liabilities;
Class 7—Revenue;
Class 8—Receipts for non-financial property;
Class 9—Financial assets and borrowing receipts.

Until 2013, budget users applied a modified accrual basis of accounting for reporting on budget execution and for financial reporting purposes. The adoption of IPSAS23—Revenues from non-exchange transactions (taxes and transfers) in 2013 resulted in financial reporting being based on a full accrual basis (Poljašević 2014).

The chart of accounts has the characteristics of a balance sheet chart of accounts and enables reporting in accordance with IPSAS according to an accrual basis as well as reporting on budget execution on a modified accrual basis. According to the balance identification, classes 0, 1, 2, and 3 are balance-sheet classes while class 4 and class 7 are income-statement classes. For reporting on budget execution, it was necessary to introduce some special classes relating to proceeds and expenditures. At the same time, within the classes that relate to revenue and expenses, special groups were formed to include accrual revenues and expenses, which do not represent the position of reports on budget execution. Within the classes of revenues and expenses, the groups of accounts 77 and 47 allocate accrued revenues and expenses that do not require an inflow and outflow. This way, the class of revenues and expenses (except for accrued revenues and expenses) and the class of proceeds and expenditures represent the class of the budget report.

According to the Rulebook on Accounting Policy, elements of the budget and financial statements are defined in the manner described below.

Assets, for the purposes of presentation on the balance sheet, are divided into non-financial and financial assets. Non-financial assets by maturity are divided into:

- non-financial assets in fixed assets—non-financial assets where economic benefits or service potential are expected for more than one year;
- non-financial assets in current assets—non-financial assets where economic benefits or service potential are expected for a period of less than one year.

Non-financial assets in non-current assets may occur as a result of the manufacturing process—produced non-current assets, and as an invention of a company, or naturally—valuables and non-produced non-current assets, and include construction in progress and advances.

Non-financial assets in current assets consist of stock stored for use, production and/or sale, including non-current assets held for sale, the property of discontinued operations, and advances for non-financial assets in current assets.

A financial asset is any asset that is:

- cash;
- a contracted right to receive cash or another financial asset from another entity;
- a contracted right to exchange financial instruments with other entities under potentially favourable conditions; or
- an equity instrument of another entity.

Financial assets are initially recognised according to their fair value plus the transaction costs that can be directly attributable to the acquisition of the property if the financial assets are not monitored by fair value through profit and loss.

Cash and cash equivalents denominated in domestic currency are measured at nominal value. Cash and cash equivalents denominated in foreign currency are measured in the equivalent amount of foreign currency. Loans are measured at amortised value—financial assets arising from planned loans are measured in the amount of outstanding principal. Accrued interest is recorded as a separate short-term receivable.

Receivables at the balance sheet date are estimated according to the possibilities of their recoverability. The uncollectable amount of the receivable is reported as expenses in the period.

The financial instruments held to maturity are measured at amortised values. Financial assets available for sale are measured at fair value. An increase in fair value on the balance sheet in relation to the initial value is recorded as revalued reserves. Financial instruments according to fair value through profit and loss are measured at fair value. Changes in fair value are recognised as income/expenses for the period. In the event of the disposal of financial assets, the net difference between the book value and the sale amount is recorded as gain/loss on the sale of financial assets.

Revenue/expenses from changes in the value of financial assets, positive/negative exchange rate differences and gains/losses on sale are purely of an accounting nature: they are presented in the income statement but are not considered budget revenue/expenses (i.e. they are not present in the report on the execution of the budget). Assets acquired through the sale of financial assets are not treated as current revenue, but as proceeds from financial assets.

According to maturity (liquidity), financial assets are divided into:

- long-term financial assets, and
- short-term financial assets

Liabilities may be classified as a present obligation (legal or derived), provisions or contingent liabilities. Liabilities are initially measured at the nominal amount which is the fair value of the goods or services for which the supplier has submitted an invoice or formal agreement giving rise to payment obligations (e.g. payments associated with social benefits). Liabilities on the balance sheet date are measured at the nominal amount or discounted value of the expected outflow of resources embodying the economic benefits or service potential of the budget user. According to maturity, liabilities are divided into: (a) short-term (current) liabilities; (b) long-term liabilities.

Net capital represents the difference between the total assets and total liabilities presented on the balance sheet. Net capital consists of permanent resources, reserves and financial results.

Expenses are decreases in economic benefits or service potential during the reporting period in the form of outflows or consumption of assets or the occurrence of liabilities that result in a decrease in net assets/equity. Expenses are recognised on an accrual basis in the period in which the obligation of payment occurred, regardless of whether payment is made. Operating expenses include current expenses and transactions between the budget units. The measurement of expenditures (excluding accrual expenses without outflows) is carried out according to the nominal value of the expected outflow of cash or cash equivalent.

Revenue is the gross inflow of economic benefits or service potential during the reporting period, when those inflows lead to an increase in net assets/equity, other than increases relating to the participation of the owner. Revenue for the purposes of budget execution reports is recognised on a modified accrual accounting basis, in the accounting period in which they are measurable and/or available:

- revenues are measurable when it is possible to express their value; and
- revenues are available when they are generated within the accounting period or shortly thereafter, based on the rights acquired in the accounting period in which they are recognised.

For the purposes of the income statement, or for accounting purposes, revenue is recognised on a full accrual accounting basis. Revenues include tax and non-tax income, including discontinued kinds of public revenues, grants, accrual revenue and transactions between the budget units. The structure of tax and non-tax revenue collected through the accounts of public revenues is amended in accordance with the amendments of the legislation in the respective areas. The measurement of revenue (except for accrual revenue) is performed at the nominal value of the expected inflow of cash or cash equivalent.

Expenditures of financial assets, non-financial assets and the repayment of debts represent a closed system of accounts used for recording expenditures for financial assets and the repayment of debt and do not represent the position of the income statement.

Expenditure is recorded when it leads to cash outflows in the corresponding balance sheet accounts. In accordance with the approved budget, accounting records of expenditure are made at the time of the commitment of the expenditure for the asset or debt service, regardless of whether cash outflow was made by the end of the accounting period or if it is expected in the next accounting period. The exception is when a reservation is going to be made for planned items in the budget for property and to pay-off debts.

The measurement of property expenditure and expenditures for repaying debts is performed according to the nominal value of the achieved or expected outflow of cash or cash equivalent. Proceeds from assets and borrowing represent a closed system of accounts used for recording proceeds from sales of property and do not represent the position of the income statement. Proceeds can be recorded before the cash flow if it comes soon after the accounting period, based on the rights acquired in the accounting period in which they are recognised. The measurement of proceeds from assets is carried at the nominal value of the realised inflows of cash or cash equivalents. Budget users are obliged to classify expenditures according to the COFOG classification of government functions published by the Department of Statistics of the United Nations.

8.3.2 *Financial Reporting*

Financial and budgetary reporting in the RS is interrelated and conditioned, but among these types of reporting there are some differences arising from the objective and purpose. While the set of financial statements presents data on assets, liabilities, net assets, revenues, expenditures, and net cash flows, the budgetary statements follow the movements of revenues/inflows and expenditures/outflows. Data should have certain quality characteristics, should relate to the same period, should have the same classification structure and should refer to the same entity in order to be comparable in these reports. Comparing them is easier if both sets of reports are drawn up on the same accounting basis. In the RS, reports are compiled on a different basis. For the preparation and presentation of financial statements for general purposes, as well as for consolidated financial statements, budgetary users use a full accrual basis, while budgetary reports should be prepared on a modified accrual basis (Poljašević 2013). In this case, a problem in comparing them occurs since, in the financial statements, prepared by applying an accrual basis, revenues are recognised when they arise, while in the budgetary reports, in accordance with the modified accrual basis, tax revenues are recognised when they are charged, or revenue from exchange transactions is recognised when it occurs. In this respect and according to IPSAS 24, in the RS, for the purposes of comparing planned and executed amounts, a special report on budget execution is compiled. Accounting for budget users is also regulated by the Rulebook on Accounting, Accounting Policies and Accounting Estimates for Budget Users (Official Gazette of RS, no. 127/11).

In accordance with this Rulebook, and in terms of the organisation and functioning of bookkeeping and accounting, budget users are divided into (Article 3):

- Budget users that fully operate through the system of treasury operations;
- Budget users that partially operate outside the system of treasury operations;
- Budget users that operate entirely outside the system of treasury operations.

Budget users have accounting in line with the standard budget classifications, which include the fund, organisational, economic, sub-economic (subanalytic), functional and programme (project) classification. Budget users whose general ledger is fully an RS treasury general ledger (TGL) are those that have all operations through an RS single treasury account. All financial transactions of these budget users, relating to the budget, including financing programmes from abroad or domestic grants, are recorded in the TGL. What is characteristic of these entities is that their financial statements do not have the character of financial statements for general purposes, and in the system their financial statements are labelled as "financial statements of individual budget users". These entities generally do not have their own property, because the property they use is recognised on the balance sheet of local governments or central government. They also do not have their own bank accounts. On a quarterly basis, these budget users fill in a report on the number and structure of employees and deliver the report in an electronic form and in hard copy to the line ministry or the line department for finance in the municipalities, cities or funds, and within 25 days of the end of a quarter they deliver the reports to the Ministry of Finance. On an annual basis, they compile the following forms: Overview of Revenues, Inflows, Expenditures and Outflows Reported in the TGL on Accounting Fund 01; Overview of Revenues, Inflows, Expenditures and Outflows

Reported in the TGL on Accounting Funds from 01 to 05; Functional Classification of Expenditure and Net-acquisition on Non-financial Assets Reported in the TGL; Overview of Assets, Liabilities and Sources Reported in the TGL; and the Report on the Number and Structure of Employees (Official Gazette of RS, no. 16/11, 126/11). These forms should be submitted by the end of February of the following year to the line ministry or to the line department for finance in the municipalities or cities.

Budget users with their own account are those whose general ledger is not located within the general treasury ledger of the Republic, municipality, city, or that are only partially located within the same. These entities make certain payments through their own bank accounts, and, in this respect, they have more freedom in cash management. However, this freedom is limited by legally adopted budget limits. These budget users compile reports on a monthly, quarterly and annual basis. The form for monthly fiscal reporting contains only the part that relates to transactions that occur using the institution's own bank account. On a quarterly basis, with the report on the structure and number of employees, budget users who do not have their own bank account also prepare an overview of revenues, inflows, expenditures and outflows disclosed outside the TGL. On an annual basis, budget users fill in the following forms: Overview of Revenues, Inflows, Expenditures and Outflows Reported in the TGL to Accounting Fund 01; Overview of Revenues, Inflows, Expenditures and Outflows Reported in the TGL to Accounting Fund from 01 to 05; Overview of Revenues, Inflows, Expenditures and Outflows Declared Outside the TGL on Accounting Fund from 01 to 05; Overview of Revenues, Inflows, Expenditures and Outflows Disclosed in the Accounting Fund from 01 to 05; Functional Classification of Expenditure and Net-acquisition of Non-financial Assets in the TGL; Functional Classification of Expenditure and Net-acquisition for Non-financial Assets Outside the TGL; Functional Classification of Expenditure and Net-acquisition of Non-financial Assets; Overview of Assets, Liabilities and Sources Reported in the TGL; Overview of Assets, Liabilities and Sources Reported Outside the TGL; Overview of Assets, Liabilities and Sources; Overview of Cash Flows that Happened Through Their Own Bank Accounts; and Report on the Number and Structure of Employees.

There are also institutions that are budget users and whose general ledger is entirely located outside the TGL. These institutions receive cash transactions from the budget which are eliminated later through consolidation.

Public sector entities in the RS started to apply IPSAS for the first time in 2006, and the new chart of accounts was adopted in 2011, by which the RS met all the preconditions for the implementation of all previously published IPSAS. Since 2013, the RS has used a full accrual accounting basis for general purpose financial reporting, which has increased the information quality of reports. In accordance with IPSAS and the accounting basis, as well as the Rulebook on Financial Reporting for Users of Budget Revenues of the Republic, Municipalities, Cities and Funds (Official Gazette of RS, no. 16/11, 126/11), the set of annual financial statements includes:

- Balance sheet (Report on the Financial Position);
- Income statement (Report on Financial Performance);
- Report on changes in net assets/capital;
- Cash flow statements;
- Interim report on budget execution;
- Interim report on the execution per accounting fund.

The balance sheet presents an overview of assets and resources on a day. The classification of assets is carried out on non-financial and financial assets, and within them on long-term and short-term assets. Ordering asset positions is based on the decreasing liquidity principle. The liabilities side of the balance sheet include liabilities that are classified as short and long term, followed by own sources.

The income statement contains an overview of all revenues and expenditures, as well as the financial result of the reporting entity on the principles of a full accrual basis. Revenues are divided into tax, non-tax, grants and accrued revenues and transactions between the budget units are also displayed. Expenses are divided into current expenses, accrued expenses and transactions between the budget units. Accrued revenues are revenues that are earned, but not collected in the observed reporting period, as well as revenues that were not planned in the budget (e.g., income from abolishing provisions). Revenues that are not collected are categorised as accrued revenues (although by their nature they should be classified, for example, as tax revenue) to allow for the more efficient preparation and control of budget execution. On the expenditure side, accrued expenditure is an expenditure that does not lead to an outflow of cash and is categorised by its nature. Currently, within the group of accrued expenditure, expenditure can be found that has been incurred, but was not planned and there are no available funds to meet the commitments associated with that expenditure. However, this situation is the result of the technical limitations of the treasury reporting system (disabled recording of expenditures by type if the funds for that purpose are not planned in the budget, and such transactions are recorded as accrued expenditures). The statement of changes in net assets presents an overview of changes in the sources in two consecutive reporting periods, classified by the causes which determined them (changes in accounting policies, errors, revaluations, foreign exchange differences, surplus/deficit for the period, reallocation between various categories of own resources, etc.).

The cash flow statement shows inflows and outflows during the reporting period and the net cash flow at the end of the period. Cash flow is compiled based on appropriate data presented on the balance sheet, income statement and additional information from the accounting records. Activities that create cash flow are divided into operating activities, investing activities and financing activities. The content and method of valuation of the positions in the statements are in accordance with IPSAS.

The interim report on budget execution represents a comparative overview of planned and actual revenues and expenses (excluding accrued revenues and expenditures), and revenues and expenses during the reporting period, stated in the General Accounting Fund 01.

The interim report on execution per accounting funds presents an overview of income and expenses (excluding accrued revenues and expenditures), and inflows and outflows during the reporting period in all accounting funds.

8.4 Audit and Other Oversight (Supervision) in the Public Sector

The financial operation of budget users in the Republic of Srpska is monitored through the activities of external public audit,[4] internal audit and budget oversight. During the last few years, capacities have been partly

[4] "External public audit" means government audit. However, due to the complexity of this public function in Bosnia and Herzegovina, i.e. the existence of a total of four audit institutions which operate autonomously and independently from one another in fulfilling their legal mandates, with clearly demarcated powers and responsibilities, the term "government" in this audit is replaced by the term "external public".

established for the organisation of an efficient and effective system of internal financial control in the public sector, covering the three main pillars of that system as follows: financial management and control, internal audit and a Central Harmonization Unit for financial management and control and internal audit (CHU).

Monitoring and control activities in the public sector concern various activities of the entities which comprise the public sector.[5] Monitoring and control of traditional budget users target activities on preparing and executing the budget, aligning the operation and financial transactions of budget users with the relevant laws and other regulations, and implementing various activities, programmes and projects in this section of the public sector in an economical, efficient and effective manner.

Monitoring and control are primarily based on financial and non-financial information presented in the financial statements. Entities obligated to submit financial statements, and the deadlines and manner of preparation, are set forth in detail by regulations adopted on the basis of the Law on the Budgetary System of the Republic of Srpska (Official Gazette of the Republic of Srpska, 121/12, 52/14 and 103/15).

8.4.1 External Public Audit

Regarding external audit's role in assuring the necessary quality of financial statements of public sector entities, it is important to take into account that external audit in the public sector comprises two independent audit functions, one of which pertains to the competence of audit companies and the other which relates to the competence of supreme audit institutions. In this, the competences set forth by law for the supreme audit institutions, regardless of their actual capacity, also cover the section of the public sector audited by audit companies.

Analysis of the relevant legal rules and professional regulations leads to the conclusion that there are many points of contact between these two types of external audit, both in the application of standards and principles which represent the basis for auditing and the auditor's work, and

[5] In addition to the traditional (direct) budget users, the term "public sector" also covers a number of other institutions and bodies, such as indirect budget users, parts of public institutions, various agencies, directorates and extra-budgetary funds, public enterprises, public institutions, quasi-public enterprises, etc.

in the scope of auditing, while on the other hand there are many evident differences conditioned partly by the characteristics of the regulations in force, and partly by the "customary" actions and understanding of the role of both. The fields in which their powers and interests intertwine the most concern auditing the financial statements of public enterprises and public institutions, and prospectively also auditing projects and programmes financed by European and other funds, public-private partnership projects, etc.

The legal framework relevant for the establishment and development of various monitoring and control mechanisms within the public finance and public administration system in the Republic of Srpska includes the Law on Public Sector Auditing of the Republic of Srpska, adopted for the first time in 1999 (Law on Public Sector Auditing of the Republic of Srpska, Official Gazette of the Republic of Srpska, 18/99, 39/03 and 115/04), and then replaced by a new law in 2005 (Law on Public Sector Auditing of the Republic of Srpska, Official Gazette of the Republic of Srpska, 98/05 and 20/14). Pursuant to the provisions of the Law currently in force, the main objective of the Supreme Office for Public Sector Auditing of the Republic of Srpska (Supreme Audit Office), as a supreme audit institution in the Republic of Srpska, is to provide, on the basis of the audits performed, an independent opinion on compliance with laws and other regulations, budget execution, financial statements, and the use of resources and management of state property by public sector institutions of the Republic of Srpska.

According to the provisions of the Law in force, the Supreme Audit Office performs financial audits, performance audits and other specific audits.

Financial audit means reviewing the financial statements and supporting accounts of the audited institutions, in compliance with the adopted auditing standards, in order to assess whether those statements are reliable and whether the balances give a true indication of budget execution. The objective is also to determine whether the regulations are being enforced, whether the funds are being used for their intended purposes, and to assess the financial management system, internal audit function and internal control system.

The Supreme Audit Office also has the right and obligation to conduct a performance audit, i.e. to review or examine an aspect of the operation of an entire institution or its part, or a programme or activity in terms of economy, efficiency and effectiveness in the institution's use of its resources. The external audit powers of the Supreme Audit Office provided by the Law include auditing the following:

- National Assembly of the Republic of Srpska;
- Office of the President of the Republic of Srpska;
- Government, i.e. ministries of the Government of the Republic of Srpska and other republic bodies, organisations and institutions financed from the budget;
- funds and other extra-budgetary institutions established by law;
- budgets of municipalities and cities;
- any other funds provided for project implementation to any of the institutions by international organisations, in the form of a loan or donation to the Republic of Srpska;
- funds allocated from the budget to institutions or organisations;
- public and other enterprises in which the state has a direct or indirect ownership share.

The powers provided by the Law include all financial, administrative and other activities, and programmes and projects managed by one or more institutions, including the procedure and proceeds of sale of property, privatisation and concessions.

Taking into account the treasury operation of budget users, and the fact that the Treasury General Ledger at the Republic of Srpska level covers almost all users of the Republic budget revenues, and that the treasury has been introduced in all local self-government units (including users of local-level budget revenues), it is important to note that, through regular auditing of the consolidated financial statement for users of the Republic of Srpska budget revenues and extra-budgetary funds, and regular although cyclical auditing of the consolidated financial statements prepared at the local self-government unit level, the audits of the Supreme Audit Office practically cover more than 90% of total funds collected as tax and non-tax revenues at all government levels in the Republic.

In conducting the audits laid down by the Law, the Supreme Audit Office applies the auditing standards of INTOSAI and the International Federation of Accountants (IFAC). The INTOSAI auditing standards used by the Supreme Audit Office are actually the ISSAI auditing standards which cover four levels of standards, guidelines and principles relevant for external audit in the public sector implemented by the supreme audit institutions as follows:

- Level 1: Fundamental principles;
- Level 2: Prerequisites for the functioning of the supreme audit institutions;
- Level 3: Fundamental auditing principles;
- Level 4: Auditing guidelines.

External public audit is conducted by audit teams headed by auditors holding the title of "certified auditor" or "certified accountant", and comprising auditors from one of a total of four levels of auditor responsibilities provided by the internal organisation and systematisation of workplaces at the Supreme Audit Office (senior auditor, auditor, junior auditor and audit assistant).

A complete audit cycle in a financial audit, starting from planning the audit to the publication of a final auditor's report, is based on the Financial Audit Guide and Methodology, while a performance audit is conducted in line with the Performance Audit Guide and Methodology. The third methodological document concerns internal audit quality control, and includes the Quality Control Guide and Methodology. All these methodologies are aligned with the ISSAI framework of international standards, guidelines and principles.[6]

All the final auditor's reports prepared by the Supreme Audit Office since its establishment until the present have been publicly available through the official website of this Office.[7]

8.4.2 Budget Oversight, Internal Audit and Internal Control in the Public Sector

Budget oversight was first established in the Republic of Srpska by the Law on the Budget of the Republic of Srpska of 2000 (Law on the Budgetary System of the Republic of Srpska, Official Gazette of the Republic of Srpska, 4/00) and it was also recognised as a form of public supervision and control in the Laws on the Budgetary System of the Republic of Srpska of 2002 (Law on the Budgetary System of the Republic of Srpska (Official Gazette of the Republic of Srpska, 63/02

[6] Methodologies were prepared and adopted by the top and middle management of the Supreme Audit Office in 2014. The Guides were adopted by the Coordination Board for Auditing the Institutions of Bosnia and Herzegovina.

[7] www.gsr-rs.org.

and 38/03), than in 2003 (Law on the Budgetary System of the Republic of Srpska, Official Gazette of the Republic of Srpska, 96/03, 14/04, 67/05, 34/06, 128/06, 117/07, 126/08 and 92/09) and in 2012 (Law on the Budgetary System of the Republic of Srpska, Official Gazette of the Republic of Srpska, 11/12, 52/14, 103/15 and 15/16).

The Law sets forth that ex post control of the legality of spending budget funds is performed by the budget inspectorate, whose operation is based on an annual work plan and unfolds continuously throughout the year. The budget inspectorate must prepare a report on its work at least twice a year and submit it to the competent body.

The Minister of Finance is authorised to issue a decision on the inspection of the intended and lawful use of budget users' funds for a certain period. The inspection is performed by a budget inspector, whom budget users must enable to inspect all available documentation relevant for the conducting of the inspection.

After completing the inspection of a budget user, the budget inspector prepares records of the established state of play. Once the oversight is conducted and proceedings are made, it is possible to issue a settlement requiring the removal of the detected irregularities.

Measures against budget users who fail to abide by the decision of the Minister of Finance are aimed at banning the use of the approved budget funds pending removal of the established irregularities.

A key problem which obstructs the expected efficiency and effectiveness of the budget inspectorate in the Republic of Srpska is seen in the insufficiently built capacities of that control function and, as a consequence, in the insufficient cooperation and coordination of operation of the budget inspectorate with holders of the activity of internal and external audit.

Internal audit in the section of the public sector consisting of budget users was first established based on the Law on Internal Audit in the Public Sector of the Republic of Srpska.[8]

This Law authorises internal auditors to conduct a systematic review and assessment of risk management, internal controls and the organisation's management, including the policies, procedures and activities of the organisation. Internal auditors assess the appropriateness and efficiency of the financial management and control system in terms of the following:

[8] Official Gazette of the Republic of Srpska, 17/08.

- achieving the tasks and set goals of the organisation;
- economical, efficient and effective use of resources;
- alignment with the established policies, procedures, laws and regulations;
- protection of the organisation's assets from losses resulting from any type of irregularities;
- the integrity and reliability of information, accounts and data, including the processes of internal and external reporting.

The Law sets forth that the internal audit function is organised and performed in compliance with the Methodology and Instruction on Internal Audit in the Public Sector of the Republic of Srpska issued by the CHU, and International Standards for the Professional Practice of Internal Auditing issued by the Institute of Internal Auditors (IIA) and the Internal Audit Code of Professional Ethics issued by the IIA, adopted by the CHU.

By their activities, internal auditors should encourage the building and functioning of a suitable control environment as a foundation for the establishment of an efficient internal control system, which requires perceiving and constantly assessing the risks that may have a negative impact on the achievement of the overall goals of the organisation, including the objectives set before the financial reporting system(s). In an organisation with an established internal audit, it is the management that should set clear and constant objectives and identify all the important risks which might lead to their non-achievement, and also adopt a plan of appropriate activities and measures to eliminate or at least minimise those risks (Šnjegota 2015).

According to budget regulations, budget users must establish an internal control system in accordance with the generally accepted standards and guidelines of internal control which should provide lawful, efficient, effective, accountable and transparent spending of public funds. Internal audit monitors and evaluates the system of internal controls, in accordance with the regulations governing the field of internal audit.[9]

[9]The Law on the System of Internal Financial Controls in the Public Sector of the Republic of Srpska [Zakon o sistemu internih finansijskih kontrola u javnom sektoru Republike Srpske] (Official Gazette of the Republic of Srpska, 91/16) defines financial management and control as a system of internal controls to be established and accounted for by the manager of the entity, and to provide reasonable assurance, based on risk management, that the budget and other funds will be used in a lawful, economical, efficient and effective manner in the achievement of the entity's goals.

Financial management and control should be organised and implemented in accordance with the international standards of internal control, in an environment comprising a control environment, risk management, control activities, information and communication and system monitoring and evaluation, as mutually connected elements.

By control activities, the legislator means in particular:

- authorisation and approval procedures;
- segregation of duties which prevents one person from being at the same time responsible for authorising, executing, recording and controlling;
- a dual signature system where no obligation can be undertaken or payment made without the signatures of both the manager of the entity and the manager of the financial service or another authorised person;
- access to funds and information;
- prior control of regularity conducted by a financial controller or another person designated by the manager of the entity;
- procedures of complete, accurate, regular and up-to-date recording of all business transactions;
- evaluation of the effectiveness and efficiency of transactions;
- supervision of procedures;
- procedures of human resources management and reporting;
- documenting of all transactions connected with the activity of the entity and in compliance with the set rules;
- procedures of monitoring financial management and control.

The Law on Fiscal Responsibility in the Republic of Srpska (Official Gazette of the Republic of Srpska, no. 94/15) sets forth fiscal rules, as well as measures and procedures constituting the basis for the establishment of a fiscal framework, limiting public spending, strengthening responsibility for efficient and effective use of budget funds, enhancing the system of controls and monitoring, etc. The purpose of adopting this Law is to ensure and maintain fiscal responsibility, transparency and the medium-term and long-term fiscal sustainability of the Republic of Srpska.

From the perspective of public monitoring and control in the budgetary system of the Republic of Srpska, in a particular manner, this Law connects the provisions of the Law on the Budgetary System of the

Republic of Srpska with the still effective Law on Internal Audit in the Public Sector of the Republic of Srpska. One of the important mechanisms of ex ante control of budget spending introduced by this Law is the statement of fiscal responsibility as a signed and certified statement to be submitted to the competent body by the responsible person of the budget user during the implementation of the procedure of the adoption of a budget or revised budget of the Republic of Srpska or of local self-government units, a budget or revised budget of funds, or decisions on temporary financing.

8.5 Challenges in Further Development of Public Sector Accounting and Auditing

The vision of the future development of accounting in the public sector of the Republic of Srpska is based on maintaining continuity in implementing the key strategic orientations and objectives that were the backbone of reform in the field of government accounting during the past period, primarily:

- consistent application of IPSAS;
- consistent application of the GFS methodology;
- further strengthening of the role of the treasury system as sound support for an efficient accounting and financial reporting system in the public sector of the Republic of Srpska.

Furthermore, the Republic of Srpska will have to undertake additional efforts to make its accounting and financial reporting system more compatible with the statistical bases of financial reporting founded on the application of ESA methodology.

Regarding the consistent application of IPSAS accounting standards, one of the main challenges in their sound application are the difficulties in providing up-to-date translations into Serbian of new standards or amendments or potential addendums to those in force, which may partly have a negative influence on the extent of education of public sector accountants or on the potential and partial divergence between the accounting methodologies and policies in force and expectations.

The degree of harmonisation of information that is or can be produced currently in the accounting and financial reporting system in the public sector of the Republic of Srpska with the requirements arising from the ESA methodology of statistical financial reporting may be deemed rather high, even more so because the system of budgetary accounting is based, among other things, also on the high level of application of the GFS methodology. In this sense, additional activities that need to be undertaken in the Republic of Srpska for the further development of a financial reporting system based on statistical foundations are completely realistic and feasible activities, although they are unavoidably connected with certain challenges, where significant technical assistance is expected also from the existing and expected new international projects in this field, mainly those financed by IPA funds.

The vision of the future development of external public audit in the Republic of Srpska is mostly based on endeavouring to conduct audit consistently in accordance with the ISSAI auditing standards framework and aimed at creating value added in the public sector by encouraging efficient and effective use of public resources, at the constant upgrading of a transparent financial management system, and at increasing public accountability for public funds management.

The main principles on which the work of external public auditors is based include independence, impartiality, political neutrality, professional capacity and competence, professional conduct, ethics, integrity, objectivity and standardisation of the approach to audit, confidentiality, commitment to the institution, and public accountability. These principles should be constantly nurtured, and measures and activities should be continually undertaken to build the strongest possible professional identity and credibility of the engaged audit staff.

Strategic goals of the future development of external public audit in the Republic of Srpska are set by the Development Strategy of the Supreme Office for the Republic of Srpska Public Sector Audit for the Period 2014–2020. The following strategic goals are identified:

- improving the quality of statutory external public audit based on international auditing standards and international best practices, which includes ensuring continuing access to up-to-date translations of all the ISSAI and other relevant international auditing standards and principles, drafting instructions on the application of the international auditing standards, etc.;
- improving the general legal framework for the statutory audit;
- improving the material basis for the functioning of the Supreme Audit Office, including the provision of adequate working

conditions, permanently safe and sufficient sources of financing, access to modern information technologies suitable for use in the external public audit, etc.;

- promoting partner cooperation and relations with the relevant local environment in order to enhance the professional reputation and influence of audit (active support for the process of educating the public about the role and importance of external public audit, formalisation of cooperation with the academic community, professional and other relevant non-governmental bodies, communication with the public by means of modern internet presentations, development of rules and procedures of communication with the media, non-governmental organisations, etc.);
- finding new forms and ways of international cooperation by formalising professional cooperation with the audit institutions in the vicinity, providing study tours and other forms of access to good international practices and exchange of experiences, participation in seminars, symposiums and congresses of international significance, etc.;
- improving the system of professional development and human resources management by ensuring permanent access by the engaged audit staff to the system of continued professional education, by encouraging the engaged auditors to take an active part in the education of others about audit and auditing tools and skills, establishing and developing a system of internal education of employees, encouraging the process of self-education, etc.;
- establishing a functional and flexible organisation of the supreme audit institution and applying new management practices;
- improving the quality control system, etc.

References

Čegar, B. (2016). Treasury System Impact on Financial Statements in the Public Sector. Banja Luka, *Acta Economica*, no. 24.

Poljašević, J. (2013). Financial Reporting in the Public Sector According to International Standards. In *8th Congress of Accountants and Auditors of Montenegro: "Prospects for Accounting and Financial Professions in the EU Accession Process"*. The Institute of Certified Accountants of Montenegro, Budva. pp. 153–171.

Poljašević, J. (2014). *Financial Reporting in the Public Sector*. Faculty of Economics, Banja Luka and FINRAR, Banja Luka.

Šnjegota, D. (2015). *Auditing Public-Private Partnership Projects.* Association of Accountants and Auditors of the Republic of Srpska, FINRAR 11, Banja Luka.

Useful Sites

www.gsr-rs.org.
http://www.vladars.net/eng/Pages/default.aspx.
www.issai.org.
www.gsr-rs.org.

CHAPTER 9

Concluding Remarks

Gorana Roje and Vesna Vašiček

This publication contains a systematic overview of public sector accounting, audit and control systems, including their development and state of play, as well as an overview of the challenges to be faced in the further development of public sector accounting and auditing in selected South-Eastern European countries. More precisely, the volume provides case studies related to Bosnia and Herzegovina (represented by two entities: the Federation of Bosnia and Herzegovina and the Republic of Srpska), Croatia, Poland, Romania, Serbia, Slovenia and the Former Yugoslav Republic of Macedonia.

A decisive influence on the shaping of public sector accounting at the country level comes from two sources: a national source and an international one. The national source is defined by the specifics related to the country's social system and economic development, the national level of education and intellectual capital, as well as the country's customs, tradition and culture. The international source relates to the

G. Roje (✉)
Ministry of State Assets, Zagreb, Croatia

V. Vašiček
Faculty of Economics and Business,
University of Zagreb, Zagreb, Croatia
e-mail: vvasicek@efzg.hr

V. Vašiček and G. Roje (eds.), *Public Sector Accounting, Auditing and Control in South Eastern Europe*, Public Sector Financial Management, https://doi.org/10.1007/978-3-030-03353-8_9

harmonisation and unification of methodological and legislative frameworks and national accounting and auditing practices, which further lead to reducing the bearing of the national specific features. Given that the development of public sector accounting, audit and control needs to be viewed in close connection with the development of the country as a whole, this publication reflects the selected countries' territorial structure, the organisation of state administration, the structure and scope of the public sector, political incentives and the extent of political and other regulations.

The country chapters show that there are differences and similarities in the achieved degree of development of public sector accounting, auditing and control systems. Regardless of the fact that the countries had rather similar starting points, they progressed at a different pace and with varying degrees of intensity. All the countries featured in this publication share the experience of a transforming social and economic environment and started their transition process in the early 1990s. All this had an impact on their public sector accounting, audit and control systems.

The fundamental feature of the budgetary system in the selected countries is the existence of many regulations and frequent amendments to normative regulation. There may be various reasons for such a high degree of public sector accounting legislation, mainly caused by the previous long period of the planned economy as opposed to a market-driven one (i.e. The public sector accounting information system was regarded as an administrative function and its full managerial impact was disregarded. The structure and content of the public sector accounting information system was viewed more in the function of achieving the goals of the state budget and not in the function of providing greater management efficiencies and better outcomes). Laws are often followed by other additional sets of regulations and guidance documents. These additional regulations, decrees, instructions and policies define and analyse certain parts of the main act more precisely and thus provide for the faster and easier qualitative adoption of the regulated solutions. However, this also results in excessively complicated administrative procedures that do not give budgetary units the opportunity to autonomously regulate their specific affairs.

The situation reported in the countries covered in this book shows that in all the countries the budget system is highly standardised. In terms of public sector coverage, all the countries follow the internationally recognised statistical framework, while the coverage includes budgetary users, non-budgetary funds and to a certain extent and under certain conditions public sector companies as well. Further, a registry of all budget users has been set up in most of the examined countries with developed classification criteria. In addition, the procedures for planning the budget and for budget adoption, as well as the budget structure, are clearly defined and prescribed. Emphasis is placed on budget classifications and on data standardisation and unification whereby comparable solutions are applied across the studied countries. The most commonly applied classifications are organisational, programme, functional, economic and classification by sources of funding. Some countries also apply classification by location, and fund accounting. The execution of the budget is organised through the Treasury system, where implementation processes of conceptually similar solutions differ across countries. The single budget account is implemented to introduce control over public consumption and to enhance financial discipline, as well as to achieve more efficient public resources management through consolidated and comprehensive liquidity management at the state budget level.

The publication also examines the challenges, possibilities and obstacles in applying the experiences of other countries or international professional authorities in the further development of public sector accounting, audit and control in the observed South-Eastern European countries. Whether or not it is possible to apply any of the developed countries' experiences and wider international trends as an example of good practice in transitioning countries depends greatly on a variety of factors that have influenced the developments so far. These factors are nationally specific, and include the capacity to meet financial assumptions that must be met for the implementation of accrual accounting, the legal and technical limitations to potential changes in the accounting model, factors affecting the dynamics of the development of national accounting, and factors hindering the reform process that lead also to political structural change. The variety of factors also encompasses certain external forces. An example of such external forces is known in public administration literature as New Public Management (NPM) which has emerged over the past two decades as the dominant public administration model. Given the evidence in this publication, NPM has begun to significantly influence the shape of present public sector accounting and has raised awareness that public sector accounting reforms need to be properly considered as an integral part of wider public sector reforms.

Previous studies on the experiences of developed countries provide evidence that public sector accounting reforms were triggered by and had the support of political structures at the time. In addition, public sector accounting reforms have been placed in the wider context of the development of New Public Management as a governance reform in the public sector of developed countries. The main reasons for public sector reforms in the developed countries were frequently public sector inefficiency and ineffectiveness and the need to improve the quality of public services while containing costs and enhancing public accountability at the same time. As for the sample of South-Eastern European countries studied in this publication, the situation is different. The strategic goals and development paths that would define the role of the individual segments in the overall general reforms are not constant, but are instead often radically transformed with political/structural change. As for the role of accounting and financial reporting as a means of strengthening public sector financial management, there is often no information regarding any future development paths as a precondition for public administration reforms enhancing governance capacity, which would further achieve the long-term sustainability of public administration. Further evidence of this comes from the regulatory framework of public sector accounting which is intended primarily for monitoring government spending at the macro level. Thus, in addition to observing the effects of the structure of the state, heritage and history of the development of the accounting system, one should also bear in mind the effects of public policy and wider reform processes that directly or indirectly have an impact on public sector accounting (budgetary processes, public sector management processes, etc.).

The field of accounting, audit and control is thus at the same time under the significant influence of the selected countries' national authorities and national characteristics, and on the other hand under the influence of the international environment and trends that require harmonisation with the international regulatory framework and standards. As evidenced in this publication, meeting these demands and expectations is no easy task, due to the fact that: (a) the gap between national and supranational solutions is very significant and seemingly difficult to cross; (b) public sector accounting systems arise out of tradition and the historical heritage of accounting and financial reporting matters; (c) accounting systems are based on law that fosters standardisation and unification and are not developed based on accounting standards and rules of accounting and the finance profession; (d) budgeting reporting is given priority over financial reporting, while financial reporting is very complex; and (e) there is a lack of tradition of developing accounting standards, implying that the introduction of IPSAS would bring significant changes and would also imply the start of the deregulation of the system and would lead to other changes.

However, given the fact that Poland and Slovenia joined the EU in 2004, Romania in 2007, and Croatia in 2013, whilst the Former Yugoslav Republic of Macedonia (having submitted an application in 2004) and Serbia (having submitted an application in 2009) are recognised as candidate countries for membership of the EU (and which are in the process of transposing or integrating EU legislation into their national regulatory framework), and Bosnia and Herzegovina is a potential candidate country which has still to fulfil the requirements for EU membership, in considering the challenges of developing a future public sector accounting, auditing and control system, and reflecting on future development paths, it is necessary to take into account the inevitable process of adjusting systems to that of the EU, as well as to the requirements of different international institutions. In Poland, Slovenia, Romania and Croatia, entry into the European Union was regarded as a very important argument and strong incentive for proceeding with further changes in the national public sector accounting/financial reporting system. In addition, EU membership has carried a number of requirements referring to reporting on state (public) finance that these countries now need to practise and comply with.

Undoubtedly, the accounting systems in the countries covered in this book show heterogeneity as far as use of the accounting basis is concerned. However, though the differences range from a cash basis, through different modifications of accrual accounting to a full accounting basis, the selected countries have, in various ways and with various dynamics (according to the specifics of each country), started or considered introducing a full or partial accrual accounting basis in their national public sector (government) accounting systems. Thus, the main challenges for the further development of public sector accounting relate to the process of transition towards accrual-based accounting and the implementation of IPSAS for the purpose of financial reporting by the general government sector. In this respect, the development of accounting and financial reporting focuses on exploring the benefits and opportunities of applying an accrual accounting basis, alongside international public sector accounting standards or the European public sector accounting standards. Furthermore, gradualism and a comparison of costs and benefits are considered key determinants of change in the implementation of public sector accounting in most of the sample countries (Romania being the exception, shifting from cash straight to an accrual basis). In the context of implementing changes within the general accounting model, it can be argued that in conditions where the government accounting information system has reached a stage of development which enables the adoption of accrual accounting, there should be no significant financial, legal or technical limitations of further breakthroughs with the full accrual accounting model and the adoption of IPSAS, except for the questionable political readiness for change (i.e. support and awareness at the highest levels of government). However, even though the budgetary regulatory frameworks of the countries studied in this publication imply future changes on the path towards European and worldwide public sector accounting and financial reporting reforms (e.g. budget regulations normatively enable and foster the application of accruals and the implementation of international public sector accounting standards [IPSAS]), the path is not being actively pursued. There seems to be a lack of ongoing projects supported by national governments to undertake rather complicated and systematic procedures for the successful implementation of accrual-based accounting (in those countries that have not yet adopted accruals) and the implementation of IPSAS.

State audit is developed in all the countries included in this publication as a form of parliamentary supervision of public spending and is based on INTOSAI standards. In practice, state audit has focused more on the audit of the financial regularity and legality of budget spending. Lately, a performance audit has been given relevance with emphasis placed on audit procedures that assess whether public funds are used economically, efficiently and for the right cause and purpose, and whether strategic and programme planning systems have been developed, together with the instruments of performance indicators, to enhance and assure efficient public sector management.

Differences between countries are more visible in the dynamics and success of the implementation of internal financial controls and internal audit systems than in the conceptual and legal framework. The successful implementation of internal control systems and internal audits in the practice of budgetary users depends largely on understanding their role and purpose, as well as on understanding the circumstances in which the system is developed and the impact of those circumstances on the opportunities and dynamics of the development of internal control systems. The discussion has also highlighted that it is necessary to observe the interdependence of these reform processes and to notice that the development of one process stimulates the development of other processes, but also vice versa that a delay in one process can slow down the continuity of reforms of a series of related processes. The internal control system is a typical example of a process or area whose development and implementation greatly depend on the level of development of a series of other processes, i.e. strategic and programme planning, budgetary accounting, reporting, the development of an organisational culture, and the strengthening New Public Management.

The country chapters also highlight that in spite of the rather unfavourable environment and the aggravating circumstances in all the countries presented in this publication, public sector accounting, auditing and control systems are being developed on an established and internationally recognised basis.

Lastly, these concluding remarks do not impose or lay down all the possible comparisons between accounting, auditing and control systems in South-Eastern European countries. The editors and authors have attempted to give the reader the opportunity to study the state of play and the directions for further development in each of the countries in the sample, to draw their own conclusions, to form judgements and to deepen their insights in the search for new solutions.

Index

V. Vašiček and G. Roje (eds.), *Public Sector Accounting, Auditing and Control in South Eastern Europe*, Public Sector Financial Management, https://doi.org/10.1007/978-3-030-03353-8

The manufacturer's authorised representative in the EU is Springer Nature Customer Service Centre GmbH, Europaplatz 3, 69115 Heidelberg, Germany. If you have any concerns regarding our products, please contact ProductSafety@springernature.com

Printed and bound by CPI Group (UK) Ltd, Croydon, CR0 4YY
30/09/2026
02225442-0011